Adulting

by Gencie Houy

for dummies®
A Wiley Brand

Adulting For Dummies®

Published by: **John Wiley & Sons, Inc.,** 111 River Street, Hoboken, NJ 07030-5774, www.wiley.com

For general information on our other products and services, please contact our Customer Care Department within the U.S. at 877-762-2974, outside the U.S. at 317-572-3993, or fax 317-572-4002. For technical support, please visit https://hub.wiley.com/community/support/dummies.

Wiley publishes in a variety of print and electronic formats and by print-on-demand. Some material included with standard print versions of this book may not be included in e-books or in print-on-demand. If this book refers to media such as a CD or DVD that is not included in the version you purchased, you may download this material at http://booksupport.wiley.com. For more information about Wiley products, visit www.wiley.com.

Library of Congress Control Number: 2022945007

ISBN: 978-1-119-90433-5 (pbk); ISBN 978-1-119-90435-9 (epdf); ISBN 978-1-119-90434-2 (epub)

SKY10057138_100623

Contents at a Glance

Table of Contents

Introduction

Everyone keeps telling you to grow up. What does that even mean? It's not like there's a manual for life. . . or wait! Is there? In this book, you'll find out exactly what skills you need to be a thriving adult. You'll discover how to keep up in an ever-changing world, how to maintain positive relationships, how to communicate what you really want, how to manage your paycheck, and how to take care of your physical and emotional needs as an adult. Your journey as an adult begins one page at a time.

About This Book

Adulting is a series of choices that require knowledge and wisdom. This book is designed to explain essential life skills you need for all areas of your life. This book includes research-based content encompassing basic human needs, your individual well-being, family strengths, community vitality, and overall wellness. This is your chance to establish the multitude of skills needed not only to function as an adult but to flourish. *Adulting For Dummies* includes plenty of real-world scenarios for situations you may encounter and high-quality illustrations that help explain concepts

I divided the content into six parts:

- Part 1: Shifting from Surviving to Thriving
- Part 2: Dating, Relating, and Communicating
- Part 3: Earning Enough to Live On
- Part 4: Maintaining a Healthy Mind in a Healthy Body
- Part 5: Completing Household Jobs
- Part 6: The Part of Tens

Foolish Assumptions

This book is written for many different audiences. Your age does not determine maturity; your actions do. Even if it is not your time to function on your own as an adult, there are still essential skills within this book that you can begin working on now. This book is relevant to everyone!

Icons Used in This Book

Throughout this book, icons in the margins highlight certain types of valuable information that call out for your attention. Here are the icons you'll encounter and a brief description of each.

TIP

The Tip icon marks tips that you can use to practice adulting skills and helpful tidbits that make certain situations easier to manage.

REMEMBER

Remember icons mark the information that's especially important to know. To siphon off the most important information in each chapter, just skim through these icons.

WARNING

The Warning icon tells you to watch out! It marks important information that may save you headaches throughout your life.

Beyond the Book

In addition to the abundance of information and guidance related to Adulting that I provide in this book, you get access to even more help and information online at `https://dummies.com`. Just go to `https://dummies.com` and search for **Adulting For Dummies** to find a handy online cheat sheet as well as books and articles on other subjects that you may find useful.

Where to Go from Here

You don't need to read this book in any particular order. You can read from Chapter 1 to the end if you'd like, but it isn't required. If you need to focus on your health, begin with Part 4. If you need financial assistance regarding budgeting or taxes, check out Part 3. If you want relationship guidance, start with Part 2.

1

Shifting from Surviving to Thriving

IN THIS PART . . .

Set achievable goals, recognize your potential, and find out how to make good decisions to go from surviving to thriving.

Speak up to advocate for yourself.

Find out what to look out for in the digital world to avoid vital mistakes and how to balance your real life and your online life.

IN THIS CHAPTER

» Realizing it's time

» Getting to know who you are

» Taking charge of your future now

Chapter 1 Experiencing the Thrill and Fear of Running Your Own Life

Everything seems like it's happening so fast! So many changes with so many new steps to take and tasks to do. Nothing seems familiar anymore. Everyone in your life sees you differently now, and you might even feel different. It's an exciting time, but it can also be a little scary. Becoming an adult happens to everyone. It happens at different times for people, but I'm guessing that since you have picked up this book, it is your time. Maybe you feel a little lost. Everyone may have been telling you it's time to grow up but they're not offering instructions on how to do so. You might be telling yourself, "Now, hold on a minute, I didn't sign up for this," which I completely understand. Everyone fears the unknown. But there's something else you should be telling yourself:

> *I am ready to run my own life, make educated decisions for myself and loved ones, and begin to thrive — not just survive.*

Running your own life is thrilling! Use this book as a guide to help you be successful in all areas of your life. Adulting encompasses everything from relationships to taking care of yourself with good nutrition, exercise, new jobs; handling first paychecks; budgeting your earnings; addressing the never-ending task of laundry; and trying to avoid some rookie mistakes.

TIP

If it isn't quite your time for adulthood, you can begin practicing the skills covered in the book no matter how old you are. After all, age doesn't determine maturity.

REMEMBER

I encourage you to come back to this book repeatedly; you might even earmark some of the chapters as you go through if you think they'll be especially useful down the road. Adulting is a forever learning experience. As your life changes, which it will, you must practice new adulting skills all the time. No one is perfect. If everyone was perfect, just think how boring life would be.

In this chapter, I touch on the many aspects of adulthood with a brief discussion, and then I tell you where you can find more information about it in other chapters. If you read a topic that you feel inclined to research deeper, go ahead and flip to that chapter!

Taking One Step at a Time

You've heard the phrase "baby steps." Well, that statement is pretty accurate for heading into the next stage of your life. It's your time to put one foot in front of the other and begin the journey of adulthood.

If you have anxiety about growing up, you are not alone. Growing up means you must face the fact that time is fleeting and you must somehow find value in your life. You have never had to do that before; most likely you have had parents, guardians, and teachers telling you what to do and what to think. Stepping out on your own means using that brain of yours for yourself.

Up until now, you have experienced the world from the lens of a child. You might have felt powerless and at the mercy of others. During childhood, emotions are the main prompt for making decisions, and as you were growing up, you might have felt helpless at times and dependent on others. It's time to step out of the shadows and step into your life.

Using an adult lens for viewing life includes the following:

- Being rational
- Setting goals
- Being proactive
- Trying to be open-minded
- Being non-defensive

- Understanding that the world does not revolve around you
- Realizing you have the power to control your thoughts and feelings

TIP

Did you know that some adults still view the world through the lens of a child? They let their emotions control their life's destiny and live in a constant state of selfishness, fear, and helplessness. One of the goals in this book is to help you refocus your lens to gain a new perspective on life.

Entering the age of maturity

As a kid, you may have said, "I can't wait to grow up!" This is normal; it gives you an incentive to learn about life and move toward adulthood. Society generally considers one of the most common signs of maturity to be age. Laws state you must be a certain age before getting your driver's license or being able to vote. But remember, just because you're no longer young in age, doesn't mean you're mature in all areas of your life.

Simply becoming an adult is not the only goal you should have. Achieving maturity should be the real goal. Maturity means reaching your full potential physically, emotionally, socially, morally, and intellectually, and not everyone matures at the same rate. For most people, personal development is a lifelong journey.

The following are a few signs of maturity:

- Living independently
- Handling your emotions
- Becoming a dependable person
- Having a willingness to work hard
- Being able to agree to disagree
- Being able to admit when you're wrong
- Realizing you still have a lot to learn
- Not getting offended about everything and taking it all personally
- Listening more and talking less
- Showing compassion
- Being happy for other people's successes rather than being jealous
- Learning to be grateful for what you have

If you just read this list and thought to yourself that you have a lot to work on, no worries. It's all laid out for you in this book. Moving toward maturity takes time and effort. It doesn't happen all at once.

REMEMBER

Age does not measure your maturity — actions do.

TIP

When you cook popcorn on the stovetop, the kernels are in the same oil, in the same cooking vessel, and are experiencing the same heat, yet the kernels still pop at different times. This analogy shows the difference between age and maturity. Just because you're a certain age does not mean it is your time to pop!

Understanding that change is inevitable

I remember sitting in my elementary school class when the teacher introduced the new vocabulary word for the week: *inevitable*. She explained that *inevitable* means that something is certain to happen and is unavoidable. To explain what inevitable means, the teacher wrote, "Change is inevitable," on a large poster board. She explained that change is unavoidable. Your body will change, your relationships will change, your friends will change, and your entire life will change. As an elementary school student, I do not think I grasped the gravity of what that meant, but I understood that I would change, and my life would change.

Your life has already gone through many changes. As things continue to change, it's important to recognize those changes, and grow *with* them and *from* them.

Although change is unavoidable, you can plan ahead for changes in your life. Start now with these tips to help you navigate inevitable changes.

- » Have a plan and a back-up plan; you will need it!
- » Look at the changes from a positive perspective.
- » Reflect and learn from the changes.
- » Create structure and routine to maintain a certain amount of normalcy during life changes.
- » Find your happy place (see Chapter 15) to relieve the stress that comes along with major life changes.
- » Be thankful for the opportunity that change brings. New situations may not feel normal yet, but make the best out them.

TIP

Change brings about a mixture of emotions. Stress is one of the main emotions that can come with it. Take care of yourself by eating right, staying active, and getting enough sleep. (Read more in Part 4.)

REMEMBER

As your maturity grows, responding to change should become a simpler process. I am not saying change is ever easy, but learning to respond to it and having a plan in place will help you feel more in control of your life.

Mapping Out Your Destination

The more knowledge you have, the more options you will have for your future. Mapping out where you want to end up might require a bit of research. You're doing that now by reading this book, and I'm proud of you for that. Your success in life will not happen by chance. If you ask any successful individual, they will say that their success can be attributed to hard work and planning.

You may have had people tell you what it means to be successful. Maybe they have said that a big paycheck, owning the most expensive car, living in a mansion, and marrying the hottest person around means success. But I would beg to differ. Success can mean something different to everyone. It all depends on your goals and priorities.

The following are a few tips that can contribute to being successful:

- Do something you love. If you don't love what you're doing, why do it? Yes, you need a job for the income, but start determining now what you're passionate about and map out a path to get there.
- Work hard. Getting to your destination takes hard work. There is no free pass in life.
- Learn from the bumps along the way.
- Remember to have fun on your journey and think positively.
- Keep moving forward. Success does not come from stagnating.
- When it is time to work, put away the distractions that keep you from focusing on the task at hand.
- Only you can achieve your goals. You cannot expect someone to step in and save the day.
- Continuously plan. Your plan may veer off track; if it does, it's up to you to steer it back on the path.
- Do not overwork yourself. Obsessing over your goal and path will likely lead to burnout. Keep your goal something you *get* to do instead of something you *have* to do.

TIP

You must stay committed to your plan and your path to be successful, but you must also be realistic. If your commitment is not showing success after a predetermined amount of time, you should readjust your plan and review your steps to success. More on this in Chapter 2!

REMEMBER

There is no right or wrong way to determine success. Whenever you decide what success looks like in your life, begin planning the proper steps to get there.

Appreciating who you are

Has anyone ever asked you who you are? Well, if they haven't, take a few moments to think up an answer now. Go ahead. I'll wait.

The answer you formed is your self-concept, which is the image you have of all aspects of yourself. If you like who you are, you will generally have a healthy self-concept. If you don't feel good about yourself, you may have developed a low self-concept.

Your self-concept is resistant to change. You most likely developed your self-concept at a young age because of what people told you, and it was likely confirmed through different social actions throughout your life.

To function at your highest potential, you must have a positive self-concept and like who you are. If you don't feel positive about yourself, there are ways to improve your self-concept:

» **Positively talk to yourself.** Think of the positive things about yourself and write them down. Then say them to yourself each day until you begin to believe them and live them. Self-affirmations are a good way to reshape your self-perception.

» **Set realistic expectations for yourself.** Setting a goal to become a professional baseball player, when you don't even know how to play, will only bring about disappointment and failure in your mind.

» **Do not compare yourself to others.** Your self-concept will suffer if you make statements such as, "I'll never be as skinny as that person," or "I'll never be as smart as my coworkers." Instead, focus on what you do well and continue to become a better version of yourself, not someone else.

» **Focus on the things that bring you joy in life.** Focusing on the negative aspects of your life can be depressing. Instead, focus on the things you love. This helps you keep a healthy mindset.

REMEMBER

Appreciating yourself can be tricky, but be proud of your personality, your heredity, and most importantly, who you are!

Improving your self-esteem takes time and effort, but you are worth the investment!

REMEMBER

"It takes courage to grow up and become who you really are." — e.e. cummings

Thinking big

Planning out your steps to success is vital when it comes to your career as an adult, but figuring out what you want to be when you grow up might be the bigger challenge. One of the first things to consider when deciding on a career path is determining what you like to do. What you do every day for your job has a huge impact on whether you feel like you're thriving in your life or just surviving.

Here are a few ways to start the process of deciding on a career path:

- Determine your interests and your talents.
- Make a list of all of the jobs you think you might be good at.
- Do research and add to your list. Chapter 8 goes into more detail on how to research prospective jobs. You may discover that there are many jobs out there that you have never heard of, and some may be right up your alley!
- Take a career aptitude test.
- Talk to a career counselor.
- Volunteer or job shadow to see if you like the day's work.
- Remain open-minded and try new things.

TIP

If people keep asking you what you will be studying or what you want to do with your life and you aren't quite sure yet, just say, "I'm exploring my options."

REMEMBER

It is OK not to know what you want to do with your life. The important part is that you get moving on figuring it out. Remaining idle stunts your growth as an individual and an adult.

Making Your Mark

Whether you're in school or starting your career, people are watching you — not in a stalking sort of way, but people take notice of your behaviors, actions, and conversations. You will begin to make your mark in society as an adult, and you want your mark to be a good one. Here are some qualities to demonstrate when you begin to make your mark.

- Act according to your values.
- Be truthful and be real. People can spot a fake a mile away.
- Be dependable.
- Control your impulsive behaviors; be patient.
- Don't give up when things get tough.
- Show discipline; use your time and resources wisely.
- Get to know the people you work with.
- Pick up the slack and pitch in when needed.
- Don't blame others and don't make excuses for your behavior.
- Don't act in anger.
- Forgive others and their mistakes. (Remember, you will make mistakes too.)
- Listen to others.
- Be kind and polite. Kindness goes a long way.
- Be respectful to others, strangers, and friends alike.
- Educate yourself before you begin sharing your opinion on hot topics.
- Have a growth mindset.
- Work on improving traits and habits you consider to be negative.
- Be good to your family.
- Learn continuously, honing your skills to reach your goals.
- Accept others just as they are. Do not expect them to be something they are not.
- Be adventurous, be bold.
- Show concern for the people around you.
- Cooperate with other people. You will need help in life; don't burn your bridges.
- Be generous. Give to others with monetary donations or by volunteering your time.

- Remain humble. There is no need to talk about your accomplishments, let them speak for themselves.
- Do not complain. If there is a problem, work to find a solution.
- Be tactful instead of abrasive. There is no need to be rude.

WARNING

People who earn a less-than-desirable reputation might have trouble repairing how others view them, but it can be done.

REMEMBER

It might seem like there are a lot of steps to make your mark on this world, so good on you for picking up this book as a guide to being a better you!

Understanding Character

Personal character develops over time, and your parents and other adults in your life may have helped you work on developing yours for your entire life. As an adult, it's time to put your values into practice in a positive way. The following are some universally honored values:

- Courage
- Fairness
- Freedom
- Honesty
- Respect
- Responsibility
- Trustworthiness

While these values are shared around the world, people prioritize them in their own way. Even with your friends and family, you might express your values differently. Demonstrating responsibility shows your character in action. This involves choosing whether to take action and accept the consequences of that choice. Here are a few ways to build character as you mature:

- Working hard
- Practicing conflict resolution
- Problem-solving

- Managing others
- Leading others
- Engaging in tough conversations with patience and empathy
- Giving credit where credit is due
- Having an attitude that no task is too small or considered beneath you
- Being nice, even when everyone around you is not

TIP

After determining your most important values, let them guide your life choices.

Navigating the Necessities

Deciding where to live is one of the most important things to consider during adulthood. Moving out of your parents' house can be an appealing aspect as you move into adulthood.

You need to consider many things as you begin looking for housing. Here are just a few:

- How much money will you have to spend on a house? Do you have a steady income so you can afford your own place?
- What type of housing will work best: apartment, condo, single-family unit, duplex?
- Will you live alone or with a roommate?
- Is renting or buying better for your situation?
- Are you emotionally ready to move out?
- Do you have realistic expectations of what it's like to live on your own?
- Can you withstand the upkeep a home of your own requires?

Transportation is another necessity that can be costly, and you have to determine whether the benefits outweigh the costs. The following are a few questions to ask yourself:

- Do you need a car, or can you rely on public transportation?
- Is the type of car you're interested in a need or a want?

» Can you afford the car payments, insurance premiums, and other associated costs (for example, gas, oil changes, and license plates)?

TIP

Determining the difference between a need and a want is one of the first things to wrap your head around. You might *need* a car for transportation, but you might *want* a Porsche. Read more about budgeting, housing, and buying a car in Chapters 10 and 11.

REMEMBER

Don't bite off more than you can chew when it comes to housing and transportation; be realistic with what you can afford.

Providing the Goods

Being an adult means you have to take care of yourself because no one else is going to do it for you. The following responsibilities can help you stay on track and thrive as an adult:

» Eating healthily (see Chapter 12)
  - Getting enough nutrients in your diet
  - Making healthy food choices
  - Drinking plenty of water

» Staying active and exercising (see Chapter 13)
  - Making exercise a habit and incorporating physical activity into your daily routine
  - Incorporating a cardiovascular workout to keep your heart healthy
  - Taking a walk to get your heart pumping

» Establishing daily habits (see Chapter 14)
  - Getting enough sleep
  - Practicing good hygiene
  - Scheduling doctor appointments regularly

» Staying positive (see Chapter 15)
  - Asking for help from other people when you're going through a tough time
  - Regulating your stress by finding a hobby or activity that you love

- Keeping a clean environment (see Chapter 16)
  - Picking up after yourself and keeping your home or room tidy
  - Doing your laundry weekly to avoid a clothing pileup
  - Repairing your clothes to save money and help the environment
- Cooking your meals (see Chapter 17)
  - Learning what appliances and equipment are around to help you be a better cook
  - Practicing safety and sanitation in your kitchen
  - Using a variety of cooking methods to keep dinner interesting

REMEMBER

Taking care of yourself properly can reduce anxiety, help you function properly at work or school, reduce your stress levels, minimize irritability, and improve your energy levels.

TIP

On days when you might not be motivated to take care of yourself properly, revisit your goals in life and where you want to be. You might need some self-care time to keep trekking along.

Stepping Up: You Got This

Throughout this book, you might read the words *You got this* quite a bit. That is because I fully, 100% believe that you can do this! You can be a successful, thriving, happy adult.

I know there might be some fear involved in becoming an adult, but many people before you have done it, and so can you. Navigating life is not easy. It's one of the most difficult things you will do, but along with the hardships adulthood brings comes long-lasting relationships, joyful memories, and proud moments.

In case you need some more convincing, here are some ways adulting is better than being a kid:

- You can literally do whatever you want when you want. Granted, you will have to accept the consequences of your decisions, but you're finally allowed to make your own choices and your own mistakes.
- You can change your circumstances. When you were younger, you were stuck with the bully in your eighth-grade math class. You had to see him every day

in class. But as an adult, you can choose to change your environment so you don't have to interact with people who cause issues for you.

- You have experienced a few things in life to help get you where you are, you have learned some hard lessons along the way, and you get to share those with others.
- You get to choose your path and how you live your life.
- You can solve your own problems.
- You can have ice cream for breakfast.

Do you see a trend here? Being an adult is invigorating because you're in charge. You make your own decisions and no one can tell you otherwise.

REMEMBER

Being an adult comes with privileges. Take adulting seriously and be responsible for your decisions.

REMEMBER

You can do this, you are worth it, and you will do great things in life!

IN THIS CHAPTER

» **Creating goals**

» **Managing the decision-making process**

» **Being your own advocate**

Chapter 2
Knowing What You Want and Getting It

You have decisions to make every day. The choices begin the minute you hear your alarm in the morning: *Do I get out of bed or hit the snooze button just one more time? What do I wear today? Should I have a donut or oatmeal for breakfast?* Sometimes, making all of these decisions can be overwhelming, especially when even the smallest choices affect your success for the day.

For example, if you decide to hit the snooze button one more time, you would definitely be late for an important presentation, which in turn could affect your performance and the way others see you. This could restrict you from reaching your goals. If you choose to leave your umbrella at home in the morning and then get caught in the rain on your walk to work, you could be stuck with soaked clothes. Maybe you decide you want the donut instead of the normal oatmeal. The donut then proceeds to give you a sugar high so you crash around 1:00 p.m. and cannot focus on your tasks for the day. Small choices like these can create a ripple effect on your entire life! You can either use the decisions you make in a day to step closer to what you want in life, remain complacent, or sometimes even move backward. Every choice you make has a consequence — good or bad.

In this chapter, I first talk about how to set achievable goals for yourself. Learning how to set goals is crucial, but you also need to understand the decision-making process and the importance of advocating for your potential, so I also cover those topics later in the chapter. With the skills I cover here, you can begin identifying what you might want in life and work on getting there!

Setting Achievable Goals

Success and self-confidence go hand in hand. Are you confident in your own abilities? Really think about your answer to that question. If the answer is no, you might not be setting achievable goals. When you achieve something, you gain confidence in yourself. You become eager to try new things and look forward to new experiences.

Setting achievable goals and meeting them takes some work, but the outcomes are often outstanding. Just think how proud you'll feel when you can tell your friends and family about a great achievement you've accomplished. The following sections walk you through setting achievable goals.

Pinpointing your potential

Potential is the possibility of becoming more than you are right at this moment. Every person has potential. Even a 100-year-old still has potential in their life! Each day is a new day to work toward being the best you can be.

Becoming the best you can be starts with knowing your potential. When you think about your potential, here are some things to help you think big!

- **Focus on what you like and what interests you.** It might be difficult at first, but try to make a list of what you like and what abilities you have. For example, maybe you are interested in all things involving animals. That is great! The next step is to match what you are interested in with your skills. Let's say you are good at taking care of animals — you know, like walking them, feeding them, and giving them the love they deserve. With this type of interest and ability, you could volunteer at the local animal shelter or dog park to further develop your skills and decide possible next steps.
- **Don't get distracted.** It's really hard to reach your potential if you let yourself get distracted. Stay focused on what interests you and the path that leads to your future.
- **Stay healthy.** Do your best to make choices that promote good health. For example, a donut now and then is fine, but you probably shouldn't choose a donut over oatmeal every day. You need to remain healthy to have the energy

needed to reach all you can be! You can learn all about healthy choices in Part 4 of this book.

- **Use your potential for good.** Whatever your interest is, put it toward creating good in the world. Returning to the animal-lover example, maybe you can gain more skills to open your *own* shelter in an effort to help abandoned animals. What a great goal to work for!

After you've thought about your potential, you're ready to set some goals.

Considering categories of goals

To set an achievable goal, it's vital to understand why goals are important in the first place. A goal is something that you want in life, such as what you plan to do, what you want to be, or what you want to have.

TIP

It's a *must* to set a goal in your own words and even write it down! Only you know yourself best, so your goal needs to come from your perspective. It also needs to be positive, realistic, and something you actually like. You'll quickly lose interest in achieving success if you don't like what you're working toward. It seems silly that someone would pursue something they do not like, but it happens all the time. People who do this don't have a plan for their life; they just fall into a path or journey they have no passion for. They might even hate it! I want to help you stay far from this so you can utilize your passions and abilities.

You may not be aware that there different are types of goals. Here's a list of some of the types of goals you need in your life:

- **Personal goals** include categories of your personal development, spirituality, and education. Examples include
  - I want to read more books, one each month.
  - I really need to get organized; I will set a timer to help me stay on track.
  - I am tired of losing time in my day! I want to get up earlier to make the most of the time I am given.
  - I will be more mentally present in every situation and give people my full attention.
- **Family goals** help to bring you together with the people you love the most in life to experience more happy moments than tense moments. Examples include
  - Let's have a certain time each week to all eat together as a family!

- Since we don't get to see each other as much as we want, let's plan a family vacation this summer.
- How about we do the laundry together? You take out the trash, and I will wash the dishes each week. That way we each have a part in the chores.

» **Career goals** tend to be more of a roadmap or path to get you where you want to be. Whether you're just having your first experience in the workforce or you have 20 years of experience, it's important to continually set career goals. Some of the goals might include

- I need to focus more on my schoolwork; I will make all As this semester.
- I intend to apply to several college programs my senior year to see what might be a good fit.
- I will earn a certification after high school that I am passionate about.
- Maybe I should go back to school. I will get my master's degree within four years.
- To better excel at my current position, I will stop procrastinating!

» **Fitness goals** are directed to the health of your mind and body, which help you achieve other goals in your life. If you're healthy and fit, you can focus on your passions and skills. Examples include

- I plan to walk 20 minutes a day for this month.
- I feel like my internal clock is off! I am setting a goal to wake up and go to sleep at the same time each day.
- I will drink at least 2 liters of water a day.

» **Financial goals** can help you stay on track with your finances. Financial goals include

- I am setting a goal to create and stick to a budget so I do not spend more than I earn each week.
- This month I will pay my brother back.
- Each time I get paid, I will save money for a rainy day.

TIP

Now it's time for you to act. Spend some time thinking about a few goals you'd like to set and write them down. Think about where you are right now in life. Are you heading toward a transition, or are you just beginning a new chapter? Either way, it's important to set goals based on what is most meaningful to you. Start with goals that are easy to achieve so you can gain self-confidence in your abilities.

WARNING Setting too many goals can cause you to lose focus and feel overwhelmed. It's perfectly OK to take a step back, slow down, and just choose one or two goals to work on at a time. Goals often have multiple steps, so it's much easier to take the steps needed to achieve a few goals at a time, and it sure feels good when you achieve one!

Creating achievable goals: The short and long of it

Understanding what your goals should be about is one thing, but how do you make them achievable? One way to do that is to create a SMART goal, which is specific, measurable, achievable, relevant, and timed:

- **Specific:** Answer the *Who, What, Where, When,* and *Why* of your goal. Being specific ensures there are no surprises later.
- **Measurable:** Your goal must include how you will measure your progress. It should answer questions like
  - How much?
  - How many?
  - How will I know?
- **Achievable:** Setting a goal should extend your abilities, but it should not *over*extend them. Ask yourself, "Is this goal realistic based on my constraints?"
- **Relevant:** To determine if your goal is relevant, ask yourself questions like the following:
  - Is this goal something I am interested in, or do other people think I should pursue it?
  - Is this the right time to set this goal?
  - Do I have the skills needed to work toward this?
- **Timed:** Include a target date for achieving the goal. This helps keep your goal a priority.

For example, a general goal might be "I want to establish an emergency fund." Great idea! But when you evaluate that goal against the SMART criteria, it needs some work. Can you measure this goal? How will you know if you have enough money for an emergency fund? A better idea would be to set a number — maybe $2,400 would work for you. Now your goal would be, "I want to put aside $2,400 toward an emergency fund." This goal is more specific, but I bet you could still be more precise by including a timetable, such as "I want to put aside $200 each month over the next 12 months to total $2,400 toward an emergency fund." Now you have something to work with!

REMEMBER

A short-term goal can be accomplished within the near future, like "Today I am going to do my laundry." A long-term goal is further in the future and will take longer to achieve. A long-term goal would be "I want to own my own business in 10 years." You achieve this type of goal by accomplishing many short-term goals that build upon one another.

Getting gritty

Grit is a mixture of perseverance, determination, and passion. When you apply grit to your goals, it means you don't easily give up when the going gets tough. The following story about Hattie is a perfect example of a person with the Grit Factor:

> Hattie has a goal to be a star on Broadway in New York City. She goes to her very first audition on Broadway, wide-eyed and bushy-tailed, then before the music for the song even begins, she gets cut! She says, "What!? I didn't even get to audition!" The person in charge says, "You're too tall for this part." Hattie packs up her things and leaves.
>
> Rejection isn't fun, but she knows it's part of the process so she moves on to the next audition, where she at least gets to sing and dance, but she shortly hears, "Thank you for your time."
>
> This pattern continues for three months. Hattie is running out of the money she saved to move to New York to follow her dream. She thinks *Maybe I should abandon my goal and just move back home to Texas*, but she remembers all she has accomplished throughout her life that has brought her here. She cannot possibly leave now.
>
> She digs deep, gets an extra job to help with money, focuses on her passion, continues to take dance and voice classes, and perseveres through her hardship and rejection for two more years, only scoring small roles along the way. Instead of dwelling on the rejection, she learns from it. She then hits it big and gets hired for the part of a lifetime!

Even though everything was rough and bumpy, Hattie carried on because she was passionate and determined. All people have a little bit of the Grit Factor in them. You just need to access it and trust yours.

If sticking with a plan seems easier said than done, you're right. The good thing about having grit and determination is that it can be learned. It's not just an inborn trait. Some people may come by it more naturally, but that doesn't mean you cannot learn. Here are some strategies to cultivate grittiness:

- Keep positive.
- Remember the big picture.
- Stay organized.
- Create a manageable list.
- Don't procrastinate.
- Keep your goals in mind.
- Remember your why.
- Watch out for distractions.
- Celebrate the small achievements.
- Choose to be successful!

Maybe you can put one of these sayings on a coffee cup or something — or maybe that's too corny for you. Either way, remember that you're telling your story, no one else's; make it a good one. I want you to know you are worth your goals, and your goals are worth achieving!

Decision-Making: It's All You!

Decisions, decisions, decisions. . . you're bombarded with them every day. The average number of decisions an individual makes on a daily basis is estimated to be 35,000 or more, and many of those are about food! It's exhausting to think about all of the decisions you make in a single day, hour, or minute.

Here are just a few of the things you have to decide each day:

- What to wear
- What tasks you have to complete
- Who to hang out with
- Whether to spend money
- When and how to complete work
- Whether you should call your family
- What you should eat

REMEMBER

Decisions, big or small, play a continual part in your life. As you progress through life, you'll make many large decisions about school, work, marriage, or children. Even when you choose to do nothing, believe it or not, you are making a decision.

Outside influences

Think about the last decision you made. Maybe it was to pick up this book and read it. Did you make that decision by yourself? Did you get help? Maybe someone said you should read this book. Many things affect the decisions you make. Some of those influences come from the people around you, like your family or friends. Those are called *external influences*. You are also influenced internally by your own belief system and knowledge. The following are a few things that can be major influences on your decisions:

- **Family:** Sometimes your family may not directly communicate their thoughts on a decision you make, but trust me, you have their ideals and expectations in the back of your mind to ensure those you are closest to are pleased. As you grow older, your family will continue to give you advice, whether you ask for it or not. They do not want to see you make mistakes that could lead to serious trouble. Part of adulting is making mistakes, but your family is there to help you steer clear of dangerous ones.
- **Friends:** The older and more independent you get, the more you may find yourself relying on your friends rather than family for advice. This is natural. But remember, your friends have about the same knowledge level as you. They may give their advice, but it's not necessarily coming from experience. Your peers can be a positive influence or a negative influence, but in the end, you have the decision-making power. You are the one who must live with the consequences.
- **Morals:** Knowing and understanding your morals or standards will help you make better decisions. Other people can tell what kind of person you are based on your decisions. Your morals shine loud and clear with the choices you make.
- **Wants:** Wants are things that you may desire but are not essential for survival. You might want chocolate cake, but you need your vegetables. You might want a designer brand of shoes, but the designer name is not essential. Your wants have a powerful influence over your decisions, so it's good to ask yourself whether you really need a thing or you simply want it.
- **Needs:** A famous psychologist, Abraham Harold Maslow, created Maslow's hierarchy of human needs (see Figure 2-1). Human beings have basic needs that must be met — the need for food, water, safety, and security. Humans also have psychological needs such as relationships, friends, feeling loved, and feeling accomplished. Self-fulfillment needs include living to one's fullest potential. The choices you make reflect the needs in your life.

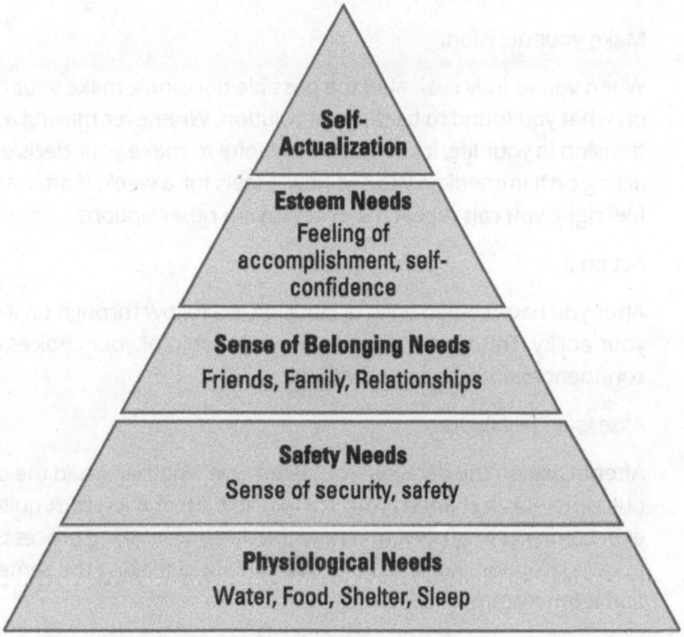

FIGURE 2-1: Maslow's hierarchy of needs.

A never-ending process

Having so many decisions and so many choices can feel overwhelming. Some decisions you make without much thought, but many larger decisions might take much more critical thinking. Don't worry, though; there is a process that can help you make those tough decisions. The following steps in the decision-making process can help you reach your goal:

1. Define the decision.

   To come up with the best possible decision, you first have to understand the situation that warrants a decision. Think about the end results you have in mind to help you make an effective decision.

2. List all your options.

   Think of all of possible alternatives or choices you have, even if some of them seem silly. The more alternatives you include, the more you have to work with to see what might fit.

3. List the pros and cons.

   List the good things and bad things about each option you come up with. Researching your options can help you assess the advantages and disadvantages of each alternative.

4. Make your decision.

   When you've fully evaluated the possible decisions, make your choice based on what you found to be the best solution. Whenever making a rather large decision in your life, it's sometimes helpful to make your decision without acting on it immediately to see how it feels for a week. If after a week it doesn't feel right, you can repeat the process with other options.

5. Act on it.

   After you have settled on your decision, do follow through on it to the best of your ability. This is your time to take ownership of your choices and be confident enough to see it through.

6. Assess and evaluate.

   After acting on the decision, you determine whether it had the desired outcome. Has it changed your life for the better? If it wasn't quite what you expected, you may need to repeat the decision-making process. It's important to evaluate your choices so that you can avoid making the same errors again and learn from your mistakes.

Here's an example of the process for a work-related decision:

1. Define the decision.

   You're unhappy in your current job, and you need to decide whether you should quit and look for a new job.

2. List all of your options.
   - Option 1: You quit your job and then look for another job.
   - Option 2: You don't quit your job and change nothing.
   - Option 3: You start looking for new jobs before you quit your job.
   - Option 4: You change your attitude in your current position into a more positive outlook.

3. List the pros and cons.
   - Option 1: You quit your job and then look for another job.

     Pro: You would leave a job where you are unhappy.

     Con: You might not find another job, or you might be just as unhappy in your next job.

- Option 2: You don't quit your job and change nothing.

  Pro: You would still have a job where you make money to provide for yourself.

  Con: You would still be unhappy on a day-to-day basis in your job.

- Option 3: You start looking for new jobs before you quit your job.

  Pro: You might feel more secure having a job already lined up before you quit.

  Con: Your current employer might realize you are seeking other positions and reprimand you. You'll still be unhappy in your position while looking for other positions, which could take a while.

- Option 4: You change your attitude in your current position into a more positive outlook.

  Pro: You get to keep your current position and practice more positive thinking and grow your mindset. You do not have to deal with the struggle of finding a new position that fits you well.

  Con: Even if you change your attitude, the atmosphere might remain toxic.

4. Make your decision.

   You choose to begin the search for a new job while staying discreet about it in your current position — maybe even changing your mindset in your current job.

5. Act on your decision.

   Begin the job search while staying in good graces at your current position. You find a new job, and it's time to put in your two weeks' notice.

6. Evaluate your decision.

   The stress of the job search really affected you, but you were able to remain in good standing with your current position, even after choosing to move on. You found a new job you might like. Congrats! Time to start the decision-making process over again to determine whether the new position is right for you.

TIP

Now it's your turn. Practice this process with any decision, big or small. At first it may seem silly or difficult to include this much detail about your choices, but in the long run, it will help you make more educated decisions.

Consequences

Consequences are a direct result or effect of your decisions. Consequences can be good or bad, can affect just you, or can affect those around you. Some consequences are minor, whereas others are life-changing. For example, you chose what college you want to go to, but it took you so long to decide you missed the application deadline. That's a life-changing consequence! Your choices can affect other people as well. If you decide last minute that you want to stay in and watch a movie instead of going out with your friends as planned, your friends are left hanging after planning on this night for a week. Not a good look on you!

WARNING

If you want the respect of people you care about, think wisely before making your decisions.

Making choices you feel good about helps raise your self-esteem and earn respect from those around you. Some decisions you make are bound to go wrong. Take responsibility for this, and don't play the blame game. Learn everything you can about your experience so you're better equipped to choose next time.

Advocating for Yourself: Scary, but Doable

Advocating means to support something or someone usually on shared values and morals. It could be making your opinion known on an important matter in public schools or standing up for better workplace conditions. It's great to be passionate about something you value, but you also need to advocate for yourself. When you value yourself and see yourself as important, self-advocating means speaking up and making your wants and needs known to help you grow and succeed.

Getting to know you

To advocate for yourself, you first need to know who you are and what you stand for. Take some time to get to know yourself.

Reflect upon these questions (go ahead, write the answers in the book if you need to):

- What are your strengths?
- What are your weaknesses?
- What do you like to do for fun?
- Where do you feel safest?

- What are you most proud of?
- What do you believe in?
- What matters most to you? Who matters most to you?
- What is your happiest memory?
- When you are stressed, what do you do?
- What are you most grateful for?
- Are you an introvert or extrovert?
- How do you learn best?
- What gives you comfort?
- How do you define success?

TIP

There are a lot of questions here, and you may not answer them all in one day. That's OK; think about one or two of them for now and then revisit them in a day or two. Once you've answered all of these questions, you're on your way to understanding yourself and what you value.

Being uniquely you

Each person has their own personality. It is formed from a mixture of heredity, the environment where a person grows up, and their cultural heritage. Personality includes behavioral qualities and the traits that make a person who they are. Who *you* are is unique, and guess what? There is no wrong way to be you! That is something I hope you can get on board with!

One idea that is important when you're learning who you are is discovering your self-concept. Your self-concept is the way you see yourself. This has been largely influenced by the people around you and their responses and behavior toward you. Your self-concept can be positive or negative:

- **Positive self-concept:** A positive self-concept is where you see yourself as likable, equal, and accepted by people.

  When the people around you approve of you or you get a ton of likes on social media, it makes you feel good about yourself. Wow, people really do like me!
- **Negative self-concept:** With a negative self-concept, you might be uncomfortable in your own skin and do not find yourself to be likable to others. You also have a significant fear of rejection because you see yourself as inferior to others.

When people have shown disapproval in something you said or did, you probably felt a small sense of personal rejection. This, over time, promotes a negative self-concept.

» **Improving your self-concept:** Feeling better about yourself is vital to growing and developing. Improving your self-concept can happen when you learn more about yourself and in the process begin to accept yourself as who you are.

  Here are some tips to improve your self-concept:

  - Develop your talents and abilities.
  - Find positive relationships with others, those who accept you for who you are.
  - Be realistic about your expectations.
  - Do activities you enjoy.
  - Have an open mind about life, maybe even a sense of humor!

TIP

Working on character traits such as fairness, respect, friendliness, trustworthiness, and responsibility can help improve your self-concept, and as mentioned in Chapter 3, maintain relationships.

Speaking up

After exploring who you are as a person, it's time to address the things you need to achieve what you want. Following are some ways that you can take action and begin to speak up for yourself:

» **Find the best person to reach out to.** Say you're having trouble at work. Would you turn to your next-door neighbor or your boss? You would turn to your boss. Maybe you're struggling with mental health. Would you choose someone to reach out to who barely knows you, or would you tell a trusted individual or professional? You would tell the trusted individual or professional. Determining who is in the best position to help you is about knowing your current situation and then researching to see who would understand and listen to your needs.

» **Figure out the best way to make contact.** Each resource has a different way to connect. Emailing, scheduling an appointment, making a phone call, or initiating a simple conversation could be warranted based on the person or resource you're interacting with.

- **Make a plan.** It's OK to feel nervous or anxious when advocating for yourself. If you make a plan with concrete steps, it will help take the stress off of the situation. Write a script and practice what you want to say. Saying it out loud for the first time can be freeing! The more you advocate for yourself, the more natural it begins to feel.
- **Be brave.** This is your life, no one else's. If you don't speak up for it, who will? Be confident with your words and actions and remember your goals.

WARNING

Not everyone has your best interest in mind, so do your research to determine who has your back and who doesn't. You might get a negative response when you begin advocating for yourself, but don't let that detour you from your end game. You got this!

Baby, you're worth it

Your self-worth is an important part of you. Let me start by saying *you are worth it!* You are worthy of love, and you are a worthwhile person. You were not created by mistake, and you have a plan and purpose in this life. Baby, you're worth it! I really hope you believe me, but if you don't just yet, that's OK. I'll show you some ways to appreciate your worth.

To improve your self-worth try repeating these sayings:

- *I am worthy of love, no matter what I have done.*
- *I am not a bad person; I just made a mistake.*
- *The clothes I wear or the car I drive do not define me.*
- *I am enough.*
- *I am allowed not to be happy all the time.*
- *I give myself time and space to set firm boundaries.*
- *Tough situations happen. It is not how they happen, but how I respond.*
- *I have empathy for others because I have been there myself.*
- *I always have something to be grateful for.*

Another way you can improve your self-worth is always to try your best. Work hard in whatever you do and finish your projects strong. Imagine this: You have just moved into a new place, and you're ready for some new furniture. Shopping time! You get to the furniture store and notice many options, but two options catch your attention:

- One option is a chair that seems unfinished. The stitching looks quickly put together and the wood is not stained or treated properly. Someone built this chair halfway and obviously cut corners; therefore, this chair has a very low price.
- The other option is an immaculate chair with beautiful stitching in the cushions, precisely stained wood, and hand-carved intricate details. It is magnificent. Someone labored for many hours on this chair, and it is properly reflected in the chair's hefty price.

Option 1 has a lower price because the person who built this chair left it unfinished; it has less value. If the builder had finished it and carried out their talent to the best of their abilities, the value would be higher.

Option 2 has a higher price because it is valued higher than option one. The person who built this chair worked to the absolute best of their ability.

REMEMBER

Knowing what you want and getting it is important in your life. Your goals should reflect who you uniquely are and what you want to achieve. The decisions you make should help lead you to a better version of yourself. Speak up and know your worth!

IN THIS CHAPTER

- » Understanding digital ethics
- » Looking at the world through the social media lens

Chapter 3 Keeping up in a Changing World

The world we live in is constantly changing. I remember sitting in elementary school and the word for the week was *inevitable.* My teacher explained the term to us by using the sentence "Change is inevitable." There was even a banner hanging in our classroom with that statement on it. We learned that change is something that happens whether we initiate it or not. Over time, things just change, and I bet if you think back to elementary school, things have changed quite a bit for you.

One thing that seems to change in our world faster than lightning is technology. It has and will continue to change the way we live, interact, and communicate. In this chapter, I discuss the rights and responsibilities you have for using various technologies that may play a big role in how you conduct your life.

Navigating the Murky Waters of Digital Ethics

Ethics are standards for right and wrong behavior, both in face-to-face interactions and online. Your character is a combination of your ethical principles and maturity. Being an adult means understanding that ethics are important in your family life, job life, and personal life. You demonstrate your character in your public life, but believe it or not, your private behavior is also a reflection of your character.

Even though you may not consider yourself a role model, someone is looking up to you whether you like it or not. As an adult, you have a responsibility to strive for ethical behavior in all that you do. In the following section, I describe some values that can help guide your behavior and actions.

Taking it at face value

Each person has a set of learned values. You learned them from your home life and from other people in your life as you were growing up. If your parents volunteered on the weekends at a food kitchen to help feed the homeless, you might have learned that having compassion for others is an important value to live by. You also may have acquired values from the schools you attended, places of worship, books, social media, and the internet. In some cases, you might have had to decipher for yourself whether values from these sources were ethically sound.

Universal values are the values that are generally accepted worldwide because most people share them. These values help to hold people together in a peaceful way. Examples of universal values include

- Love
- Equity
- Courage
- Truth
- Respect
- Trustworthiness
- Peace and nonviolence

The people around you place different levels of importance on each of these values. While you may have similar values as your friends and family, each person may express them differently.

Understanding rights and responsibilities

Whether you're behind a screen or face to face with someone, you have rights and responsibilities to other people. What you value comes out in your character as a person. On social media or in a group of friends, here are some character traits that are a must:

- **Integrity:** Always act according to your values. Don't waver between what you think is right and wrong.
- **Self-control:** You have control over your actions. Tame that temper!
- **Honesty:** Tell the truth with compassion and tact. Don't be fake and hide behind a computer screen; stay true to who you are.
- **Patience:** Don't be impulsive. Reread that angry email before you send it. Wait your turn and keep the needs of others in mind.
- **Perseverance:** Don't get discouraged easily. Stay the course and work toward your goals.
- **Dependability:** If you say you are going to do something, follow through and do it. Can people count on you?

TIP

Responsibility is the way you show your character to others. Owning up to your mistakes shows what type of person you are. A simple email apologizing or owning up to an error is always a better choice than trying to hide a mistake.

Think of a time you've messed up. Did you own up to it, or did you try to hide it? Make a plan based on your values for how you can handle mistakes in the future. You have a right to say, post, or text what you want, but do not stray from your own personal values.

Being cautious: Don't be quick to click

There are many freedoms and benefits that come with communicating electronically, but there are also some major distractors and even dangers lurking behind your screen. Being cautious with the websites you visit and the emails you interact with will help you navigate through online communications and possible scams.

Cybercriminals are quite resourceful when it comes to attempting to lure you to click on a link or attachment. A malicious email can seem convincing because it might look like it came from a bank, a government agency, or a business you are familiar with. But don't be too quick to click; the cybercriminals are counting on that. They might make the email seem urgent "because your account has been compromised!" If you are unsure whether the email is legitimate, check with the company directly by calling or reaching out via the contact form on the website. Do not reply to the email or click any links in the message, though.

Here are a couple of common forms of malicious electronic communications:

- **Spam or junk mail:** Items that are sent to you without you having asked for them. Your email account usually comes with a junk folder where these types of messages are routed. Unfortunately, sometimes emails you need get sent to that folder, too, so you do need to check it periodically. After you have checked that folder for important emails, delete the spam.
- **Phishing attacks:** Criminals may try to collect personal or financial information from you by sending emails that look like they come from a trustworthy source. Beware, don't give it to them! Spam and phishing attacks can also be found on social networks. Facebook, Twitter, YouTube, and many others are susceptible to the "bait and click" factor. Don't fall for it. If it seems too good to be true, it probably is.
- **Smishing attacks:** Criminals can also obtain your cell phone number. They will SMS text you a compelling link. When clicked, a malicious program downloads to your smartphone and sends the attacker your personal information. If you get a link texted to you from an unknown number, block the number and delete the text. Do not click on the link!

When you use the internet, you are connected to other computers and smartphones where data is exchanged. Because of this, it is very important to make sure your device and your information are as private as possible. Here are some suggestions for keeping yourself safe online:

- Never reveal personal or financial information online unless you have checked the security of the website. You can do this by looking at the URL. Malicious websites try to look just like the site they are imitating, but there is always something off, like a misspelling or an incorrect domain (.com, .net, or .gov).
- If you are online shopping, make sure it's a trusted source. If it's a new shopping site, check for customer service information and possibly call before ordering.
- Keep your smart device up to date with the proper malware to protect your online activities.
- When in doubt, delete it! If it looks even the slightest bit suspicious, just throw it out. If someone really wants your attention and needs to get ahold of you, they won't try sending a link. They will email or contact you directly.
- Every time you create an account online, use a unique password. This makes it harder for someone to hack into your account. A strong password includes:

- A mixture of uppercase and lowercase letters
- At least 12 characters
- No parts of your first or last name
- A mixture of numbers and letters
- At least one special character, such as @ ! # $?

Evaluating Appearances: Social Media Isn't Always What It Seems

Social media offers us a whole new world to present ourselves, communicate, and research information. But not everything about social media can be seen with the naked eye. You may find that social media is changing your perceptions of yourself, others, and the entire world. How can you tell what is real and what is not?

There are many different social media platforms. All have their own purposes. Here are a few of the different platforms you are probably familiar with:

- **Social networks:** Facebook, Twitter, LinkedIn
- **Social media sharing networks**: Instagram, Snapchat, TikTok, YouTube
- **Discussion boards:** Quora, Digg, Reddit
- **Content creation networks:** Flipboard, Pinterest
- **Consumer reviewing networks:** TripAdvisor, Yelp, Zomato
- **Blogging networks:** Tumblr, Medium, WordPress
- **Social shopping networks:** Etsy, Polyvore, Fancy
- **Interest networks:** Goodreads, Houzz

People have never been more linked, connected, or bound to technology as a society. Is this virtual reality something you could live without? Your answer might be no, especially if your school or workplace requires that you engage in some form or fashion of social media. Even in elementary school, students prepare avatars of themselves to participate in online lessons. It's hard to get away from social media, and I do not see it going anywhere anytime soon, so I want to have an honest conversation about how to manage its role in your life.

Finding a balance

In the social media world, you may feel bright, pretty, and shiny by posting all of the perfect pictures and great news in your life. But is everything you post your true self, or just a fantasy you are expertly preparing for the world to see? If you find yourself making your 20th carefully curated post for the day, you might think twice before posting it. You must maintain a healthy balance between the virtual world and the real world. You cannot lose your sense of self. If you do, you will lose all of your hard work regarding your goals, values, character, and your real priorities. Some people use social media to create something that they are not. Life is not about the number of likes you get; it's about authentic relationships.

WARNING

Be careful! Social media may become distracting enough that you will want to avoid all of your actual life issues.

TIP

If you feel yourself beginning to slip too far into the cyberworld, try to "unplug" for a day or so to reset your true identity.

Here are some tips to keep it real as you're using social media:

- Don't compare yourself to others' posts on social media, especially celebrities. They have a whole team working to make them look amazing in all of their posts. Ever heard of filters?
- Set a limit to your time on social media. Most of us probably spend at least an hour a day on social media, a little bit here and a little bit there. If you had that time back, you could work on the bigger goals you have in life. Most devices have a timer or alarm you can set to tell you when you have gone over your allotment for the day. Go ahead, set it up today!
- Being "liked" is not the be-all and end-all. It's OK to want people to like your posts, but it is not OK to keep refreshing your feed every 30 seconds to see who has liked your post. Don't try to gain all your confidence and approval from social media. Remember, you need to be happy with yourself first before giving that control to others.
- Those you love and care for the most deserve your attention first. Put your real-life roles before social media. When you are out to dinner with your family or friends, put the phone away. Stay in the moment, or you might miss the best time of your life.

REMEMBER

Social media has many advantages, but with those advantages come just as many disadvantages. Make sure you balance the positives with the negatives.

Capturing your success

Social media and having an online presence is not going away. If anything, it is more important than ever to have a version of your real, authentic self online. Way more people than you think are looking at your social media account.

For example, if you're applying for a job soon, the first thing the company will do is look you up on social media. I don't know about you, but I want potential employers to see me in a positive light. Here are some things to remember about crafting a presence on social media platforms:

- **Your online trail will follow you for the rest of your life.** If you have any inappropriate posts, delete them from public view immediately. If you want to save them for the memories, you can always archive them on Instagram or save them to your memories on Snapchat. Ask yourself, "Do my old posts mirror the views I have today?" If the answer is no, you have some cleaning up to do.
- **Deactivate old accounts.** I am so glad social media wasn't around when I was in middle school, but it might have been when you were. You could very well have a YouTube account from middle school. If this makes you cringe, a future employer will probably cringe as well. Deactivate it immediately!
- **The first thing that pops up when people search for you online is your cover photo or profile photo.** Make sure it's appropriate. It doesn't have to be a professional photo or anything like that, but something presentable is perfect. As you become more of an adult, avatars are not a good look either.
- **Update your email addresses and handles.** `Lovergirl94@gmail.com` or @toughguy99 is not the best representation of yourself in the adult world and looks pretty out of place on a resume. Something with your actual name in it is best.
- **Remove any accounts you have with shady websites.** We are prompted almost daily to create a new account for something. If you created an account with a website without intending to do so, delete that account.
- **Don't be too quick to "share" that controversial article or post.** The whole internet doesn't need your opinion on controversial topics — especially ones that a future employer might look down upon. Again, finding that balance is crucial.
- **Update your "friends" and who you follow.** People make judgments about you based on who you hang out with. Ever heard of "guilty by association"? It's the same idea online. Instead of following the friend from a long time ago who constantly posts inappropriate content, find someone who fits more into your adult view on topics. I have seen employers pass on individuals solely based on who their friends were and who they followed. Yikes!

» **Share positive times in your life.** Do you like to volunteer? Share that! I am not saying that you should carefully create fake positive events, but you can share content you are proud of. Doing this can help build respect.

Staying linked

LinkedIn (`https://linkedin.com`) is possibly the most popular website for professional profiles. LinkedIn offers job searches, networking, the ability to follow entities of your choosing, and much more. Employers choose LinkedIn to look for potential employees, investment ideas, and networking opportunities. It's important to have an online professional presence on a site like LinkedIn.

Here are some ways to succeed with a LinkedIn or similar professional profile:

» Make sure your profile picture is a recent picture of you. This is a place where a more professional photo would be appropriate.

» Have a headline and a summary of yourself. This is your chance to brag about yourself and your abilities.

» Grow your network. Most sites like LinkedIn allow you to link your email address book. This way you can find those you already know on the network.

» List the relevant skills and services you offer.

» Reach out to other professionals to endorse you on the site.

» Complete LinkedIn learning courses. This shows you are willing to continue to learn and grow as a professional.

» Share and add comments on the LinkedIn feed. This shows you play an active part in the online networking process.

REMEMBER

Keeping up in a changing world can be overwhelming at times, but it is important to consider. Within the real world and the virtual world, you have rights and responsibilities as an adult. Don't take that lightly. Guard yourself by understanding and applying online safety tips. Most importantly, stay yourself. You are the only one of you in the world, so stay real!

2

Dating, Relating, and Communicating

IN THIS PART . . .

Find out how to make new friends and maintain old friendships with people who have your best interest in mind.

Figure out your new adult role within your family and figure out how to create a strong bond for life.

Figure out how to create purposeful romantic relationships by showing trust, openness, and reliability. Navigate the world of dating through dating apps and organized events or in your day-to-day life.

Use your body language, your voice, emails, texting, and social media to communicate your message to others.

IN THIS CHAPTER

» Understanding why friendship is important

» Identifying people who aren't true friends

Chapter 4
Making New Friends While Keeping the Old

Humans are social creatures. Friends can offer much needed companionship and support as well as help improve your self-confidence and worth. Having friends helps increase your sense of belonging and purpose in life. I know it is not always easy to develop new friendships and maintain old ones, but it can be done. In this chapter, I cover how to develop and nurture long-lasting relationships.

Recognizing the Importance of Friendship

Friendships can enhance your life in various ways. Good friends can help challenge you to be a better version of yourself. Friends can encourage you in many aspects of your life and support you when times get tough. Friendships are good for your health and well-being, can provide emotional support, help build your confidence, and help combat stress.

I'll bet throughout your life you have had many friends. Some friendships may have been long-lived, whereas other friendships have trailed off as you've grown apart. The important factor is not about the quantity of friends you have but the quality of friends. A good friend will stick with you through thick and thin. They also allow you to be your true self around them and love you for who you uniquely are. It's great when you can find a friend like that.

Friendships fall into different categories based on the strength of the bond between the people involved:

- An *acquaintance* is someone you know and communicate with but do not have a close bond with. You probably do not spend much social time with an acquaintance.
- A *good friend* is someone with whom you share common interests. You like to hang out socially with good friends and enjoy spending time together.
- One or two of your good friends might turn into *best friends*. These friends are the ones with whom you share your deepest thoughts and feelings. You also seek their advice when you face tough times.

The work of being a good friend

Most of the time, making friends will come naturally. Friendships will develop wherever you spend most of your time. If you spend several days a week at the gym, you will meet like-minded people there. This statement is also true of the workplace, schools, places you volunteer, and social scenes.

You are likely to form a friendship with someone who has the same personality type as you. When people think and act alike, they usually enjoy being together. You want to develop friendships with those who have similar personal priorities as you. Being a good friends means you must demonstrate

- Kindness
- Empathy
- Dependability
- Loyalty

WARNING

Peer influences can be very strong. Consider your current friends and whether they have a positive influence on you or they persuade you to go against your morals. Friends should be mutually beneficial rather than dragging each other down.

The art of meeting new people

You have to put some work into making friends. In other words, you have to be open to meeting new people and forming friendships with people from different backgrounds. Through these friendships, you will learn more about each other's cultures, religions, beliefs, and customs.

One way to make friends is at an event where you don't know anyone. It can be stressful, but try to make yourself approachable. No one wants to be rejected, so if someone makes an effort to talk to you, make sure you receive them warmly.

Here are some things to remember when meeting new people:

» Show others you're interested in them.

» Focus on the conversation.

» Ask questions.

» Remember names when people introduce themselves.

» Provide feedback to keep the conversation going.

» Remain open-minded.

» Be yourself.

» Don't give up!

TIP

You do not have to wait for someone to make the first move to strike up a conversation. You can approach other people. Who knows, maybe a lifelong friendship will begin!

Squad goals!

Can you imagine living alone for the rest of your life? Or even worse, being the last person alive on Earth? How long would you last? Human beings are not meant to be alone. Companionship has always been a part of human nature. The older you get, the more you realize that friends are not just people you hang out with for fun. Friends can become more like family — people you do life with. Friendships can increase your life expectancy and help you survive tough times.

There are many benefits — too many to count — to having a true friend. Here are a few:

- You have someone to share your life experiences with. When something awesome happens, you naturally want to tell someone. A true friend is genuinely excited for you.
- A good friend is a confidence booster. Friends will realize if your full potential is not being used. They will help you believe in yourself.
- Laughter is the best medicine. A friend will help you overcome your stress, let you vent your anger, and help you laugh it off.
- A friend can help you maintain good habits. Research shows that positive support from your friends can even help you quit bad habits like smoking and drinking.
- You have someone to help make tough decisions. Seeking a friend's advice can give you a different perspective.
- There is someone there during times of grief. When a sad event occurs in your life, having the comfort of a friend reminds you of a bigger picture and can help you adjust to a new normal.

A friend in need is a friend indeed

Treating people the moral way is vital to any relationship. That means treating your friends with honesty, kindness, and compassion goes a long way. Remember the golden rule: Treat others the way you want to be treated. If you treat people with respect and go out of your way to help your friends, they will return the favor. The following scenario illustrates what it means to be a true friend to someone:

> Scott is a schoolteacher who goes above and beyond to help his friends in need. Just the other day, Scott's friend needed help with academic work. Scott took time out of his day and used his talents as a schoolteacher to ensure his friend was tutored to an A+. The next morning, Scott's car would not start. Bummer! It just so happened that the friend Scott tutored on schoolwork is a mechanic. Scott called up his friend, who took time out of his day to help get the car started.

The mechanic friend might not have taken time out of his busy schedule to help Scott if Scott hadn't made time to tutor him the day before. Friendship is about giving of yourself. Eventually, you will form a network of support around you with friends you live your life with.

TIP Sharing your talents and abilities with your friends pays off in the long run.

A healthy friendship

A healthy friendship requires mutual effort from both sides. Here are some tips for maintaining a healthy friendship:

- Communicate with one another, truthfully.
- Give each other space if needed or when requested.
- Make an effort to be there for your friend when they need you the most.
- Don't call your friend out in front of people; wait until you are alone with them to give constructive criticism.
- Be transparent with your intentions.
- Do not judge your friend.
- Listen.

REMEMBER Being yourself and treating others the way you want to be treated is a vital part of having a healthy friendship.

Recognizing Fake Friends

The world isn't full of only people who can be your friends. In fact, some individuals might be just the opposite. Some people do not want to see you succeed and do not treat others with respect.

There are some telltale signs that people might be using you. Here are some red flags that someone is a fake friend:

- They speak to you in a demeaning way and are discouraging.
- They never really listen to anything you say or your point of view. They only want you to listen to them and their issues.
- They are not there when you need them most.
- They magically show up if they need something from you.
- If you have a great achievement, they are jealous.
- You feel drained or exhausted after hanging out with them.

- They share your secrets and talk about you behind your back.
- They are disrespectful to you.

Do any of your friends exhibit these signs or behavior? If they do, they might be "fake" friends. It's probably time to move on and end the friendship. Not all friendships last forever. If you're in a friendship that is not healthy and constructive, be direct. Giving honest reasons about leaving the friendship instead of blaming the other person can help it end positively. Focus on you and your feelings, not on the other person and what they have done. After all, you might have to continue to be around this person, now in the form of an acquaintance.

Peer influence

Have you ever been in a situation where you felt uncomfortable with what was happening in your friend group, but you went along with it anyway, just to fit in? Or maybe a friend posted their engagement pictures on Instagram, and you immediately thought to yourself, *I am behind in life; all of my friends are moving on and great things are happening for them.* You may have either gotten anxious and immediately started working on a plan to be like them, or you got depressed.

Unfortunately, it's easy for people to get caught up in comparisons with other people, which only leads to a negative self-image. It's time to stop the comparison game. Everyone is on their individual path, running their own race. Yours will look different and be unique from anyone else's. Do not get caught up with comparing yourself to others. You will end up chasing invisible standards that are set by other people trying to run a different race than you.

TIP

It's great to have friends who are older than you. They can provide life experience and help guide you if you get off track. After all, they have already been through it.

The friend/acquaintance paradox

You may be wondering what the difference is between a friend, an acquaintance, a colleague, a classmate, and a boss. Each classifies as a different type of relationship:

- **Friend:** This is where you get to let loose and relax. With your friends, you get to hang out and be social. This is a very casual relationship.
- **Acquaintance:** You might be a little more reserved around an acquaintance. This is your favorite barista at your morning coffee shop. You make small talk and enjoy pleasantries, but the relationship doesn't go much further than that.

- **Colleague or classmate:** This might be someone you spend a lot of time with at work or school, even up to eight hours a day! You enjoy their company and like working with them on projects, but you remain professional because you are at work. The people around you at work and school are important to your sanity. Sometimes colleagues might grow to be good friends outside of work; but maintain that professional relationship with them inside of the workday.
- **Boss:** First and foremost, your boss is your boss, not your friend. You are there to work. You need to maintain a line that shows professional respect toward your boss. Do not cross that line at the expense of being funny or trying to be liked. Your boss has a responsibility to the company, and crossing the line can be detrimental to your career.

TIP

Make mental notes of the standards expected of you professionally and the ones you have set for yourself personally. Let these notes guide your behavior in the many types of relationships you have.

Energy vampires

In your life, you will have many types of friends, all with different personalities. That is a good thing. Being around people who are different from you can help you learn about yourself.

But you may find that some friends or other people you're around have some undesirable qualities. Friends and family you love to be around might also have some needy or clingy tendencies, which can grow to be exhausting at times. Following are some techniques you can use to help keep needy friends at bay, while still having a close friendship:

- **Don't feel required to answer your phone calls immediately.** You have a life, and you're busy. I have seen people in line at the store with their hands full of groceries, or people in the middle of a conversation, but they still pick up their phone immediately when it rings. Maybe it was an emergency, and that's OK, but it's also perfectly fine to be busy doing something else and call back later. This shows your clingy friends and family that you value your time and will call them back when you can give them your full attention. Stay in the moment as much as you can.
- **Text messages can also wait for a response.** If you have a needy friend who constantly texts you with their issues, don't respond right away. Waiting at least 30 minutes to an hour before responding shows your friend that you have other priorities in your life.

- **Empathy, or the ability to put yourself in someone else's shoes, is a wonderful quality to have.** However, if you have a friend with a clingy personality, it's not a good tactic to use. Being nice is great, but don't be so nice that others take advantage of you. Don't cross that line.
- **Don't succumb to guilt.** A needy friend might want to hang out on a night you're busy or when you just don't feel like it. Feeling guilty is unnecessary. Being able to say no is freeing.
- **Say "no."** *No* is a complete sentence. You do not have to explain or apologize. People tell you no all the time, so don't feel bad about saying the same thing.

REMEMBER

Beware of the vampires! Those are the people who like to suck the life out of you. If you have people in your life who are needy and clingy, use the above techniques and come up with some on your own to help you manage those friendships. Friendships should be uplifting and encouraging. If you have tried different techniques to curb the clinginess and the person still refuses to be respectful of you, it might be time to move on.

Time to move on

Ending a friendship might be hard, but there are reasons friendships need to draw to a close. If you're unhappy or feel like the friendship is taking from your life rather than adding to it, you may need to walk away. It might even be that you just don't feel like you have the same connection with a person as you had in the past.

Ending a relationship with someone you've considered a real friend can be challenging. The following behaviors in a friendship scream, "It's time to end the friendship!"

- **The friendship is one-sided.** You are working at the friendship, pouring out all your energy into social invitations, moral support, and so on, only to realize that the energy does not go both ways. A mutual friendship is a two-way street.
- **The friend betrayed you.** Any relationship has minor incidents that affect trust. If the friend is remorseful, you may want to give them another chance, but a lot of minor incidents can add up. Major incidents are red flags, and most likely you will want to disconnect immediately. If the betrayal is big enough, ghosting, not speaking to the person, is effective.

REMEMBER

If one person in the friendship is hurt by the other, it's extremely difficult to gain back trust. Make sure that you're treating your friends with the same respect you expect of them so that you are not the one doing the betraying.

- **You have nothing in common.** People grow and change. You might be the exception, but I did not remain best friends with my kindergarten bestie. Our likes and dislikes change; therefore, the people we are around change. It's normal for friends to drift apart.
- **Drama, drama, drama.** You know those friends who drama follows wherever they go. If there is no drama or conflict, they create it, and guess who is inevitably sucked into it. *You.* You will get to a point in your adult life where drama is a waste of your time. (Hopefully, after reading this, you can recognize drama in people a little easier.) Living in this chaos can be unhealthy and overwhelming. You do not need the extra drama in your life. Adulting is hard enough on its own.
- **You feel worse after being around them.** You may have a friend who constantly throws verbal jabs at you. They may mock you but then say, "JK." If you're at a point where your friend has turned completely negative and pessimistic, it might be time to end the relationship. You should feel better after being with your friends, not worse.

When it's time to end the friendship, what exactly do you say? While it could feel awkward, it's important to talk about it and make your feelings known. The following phrases can help you move on:

- "Thanks for inviting me to the party, but I feel like it just isn't my scene anymore."
- "I need to start putting myself first; this friendship isn't healthy."
- "The past few times we have hung out together, I have left feeling exhausted and angry. I think it's time to spend some time apart."
- "In the past year we have both grown and changed, but in different directions."
- "I just need some space right now."
- "I still care about you, but I cannot focus on our friendship right now. I have to put myself first."

REMEMBER

Be direct with your words. Speak up for yourself. (Read Chapter 2 for more about that.) You're worth it! If a friendship is causing you more harm than good, it's time to move on.

WARNING

If you find yourself in an emotionally or physically abusive friendship, seek professional help immediately at the National Domestic Violence Hotline, `https://www.thehotline.org/`.

IN THIS CHAPTER

» Understanding family roles and accountability

» No two families are alike

» Working through crisis in the family

Chapter 5
You'll Always Be Their Kid: Family Dynamics

I don't know about you, but I'm getting a little hungry, so let's make some sugar cookies! You need butter, sugar, flour, eggs, vanilla, salt, baking soda, and baking powder. Here is what each ingredient is used for:

- The butter provides tenderness in the dough.
- The sugar is for flavor and browning.
- The flour is for structure.
- Eggs bind the ingredients together and provide leavening.
- Vanilla and salt are for flavor.
- Baking soda and baking powder are to ensure the cookies rise and do not stay flat.

You need more than just the ingredients to make a cookie, though. Each part must be intertwined and mixed together to form a whole cookie. If even one part does not do its job or is forgotten, the cookie will not be the same and will not come together as it should.

The cookie is an analogy for how you can think about families. Each person has a role and responsibility within their family. If each role is not carried out, families could suffer. In this chapter, I talk about families and the part you play to make yours a whole. (If you want to make some cookies or snacks, check out Chapter 17!)

Understanding Roles and Responsibilities in Families

A family works together to be better as a whole, and each person is a special part of their family that makes it unique. While you're with your family, you laugh, you cry, and you learn together. Young children are very egocentric; everything is about them and they don't give much consideration to others. That is the nature of human development. The older you get, the more you should try to think of yourself as part of "us" and not just "me." Whatever you do affects other people in your life, especially your family.

TIP

Think about some ways you can make your family's day a little bit brighter. Once you come up with an idea, try it out! It might make your day brighter too.

One truth of every culture is that families are the building blocks of society. Families have children and help them grow and learn to become independent adults who form their own families. The process of growing individuals doesn't just happen overnight. Here are some functions families perform:

- Providing basic necessities
- Giving emotional support to one another
- Teaching values
- Passing on traditions and culture

REMEMBER

There are many different types of families. You may not have a biological family that has provided basic functions for you, but you may have found a family within your friends. Each family is different, and your upbringing is part of what makes you unique.

Playing your part

People within a family have certain roles and responsibilities. Mother, father, child, older brother, and younger sister are all roles you might play. Within a family, a person has multiple roles. You can be a son and also an older brother and also a student. You could be a mother and also the primary wage earner. Each role has expectations associated with it. As you move into adulthood, your roles and responsibilities within your family will likely change. For example,

- If you live at home with your parents, your role might be to pick up after yourself and pitch in with chores and cleaning and other responsibilities deemed necessary regarding your family situation.
- When you do not live at home anymore, your responsibility to your family may be to check in at least once a week to discuss what has been going on in your life and see what has been happening at home.

REMEMBER

Even if you have begun your own family, it's still important to stay connected to your guardians and those who raised you. Sharing parts of your life with them once a week means more than you know.

TIP

You can add a positive aspect to your family through your actions and behaviors.

Navigating the family life cycle

Families are constantly changing. There are five stages that families go through.

The beginning of the life cycle stage is the *independence stage*. Being single and independent on your own is the most common lifestyle for people in their 20s. To some, this independence is the first sign of adulthood. You live on your own for the first time, have a steady job to earn an income, buy your own food, purchase your own car, and do most life-management tasks on your own for the first time. You also begin to emotionally separate from your parents and develop unique qualities that define who you are. During this stage

- You realize your parents were smarter than you'd previously given them credit for (and maybe are even geniuses!).
- You begin to see yourself as separate from your family and extended family.
- You begin to develop intimate relationships with people outside your family.
- You set your own goals and establish yourself in your work or career.

TIP

Once a person has emotionally separated from their parents, they may choose to skip the coupling, parenting, and launching stages. Remaining single is a popular and perfectly acceptable option!

The middle of the life cycle stage includes three stages:

» **Coupling or marrying:** During this stage, a person finds a romantic partner to settle down with, most likely moving in together. All of the new skills and qualities you learned about yourself in the independence stage are now addressed in your ability to commit to a new family. Some views and habits you might need to adjust include

- Putting someone else's needs first
- Handling finances
- Engaging in activities and hobbies
- Managing in-law relationships
- Expressing sexuality
- Interacting with friends and friend groups
- Lifestyle

» **Parenting stage:** You and your partner have children. This stage is seen as the most difficult stage in the life cycle, but hopefully you have developed the skills you need in the previous stages to help your children learn them as well.

Adding children to the household brings about a large change in roles. Your identity begins to shift and how you relate to your partner and others adjusts as well. Joy comes with having children, but raising children also adds much stress. Your child's development, health, and safety depend on you. Here are some changes that will happen in this stage:

- You move into a parenting role.
- You adjust your relationships to make space for children.
- You must realign and reform relationships with the extended family including aunts, uncles, and grandparents.

» **Launching adult children:** This stage begins when the oldest child leaves the household and ends when all children have left, and it's otherwise known as the empty nest. Your parents may be in this stage as they watch you leave the house for the first time.

Parents in this stage need to adjust to an adult relationship with their grown children. It might take some time to form this adjusted relationship, but be patient; it will happen by as you and your parents reprioritize goals and roles. Some goals to focus on during this stage include

- Moving into an adult relationship with children
- Realigning life without children

- Shifting the lens back to yourself and your partner
- Properly caring for your elderly parents

The end stage of the family life cycle includes the retirement or senior years. This stage is looked at as a time in your life where you are free from the responsibilities you once had with children, and you can focus on the fruits of your labor throughout your career. Some goals for this stage in life include

- Rediscovering your interests on your own and with your partner
- Maintaining health and safety as your body ages
- Providing connections and support for your adult children and their families
- Caring for your elderly parents and supporting them as they grow older
- Dealing with the loss of loved ones, possibly including your partner
- Providing care and advice for others going through the same experiences you have gone through during earlier stages of your life

TIP

Understanding the family life cycle (see Figure 5-1) will help you recognize your own point of view as well as gauge the point of view of others who are at different places in life.

REMEMBER

You are in charge of your life. Choosing to remain single without children might be the best option for you, *or* you may choose to have a large family. Each person is unique and has different goals in life. Do what makes you thrive!

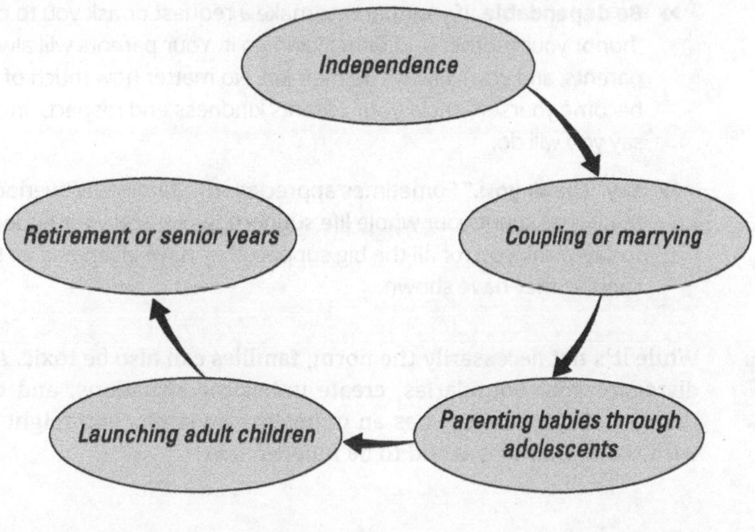

FIGURE 5-1: The family life cycle.

Getting Along

The differences within families can be a challenge to building a strong family. Within your family, I bet there are people of different ages, different genders, different likes, dislikes, activities, hobbies, commitments, abilities, and so on. When you put all these disparate pieces together within one unit, the dynamic can quickly get chaotic. How do all of these parts work as a whole and function properly?

It starts with you and your attitude. You can only control yourself, no one else. Having a positive outlook, controlling your anger, and taming your tongue will go a long way with your parents, siblings, and extended family.

The mother of all battles

At times, it may feel like a challenge to get along with your parents or guardians, especially as you grow into an adult yourself. It's important to find ways to stay close. Here are some ways to do that:

- **Take time to understand others.** You are now moving into adulthood and are ready to understand your parents as people — not just as Mom and Dad but as actual people with beliefs, values, and their own experiences. Believe it or not, they were kids once, too. Take the time to find out about your parents' lives. It will help you see them as individuals. They are not just there for you and what you want. Listen to their experiences. You will quickly realize that they are experts, and you will need their help!
- **Be dependable.** If your parents make a request or ask you to do something, "honor your mother and father" and do it. Your parents will always be your parents, and you'll always be their kid. No matter how much of an adult you become yourself, show your parents kindness and respect, and do what you say you will do.
- **Say "thank you."** Sometimes appreciation in families is overlooked. Your family has spent your whole life supporting you and your endeavors. It's time to say thank you for all the big support they have given and all the small daily support they have shown.

TIP

While it's not necessarily the norm, families can also be toxic. A toxic family may disregard your boundaries, create unhealthy situations, and cause more stress than joy. If your family has an unhealthy dynamic, you might have to sever ties with them. Don't be afraid to be independent.

REMEMBER

You can seek help from a professional if your family situation is toxic and unmanageable. It's hard to cut necessary ties with people we love; a family therapist might be beneficial. You can find more information at this website — `https://www.psychologytoday.com/`.

Rivalry in the family

Rivalry in the family is common, and sibling rivalry involves competing for attention and love from parents. As with any relationship, it's important to try to have a positive outlook if you find yourself in this situation.

REMEMBER

You are your own person, so try not to fall into the trap of keeping track of siblings' awards and the treatment and compliments they receive from others (especially your parents). Siblings provide a unique relationship as you move into adulthood. They grew up the same way you did, so remember you are on the same side, and you can help guide each other through life.

Appreciating Families' Uniqueness

Your family may look different from other families. That is OK because each family is unique. Families vary depending on their cultural background and traditions. Some cultures have multiple generations living in one location and are more close-knit. Other families might value independence by encouraging their children to move out and live on their own.

Families who emphasize cultural history teach their children to carry out their traditions and beliefs as they grow more independent and teach them to stay in touch with their cultural heritage. If you learned family traditions, it's worth remembering them and passing them on to your own children if you have them one day.

Every family situation is different. Within these topics, "interprelating" is a good idea. That means to interpret the information according to your family experiences, then translate your goals to be applicable.

Differences in people's upbringing and families are what make life interesting. Can you imagine if we were all brought up the same? Life wouldn't have the same challenges, and might be — dare I say — boring!

Establishing strong families

Strong, successful, loving families do not just happen by mistake. It takes some effort on your part and your family's part to create a strong family. The following are some qualities of loving families:

- Have a growth mindset toward life and family
- Genuinely enjoy being together
- Demonstrate appreciation one another by showing it and speaking it
- Share the same values, morals, and goals
- Show commitment to one another
- Respect each other
- Listen to one another
- Give emotional support

TIP

You can add a positive aspect to your family through your actions and behaviors.

Appreciating the wisdom of your elders

Utilize your resources! No one understands a challenge or experience better than someone who has already been through it. Seek the advice of an older generation to help avoid crucial mistakes. Sometimes it's just nice to have the comfort of knowing that you will come out the other side of a challenging life event alive!

Here, I have compiled a list of advice from the older generation to create some "silver-haired wisdom":

- Don't be afraid of getting older.
- Always allow time for your family; there is no substitute for family.
- Don't let the sun set on your anger.
- Keep your mind sharp by continuing to learn new things.
- Travel, travel, travel while you can.
- Save money for retirement.
- If you do not like your job or career, leave and find a different path. Being happy is important.
- Stay healthy and treat your body well. You will wish you did later in life.

» Live your own life. Stop comparing yourself to others.
» Look a person in the eye when communicating with them.
» Treat others the way you want to be treated.
» Laugh it off.
» Give of your wealth and time to serve others.

Navigating Crisis in the Family

Changes and challenges are part of the normal highs and lows of life. Some changes can be exciting, such as a new job or promotion, whereas others can be scary, such as financial changes and illnesses.

Families experience major problems that can deeply impact family members. This is normal and you are not alone. Families might experience any of these issues in a lifetime:

» Adding new family members
» Moving
» Unemployment
» Homelessness
» Financial hardship
» Illness
» Death
» Separation or divorce
» Addiction
» Substance abuse
» Domestic violence
» Mental health
» The effects of infidelity
» Abuse or neglect
» Arguing parents
» Jealousy within the family

- Crime
- Adjusting to stepparents, stepbrothers, and stepsisters
- Generational differences

If these are happening or have happened in your family, you are not alone. It's not your fault. There are ways to cope with family challenges and to thrive in your life as an adult.

WARNING

If you are in an emotionally, physically, or sexually abusive family situation, seek solace from a trusted individual. Seek professional help immediately through the National Domestic Violence Hotline at `https://www.thehotline.org/`.

Functioning in the dysfunction

When families experience struggles, it's important to know strategies to handle difficult problems. Learning to cope takes time and effort, but it can be done. The following are some common situations that can take a toll on families, as well as some ways to keep moving forward:

- **When unemployment happens to yourself or a family member, normal feelings include anger, sadness, frustration, and low self-confidence.** These feelings are usually temporary and dissolve as the job hunt begins.
- **Homelessness exists all over the world and has become more common in recent years.** Poor economic conditions can lead to job loss, but it can also happen due to natural disasters. Some communities can help those with nowhere to go. Homeless shelters, food kitchens, and charitable organizations, such as the Red Cross and the Salvation Army, can offer a safety net.
- **If a family member becomes seriously ill, everyone in the family can become stressed and anxious.** One of the best ways to cope with a serious illness is to educate yourself about the illness and situation. This can help you better cope with and contribute to the daily needs of individuals. Pulling together as a family and showing compassion can create a stronger, unified family.
- **Separation and divorce cause the original family to undergo some major changes.** Children usually blame themselves for their parents' separation or divorce, but it's not the child's fault. Adults and children might feel isolated and lonely during this time, but many other people have experienced the same feelings. You are not alone.

  If you feel torn between two parents, do your best to spend the same amount of time with each one. Roles and responsibilities within the family might change. For example, if you are the oldest child, you might need to contribute to helping younger siblings more and complete more duties within the home. Sharing your feelings with parents or a counselor can help you come to terms with the new normal.

- **Addiction and substance abuse can break down a family quite quickly.** Some people who are dealing with addiction will do anything to get the drug they crave — even hurting their own family. Dealing with addiction is very trying for any family. You might live in constant fear, walking on eggshells, never knowing when abusers could begin irrational behavior. Financial issues become a problem and crime might ensue so that a person can gain the next hit. Recognizing the signs of addiction is the first step in getting help and coping with addiction. Staying detached from family members while also continuing to love them is sometimes necessary for them to get the help they need.
- **Abuse in the family is unfortunately common.** Jennifer grew up feeling worthless due to the emotional abuse from her mother. William physically abused his wife by punching and hitting her when he was angry. Sexual abuse happened when Julie was forced into a sexual activity with an adult, and neglect occurred when a toddler and baby were locked in an apartment alone with no food. There is no excuse for these types of abuse, which are severely damaging to the victim. If abuse is happening, speak up. Find sources within your community to contact in cases of abuse.

Family members can provide the help and support through their love and care, but sometimes gaining help outside of the family is just as important. The following list offers suggestions of people and places to turn to when you need to find help outside of the family:

- Extended relatives and friends
- State family violence programs
- The National Domestic Violence Hotline (https://www.thehotline.org/)
- National Child Abuse Hotline (www.childhelp.org)
- National Sexual Assault Hotline (www.rainn.org)
- National Center for Victims of Crime (www.victimsofcrime.org)
- National Coalition for the Homeless (www.nationalhomeless.org)
- National Center on Domestic Violence, Trauma & Mental Health (www.nationalcenterdvtraumamh.org)
- National Suicide Hotline (https://988lifeline.org/talk-to-someone-now/)

REMEMBER

Speak up to be an advocate for yourself. You *are* worth it!

Receiving a dreaded phone call

The monotony of the day ensues. You wake up, start the car, and drive to work. Same old, same old. You think to yourself, "I can't wait until the weekend. I am ready to see my friends and family and just relax." Life is good, work is good, family is good . . . then the phone rings. "I'm sorry to interrupt your day, but I have some news for you, and it isn't good."

How is it possible that with just one phone call, your life could drastically change? Life as you know it will never be the same. You can never really fully prepare yourself for a dreaded phone call. Death, a poor medical diagnosis, a miscarriage, a breakup, a job loss, or any other serious piece of bad news can cause a jarring and shocking effect in your life. How can you react and what can you do?

- **Let yourself be upset.** Do not avoid your emotions. Pushing them away and suppressing them can lead to much more stress later on. Your brain is equipped to handle bad news. Setting such news aside could add more tension.
- **Change your perspective.** After the bad news has sunk in, try to reframe your thinking to the more positive side of the situation. Identify the brighter side instead of only the negative.
- **Acquire resiliency.** If you tend to crumble when hearing bad news, don't worry, resiliency can be learned. Read Chapter 2 to see how goal setting and the grit factor can help.
- **Focus on your health.** If you have a healthy body, your mind can react to bad news more clearly.
- **Seek help and support.** There are people who love you and care for you. Open up to them and use their help and support when bad news happens.
- **Make a plan.** After coming to terms with the bad news, make a plan for moving forward. Every situation has different first steps, but being organized and having a plan will ease the chaos.

TIP

If you get bad news, take a deep breath and give yourself time to process.

WARNING

Try to stay calm to ensure you don't become impulsive and possibly worsen the situation.

IN THIS CHAPTER

» Working on changing your relationship status

» Knowing when it's love

Chapter 6

Bumbling through the Dating Scene

Changing your relationship status is a big deal. It takes time to master the art of relationships. It means learning about yourself first and what you believe in, then figuring out how your values relate to the people around you.

Finding the right person to walk through life with can seem overwhelming, but the strategies I share in this chapter can help you feel confident in your relationships. Let's first look at the complexities of finding and keeping a significant other.

Getting Out of the Friend Zone

Do you ever wish the love of your life would come sweeping through your door declaring their love? Don't we all! Instead, you are left to sort through multitudes of dating apps on your phone and comprehend a whole dictionary of dating lingo. It can be confusing and hard to figure out, but it all leads to the same thing: establishing a relationship.

Many relationships begin with people who start as friends, so the age-old adage of "love at first sight" may just be a dream. You are likely to make friends with people who have the same core values as you and your outlook on life, goals, and priorities are similar, which makes a great foundation for a romantic relationship. Being friends before dating allows you to get to know the person before stepping out of the friend zone and into a committed relationship.

Engaging in purposeful dating

Whether you're dating a friend or meeting someone for the first time, you need to understand your purpose for dating. Are you dating with marriage in mind? Are you dating for companionship? Most of the time dating helps you with the following things:

- Learning what you want in a relationship — what you do and don't like.
- Recognize your values. Sometimes you don't realize what is especially important to you until you compare it to someone else or find that someone is lacking in something that is significant to you.
- Meeting new and interesting individuals.

Figuring out where to meet people

When you've decided that you're ready to launch yourself into the dating scene, you have to figure out where to meet people to date. The following are some places you can meet new people:

- Use online dating apps. The vast array of online dating apps are a great place to meet other people who have the same intentions of dating, which takes some of the guesswork out the process. Bumble, Tinder, and Hinge are more casual in their approach. eHarmony and Match are the more serious relationships apps.

  Regardless of the app you use, beware that some people pretend to be something they are not. Catfishing, or creating a fake profile to mislead others, is a real thing and it happens more often than you think. Keep the following things in mind:

  - Avoid connecting with profiles that are halfway filled out, have only one photo, and include little information. This is a sure sign that it is a fake profile.
  - Before you go on a date with someone you have connected with, do a little research. Look them up on social media to see if you have mutual friends. A video chat with the person can also help confirm that what's in the person's profile is accurate.

- If you have a match and want to meet in person, tell a friend where you are going, make sure it is a public place, drive yourself there so you can leave if you need to, and trust your first impression. If you sense red flags at any point, get yourself out of there!

» **Notice the people around you when visiting your daily spots.** When you're getting coffee, put the phone down, look around, and strike up a conversation with someone. When you visit your regular dog park, put yourself out there and converse with others. If you aren't sure what to say to a stranger, start with a compliment. If you begin paying attention to your surroundings, you will be surprised by how many chances you have to interact with others. Don't let them pass you by.

» **Interact in class or at work.** You spend a lot of time in class or at work, so those are great places to interact with others. Most likely, the people you meet in those places have some of the same interests as you, so beginning a conversation should be easier than approaching someone in public. You'll most likely be assigned to work collaboratively on projects, which gives you time to get to know people.

» **Speak with people at social events.** Worship services and events, weddings, concerts, art shows, a friend's party, a 5k fun run, and really anything you like to attend that has other people are places to make an effort to meet someone. Any time you have an opportunity to meet new people, a new relationship can develop (see Figure 6-1).

FIGURE 6-1: Being open to meeting new people helps form new relationships.

WARNING

Using your phone to *find* a date is one thing, but overusing your phone when you are *on* a date is a turnoff. If you are face to face with a person, put your phone down, make eye contact, and truly listen to them.

TIP

Ask the person you are on a date with questions to get them to talk about themselves. This does two things:

» It allows you to get to know them better.

» Everyone loves to talk about themselves. Your date will associate that pleasant feeling with you and remember that they enjoyed your company.

  Here are a few questions you could ask:

  • Will you tell me a little bit about yourself?
  • Who are the special people in your life?
  • What is something fun you like to do?
  • Where is your favorite place on Earth?
  • What goals do you have in life?

TIP

Remember to ask open-ended questions, which means questions that leave the other person room to explain rather than simply answering yes or no.

WARNING

If you decide to pursue a relationship outside of the friend zone with a close friend, the friendship will never be the same.

Getting what you give

In any relationship, you get out of it what you put into it. In fact, for the relationship to be successful, mutual respect, or regarding each other with honor and admiration, is required. You cannot expect to agree on everything, but you can respect each other's right to differ. Building mutual respect is simple. Be kind, courteous, and thoughtful. Other ways to build respect for one another include

» **Trust:** Having confidence in people means you trust them. In a successful relationship, trust is a given. If trust is broken, even in the smallest way, it is hard to repair the relationship.

» **Openness:** When you are dating, it is important to create an atmosphere of openness. In other words, you and your significant other feel safe and free to share thoughts and feelings. It is hard to grow into a deep relationship with anyone if you are unwilling to tear down your walls and show them the real you.

» **Reliability:** If you say you will do something, do it. If you say you will be somewhere, be there. It is disrespectful to back out of your commitments.

WARNING

If the person you are dating does not show any of these qualities, it's time to end the relationship.

REMEMBER

Respect can mean giving others the benefit of the doubt. This also means not being too quick to judge.

Knowing When It's Time for Those Three Little Words

I love you.

Whoa, whoa, whoa! Let's slow things down a minute. I love you . . . already? We just met! I mean, I like you and all, but are we really in love?

There are some ways to tell the difference between love and other feelings. You probably get tired of people telling you, "When you know, you know." How can you tell you're in love if you don't know what to look for? There is plenty of information that can help you decipher the emotions you are feeling and determine whether they equate to those three little words.

"Stupid Cupid, stop picking on me!"

I bet at some point in your life you have felt like Cupid is picking on you. Your emotions are a jumbled mess, you find yourself thinking about one person *all* the time, and you cannot concentrate on your responsibilities. Is what you're feeling the real deal?

You may have done some group dating and some casual dating but find yourself wanting more. One thing you need to understand is the difference between love and infatuation. Infatuation is a short-lived, highly passionate admiration for someone. Here are some examples of infatuation, which can be one-sided or may be mutual:

» Having intense feelings for a social media influencer, a celebrity, or someone you have never met

» Being "in love" with what you imagine a person is like

- Centering on just a few admired traits of the person rather than the whole person
- Lacking reason
- Being selfish and possessive of the other person
- Occurring shortly after breaking up with another person — being "on the rebound"
- Being blinded to the truth and later wondering why you had those intense feelings for the individual

With infatuation, you want to spend every waking minute with someone, but if you're losing part of your independence, the infatuation is going too far. "I must have you with me every minute" is indicative of an infatuation, whereas "I cannot wait to spend time with you" speaks of love.

However, infatuation can lead to love. Relationships usually begin with a little bit of infatuation, but when the extreme feelings wear off, a relationship based on trust and respect can follow.

Love can be hard to define, but here are some examples:

- Love is
  - Committed
  - Positive
  - Kind
  - Selfless
  - Patient
  - Truthful
  - Hopeful
  - Faithful
  - Strong
  - Healthy
- Love is *not*
  - Jealous
  - Angry
  - Controlling

* Abusive
* Anxious
* Insecure
* Suspicious
* Toxic
* Harmful
* Prideful

Think about a relationship you might currently be in or one you have had in the past. Was it love or infatuation? Understanding the difference can help you recognize real love when you find it!

TIP

Rejection is a normal part of life and everyone will experience it one way or another. It is never fun, but it is only as hurtful as you let it be. Talking to someone about your feelings and being kind to yourself can help you move on. Rejection in dating can help you deal with other adverse situations in your life.

REMEMBER

Real love takes time and grows out of friendship and trust.

Types of love

Love is not just a feeling; it is a choice. Every day you wake up, you either choose to show love or choose the opposite.

When you are in a committed relationship, there are different types of love. Learning to love will help you prepare for a lifelong partner. The following types of love work together in a committed or marital relationship:

» **Altruistic love:** This type of love is compassion toward the well-being of another person or being present in a time of need.

» **Companionate love:** This is a type of love that includes a feeling of deep friendship. Mutual respect for one another and daily affection are priorities in this form of love.

» **Romantic love:** This is an emotional love where couples become devoted to one another through creating their own peace and happiness.

» **Sexual love:** This type of love is a physical extension of the intimacy and communication that a couple shares.

REMEMBER

All four of these types of love work together in a relationship to create a long-lasting unified connection.

WARNING

Don't confuse sexual love with casual sex. Casual sex is a physical act that does *not* include the intimacy and commitment of love. If you are partaking in sex, make sure you protect yourself against sexually transmitted diseases (STDs) and unplanned pregnancy. Casual sex is also known to take a toll emotionally on an individual. Take care of yourself!

Acts of love

When you love someone, whether it's romantic love or compassionate love, there are some great ways to demonstrate how you feel. It is not always easy to know how to act when you love someone, but here are a few ways to start.

- Give a gift. It doesn't even have to be a gift that costs money. A little something to let someone know you were thinking about them will do the trick.
- Brag about the other person to others.
- Learn how the person understands love the best. For example, do they like when you do something for them, or would they rather you spend quality time with them (see Figure 6-2)?
- Support them in their successes, decisions, and failures.
- Give a hug.
- Leave them a special note.
- Tell them you love them.
- Speak positively to them and use kind language.
- Say please and thank you.
- When the person gets home from work or school, actually get up, greet them, and say, "Hello, how was your day?"
- Try their favorite hobby with them.
- Be patient.
- Be there when times are tough.
- Accept them each day for who they are, not who you wish they were.
- Communicate often.
- Say you are sorry when you make mistakes.

- Put the phone down and spend quality time with them.
- Make eye contact.
- Recognize what they need and do it before they ask for it.
- Watch their favorite show with them.
- Give them time for self-care.
- Try new things together.
- Trust them.

FIGURE 6-2: Happily spending time together is an action of love.

REMEMBER

Love encompasses many emotions, including a feeling of warm, personal attachment and deep affection toward someone. Never take those you love for granted. Spend as much time showing your love to them as you can!

TIP

Make yourself available for love. Open up and work on showing your true self so others know how to show *you* love!

IN THIS CHAPTER

» Communication 101

» Sending unmixed messages

» Working through problems

Chapter 7 Saying What You Mean

Have you ever had a word or a phrase on the tip of your tongue, but you just can't remember what it is you want to say? Or maybe you needed to have a heart-to-heart conversation with someone, but you didn't know where to start.

Communicating is expressing what you feel, what you want, or what you need in a variety of ways. Maybe you are excited, so you shout from the rooftops! Maybe you are sad, so you slouch down in your seat, or maybe you are tired so you let out a huge yawn. All of these things send a message. It is up to you to decide if you want to send a positive or negative message.

In this chapter, I cover the basics of communication, including the different ways to communicate, conversation starters, email etiquette, solving conflicts, and texting and snapping. No matter how you communicate, it is important to look out for mixed messages.

Understanding the Basics: Communication 101

Verbal communication is speaking to communicate your thoughts. To some, verbal communication comes naturally, but others may not feel comfortable speaking in certain circumstances. You might get nervous speaking in front of large groups of people, or maybe you would just rather listen and observe when you're with your friends. This is perfectly normal, but for those situations when you *have* to talk, you need to be able to communicate what's on your mind.

The following are qualities of effective verbal communication:

» **Holding your tongue until you have thought about what you want to say.** Consider what points you have to share before opening your mouth. Steer clear of embarrassing yourself or hurting someone with your sharp tongue when you speak without thinking.

» **Speaking clearly.** When you have something to say, make sure you say it understandably. If you are in a habit of mumbling, try to pronounce each syllable carefully so others get what you are trying to say. Otherwise, people will tire of trying to decipher your words and will move on. Also, be respectful of the environment you are in. Do not talk too loudly when it is not warranted. Be mindful of the speed at which you are talking, as well. People will not be able to follow along if you are a speed talker and leave them in the dust!

» **Exuding a positive vibe.** Express yourself in a welcoming manner — warm and enthusiastic (see Figure 7-1). You do not want to be the negative person who is always complaining or criticizing others. Other people can find that exhausting to be around. People want to hang out with you if you are positive when you talk.

FIGURE 7-1: Exude a positive vibe when talking to others.

- **Knowing your audience.** I am willing to bet the way you talk to your close friends is different from the way you talk to your boss. Keep this in mind when communicating with different people and remember to remain appropriate with each audience.
- **Asking for feedback during conversations.** The only way you are going to know if someone is following along with what you say is by asking occasionally if they understand your point. You might say, "Does that make sense?"
- **Being aware of the give and take of a conversation**. There is a delicate balance between talking and listening. If you begin to hog the conversation and talk too much, your listener might get bored and stop paying attention.

Brushing up on conversation starters

It can be a little scary to begin a face-to-face conversation, especially with someone you just met. Beginning a new conversation by asking a question is a great way to show someone you are interested in them and to get the conversation flowing. Making "small talk" could lead to a more in-depth conversation. Questions to initiate a conversation include

- How is your day?
- What brings you here?
- Can you believe this weather?
- What type of music do you like?
- Seen any good shows lately?
- What is your favorite food?

If you show genuine concern for and interest in another person and how they answer the questions, a great conversation could begin flowing because they will feel like they are heard and in turn listen to you!

TIP

Believe it or not, everyone likes to talk about themselves. If you aren't sure what to say in a conversation with someone you just met, get them talking about themselves by asking questions. Before you know it, you'll have gotten to know that person on a deeper level, and they'll feel edified in the conversation with you.

Speaking without words

You don't need to talk to communicate; a smirk or a smile can say volumes! Communicating without words is called *nonverbal communication*. Body language is what your body is involuntarily or voluntarily doing to communicate. Facial expressions, body posture, arm gestures, and eye movement can show your true feelings about a topic.

Here are some examples of things body language can communicate:

- » Smiling with arms by your side means you are happy and ready to contribute.
- » Crossing your arms gives off a vibe that you are not interested in a topic, disagree, and are closed off to what is being said. I cross my arms a lot when I'm cold. If you're like me, it's important to be aware of what your posture might be conveying to other people.
- » Biting your nails or playing with your hair shows others that you are nervous or anxious.
- » Resting your hand on your cheek shows you are eager for knowledge or you are evaluating your thoughts.
- » Rubbing both hands together can mean that you have lost your patience or are nervous about what is to come.
- » Avoiding eye contact shows you could be guilty, shy, or bored.
- » Resting your head on your palms shows stress, sadness, or exasperation.
- » Tilting your head to one side shows interest in the topic being presented or curiosity.
- » Placing your hands on your hips show confidence and authority.
- » Be mindful the direction your feet are pointing. If they are facing the person you are talking to, it means you are interested. If they are facing away from the conversation, it means you are trying to get out of there!
- » Leaning away or back could mean disinterest or even fear.

WARNING

When your words do not match your nonverbal cues, you could be giving off mixed messages. What you truly think and feel will always find a way to show. After all, actions speak louder than words. However, if a physical or mental impairment keeps you from mastering these body language expectations, just do the best that you can.

Polishing your email etiquette

Whether in school, at work, or in personal life, you will need an email address to stay connected. You need an email address for most online accounts and activities, and, let's face it, you probably already have one email address, if not more. But if you haven't actually taken the plunge into the world of email, it can be tricky.

Emails are a way to send information to a person in a quick manner and are seen as more professional than a text. Emails can be used to send information or inquiries to your boss, ask your professor questions on assignments, or give life updates to your family. Whatever it is you are writing about in an email, you must remember your audience.

Here are some steps to help guide you with writing a proper email:

1. **Ask yourself if the information you are sending is appropriate in an email.**

   Should you communicate in person, via FaceTime, or make a phone call instead? For example, if you have bad news to communicate, a face-to-face conversation would be better.

2. **Use the subject line.**

   You should include a short purpose for your email in the subject line so the receiver knows what to expect. This could help you get a faster response because the recipient will be more apt to read your email if they have an idea of what it is concerning.

3. **Use proper titles for who you are addressing.**

   Formally address others unless they have given you permission to do differently. Use Mr., Mrs., Ms., Dr., Professor, and so on.

4. **Do not assume the receiver knows who you are.**

   Identify yourself and the purpose of reaching out.

5. **Organize your email logically.**

   Start with a greeting first; then have a beginning sentence that expresses the purpose of your message. List your key points, including your important ideas first, and then conclude by showing appreciation for their time.

Writing a good email requires more finesse than just knowing how to write the beginning, middle, and end. The following are characteristics of and guidelines for well-written email communication:

- **Have one topic per email.** Long-drawn-out emails are more likely to get buried in an inbox.
- **Avoid using all capital letters to get your point across.** ALL CAPS IS THE EQUIVELENT OF YELLING. This is very rude in an email.
- **Use diplomatic, positive, and professional language.** Carefully craft your email when you have had time to think and reflect on what you want to say.

- **Never compose an email when you are upset or angry.** Wait until you calm down before writing or sending an email. If you need to write out your feelings, do so on a piece of paper to get them out of your system.
- **Items you write in an email should also be things you would say in person.** If you cannot say something to someone's face, you shouldn't write it either.
- **Check your spelling and grammar.** Nothing screams *unprofessional* like misspelled words, incorrect grammar, slang, or emojis. Reread your email before you send it to make sure it gets your message across.
- **Review who it is addressed to.** Is it the right person? Did you include the attachment? Are you sure you want to send it? Once you send it, it's gone.
- **Give plenty of time for a response and be patient to hear back.** People are often busy, and they may not be able to reply to your email immediately after receiving it. If you haven't heard a response within three to four days, it is OK to send a polite reminder email.

REMEMBER

Use good judgment when deciding whether to send an email or speak in person.

Texting, snapping, and chatting

You have the world at your fingertips and can stay in constant contact by texting or using other apps. Texting is usually pretty informal; you might text your friends or family throughout the day. It is important to take into consideration who you are texting and communicating with. Incorrect grammar, slang, and emojis are acceptable with some people, but your parents might need proper grammar and less slang to understand what you are trying to say. Don't let your message get lost in translation.

Apps for communicating with other people are constantly changing and improving the way we communicate with each other. Apps make it very easy to send videos, stories, and photos with the press of a button. But beware, whatever you choose to send should still be thought out completely because once sent, it remains in rotation forever.

WARNING

You may send a text, video, or photo to one person, but they may not be the only person to see it. People often forward messages on to other people, and that's how photos and videos become viral. If you are sending sensitive information, make sure you trust the receiver to save it for their eyes only!

Hearing AND listening

Half or more of any conversation is listening. I mean truly listening, not just thinking about what you are going to say next. This skill takes some work, but it is imperative for anyone with good communication skills. Hearing is the physical act, but active listening is absorbing what you're hearing and responding with your full attention. Active listening includes both verbal and nonverbal feedback:

- » Verbal feedback is saying things to the speaker like "Yes," "Okay," or "That sounds good."
- » Nonverbal feedback involves nodding your head in agreement, making eye contact, or shaking your head when you are not sure what is being communicated.

TIP

People will begin to converse with you more and feel like they can trust you if you learn to show that you are genuinely interested in what they are saying. This is done by giving verbal or nonverbal feedback during conversations.

If you think you might be struggling as an active listener, here are some ways to improve your skills:

- » Really hear what is being said. Don't sacrifice listening by thinking of your comeback while the other person is talking.
- » As the speaker is talking, try to interpret what they are saying. If you have interpreted their message correctly, then you fully understand what they are trying to say. This is very important in any relationship. Many times we "interpret then translate" (or "interprelate," as I like to say) it into what we *want* to hear instead of what is *actually* said. This could be dangerous.
- » Evaluate the words spoken. Do not evaluate the person. Preconceived ideas or stereotypes should not get in the way of your evaluation.
- » Responding to the speaker is vital. Something as simple as nodding your head helps edify the speaker and lets them know you are following along. If you aren't quite sure what the speaker means, try rephrasing and repeating back what they said in your own words to see if you are still tracking correctly.

Sending Mixed Messages

Many messages might include interference for a multitude of reasons. It's up to you to remove any barricades that might block effective communication. Watch out for the following things in your communication:

- Lies, gossip, threats, or insults will close the line of communication and often ruin relationships.
- A preaching or a fault-finding attitude can include statements such as "Why can't you just get it together?" or "Why don't you ever take out the trash?" This is the verbal equivalent of someone pointing their finger in your face while tapping their foot. Always having something negative to say will cause people to avoid you at all costs.
- An egotistical attitude means that you are not open to other people's thoughts and ideas. If it isn't about you, then you are not interested. Keep in mind there is always more than one way to look at a situation and be open to other people's perspectives.
- Sarcasm can confuse listeners; it expresses a tone the opposite of what you are saying. Sarcasm usually ends up hurting people and prevents open communication. It is especially hard to decipher in written communication. Just say or write what you mean how you mean it!
- Interrupting is very rude. I bet you've been interrupted at some point and know that it's hurtful and frustrating. Let others finish what they are saying before butting into the middle of their point. If you find yourself being interrupted by others, say, "Thanks for your input, but I would like to finish what I was saying first." Hopefully, they will get the idea and stop interrupting.

It's all in the delivery

The way you speak is just as important as what you say. The same sentence can mean different things when you emphasize different words.

Try saying, "I want to rest all day on Saturday," out loud four times but emphasize a different word each time:

- "I" the first time
- "Rest" the second time

- "All" the third time
- "Saturday" the last time

Did you notice the meaning of the sentence changed each time you said it? Your tone of voice also changes the meaning. Control your emotions when you communicate to help other people receive your message more clearly.

TIP

As you talk, try your best to make people feel welcomed and comfortable. This is called establishing rapport with your listener. For example, smiling and having your arms open while maintaining a respectful and enthusiastic tone creates a calm and pleasant atmosphere.

Arguably the best

Conflicts arise in everyday life (see Figure 7-2). Whenever your values clash with another person's values, it can create conflicts or disagreements. Sometimes it's hard to see another person's point of view, but that's exactly what is needed to help resolve conflicts positively. Otherwise, the results of the disagreement might become very negative. To gain positive results in an argument, each person must have mutual respect for the other, really try to listen, and have a commitment to solving the issue. Conflicts can sometimes even bring people closer together.

FIGURE 7-2: Conflict arises in everyday life.

Some causes of conflicts can seem trivial, whereas other conflicts brew for a while and become significant. The following list includes some possible causes of conflicts that you should be on the lookout for:

- Power struggles
- Environmental influences
- Personality differences
- Jealousy
- Prejudices
- Revenge
- Misunderstandings and poor communication
- Stress
- Drugs and alcohol

If you're attentive, you may be able to identify the early signs of potential conflict. Here are some changes in people that might indicate a conflict is brewing:

- **Body language and facial expressions:** Does the person seem more aggressive lately? Do they make faces of disgust or disappointment?
- **Behavior changes:** Does the person remain silent when they would normally be outgoing?
- **Lack of tolerance:** Does the person no longer care about respecting other people's views and values?
- **Out-of-character remarks:** Does the person make strange comments that don't make sense to you?
- **Cliques forming:** Does the person hang out with different people and begin to exclude others from that group?
- **Emotions spilling Out:** Does the person seem more emotional than usual without being able to explain what is wrong?
- **Starting arguments:** Does the person try and initiate arguments with blatant name-calling or threats?

When you can answer yes to these questions about another person or yourself, there could be external or internal conflict brewing!

REMEMBER

Sometimes the conflict might not be about you at all, but rather an internal conflict of another person spilling out onto you. Getting to the root of the issue is what is needed for all parties to move forward.

Peacekeeping

If there is an argument, fight, or conflict, what is the best way to approach solving the issue? Well, first you need to ask yourself, "Is this worth the fight?" For example, if you are never going to see the person again, a difficult situation is probably worth walking away from. Walking away is not a cowardly position, especially if you are in danger of some sort. Arguments might become violent if they are left to escalate, so walking away in that instance is best for your health and well-being.

Here is a common conflict scenario:

> Elsie and Bonnie have been living together as roommates for the past two months. Unfortunately, things have been a little bumpy. The two have been best friends for many years, but have never lived together, so they are continuing to learn new things, good and bad, about one another. Elsie values a clean and tidy apartment, but it is not a priority for Bonnie. Bonnie leaves her clothes and dirty dishes all over the place. But whenever Bonnie brings home her groceries, Elsie digs in and eats them as her own. Bonnie even caught Elsie enjoying the last scoop of ice cream! They still have ten more months on the lease, so they need to resolve these conflicts.

Conflict resolution allows both people to come to a solution together. Let's walk through this process using Bonnie and Elsie's situation as an example:

1. **Define the problem.**

   Each person shares their version of the problem. Elsie and Bonnie see each other as disrespectful when dishes are left everywhere and food is eaten without permission being asked.

2. **Suggest solutions.**

   Each person gets to say what they think should happen to solve the problem. Elsie thinks Bonnie should pick up after herself and keep everything clean. Bonnie thinks Elsie should eat her own food.

3. **Evaluate solutions.**

   Each person evaluates the presented solutions to see if they are plausible. Bonnie doesn't see an issue with keeping the common spaces clean but would like to leave her own room messy if she wants. Elsie understands that she should only eat the groceries she buys, but if she is in a bind, she can ask Bonnie.

4. **Compromise.**

   If each party is close to an agreement, they can compromise. In other words, Elsie might compromise by agreeing to allow Bonnie to keep her personal room messy, and Bonnie might compromise by allowing Elsie a snack now and then.

5. **Work with a mediator.**

   If both groups cannot reach a compromise, a mediator can come in to bring a fresh approach. In this case, Elsie and Bonnie bring in a friend to help them agree on a plan moving forward. The friend even suggests they create a roommate contract that will help them both feel respected and heard.

REMEMBER

It is perfectly normal to get angry during a conflict. Try to control your anger by exercising, talking it out, or taking some deep breaths. Wait until your anger has calmed before working through the conflict resolution process.

Solving Problems: It's a Process

Houston, we have a problem. OK, it may not be that dramatic, but when an issue arises, do you know what to do? Imagine you locked your keys in your car. You could just sit there and wait for it to unlock magically, or you could problem-solve by calling a family member with an extra key to come help.

Problem-solving is about taking charge of your situation. You can control how you react to the things happening around you and form your next steps by applying the problem-solving process. Here's what you need to do to take initiative and to problem-solve issues big and small:

1. **Define the problem.**

   What exactly is the problem? How long has it been going on? How did you discover the problem?

2. **Find clarity.**

   What extra information do you need to understand the problem fully, and how can you get that information? What is your end goal in solving this problem?

3. **Identify possible causes of the problem.**

   List all of the possible reasons you have an issue to help you determine what is the root of the problem.

   WARNING

   If you skip this step, the problem might only get a bandage, not a full fix.

4. **Create an action plan.**

   What actions can you take to address the problem and keep it from growing? Assign yourself a timeline for taking action.

5. **Take action.**

   As hard as it might be, put one foot in front of the other and step out of your comfort zone. Taking action is hard to do. Many people like to sit around and talk about their problems, but actually executing plans to solve the problem is another story. Here are some tips for taking action:

   - Keep the end in mind. Just think how great it will be when you have this problem behind you!
   - Start small. Even a small step is a step in the right direction.
   - Stop waiting until everything is perfect. Life isn't perfect and it never will be. That is what keeps it interesting.
   - Don't overthink things. If you begin to overanalyze the situation, it could paralyze you from moving forward. There are always a million reasons not to do something.

6. **Keep the momentum going.**

   Once you take action, keep moving in the right direction by reminding yourself that you are in charge of your choices and actions. Problem solving is never an easy path. Stick with it!

7. **Evaluate the results.**

   Did everything go as planned? What could you have done better?

8. **Keep improving.**

   Things might not have gone as planned when you were solving the problem; that's OK. You are going to make mistakes, but the key is not to repeat the same mistakes.

REMEMBER

Problem-solving is a process. It takes time, effort, and hard work. Just when you think you have life figured out, another curveball comes your way, and you have to start the process all over again.

WARNING

If you do not handle a problem when it arises, the problem could grow into a dangerous situation. Now that you have the tools to problem-solve, tackle your issues head-on so you can move forward.

3

Earning Enough to Live On

IN THIS PART . . .

Get out into society and contribute to something you love doing! Discover options available to you for careers and figure out how to snag a job that's right for you.

Understand the ins and outs of the career world so you can make a difference in your field.

Understand the particulars of receiving a paycheck, where your money comes from, how to handle it, and how to give back.

Create a budget for your money so you can determine what you can afford.

IN THIS CHAPTER

» Being the best you can be

» Making good career choices

» Getting hired

Chapter 8 It's Called Work for a Reason

What do you want to be when you grow up? That is the age-old mystery. Think back to kindergarten. Did you answer that question by saying a police officer, a teacher, or a doctor? Are you still on that path? Our kindergarten selves might not have realized the commitment and work it would take to become a police officer, a teacher, or a doctor, or maybe we just didn't know what would make us happy yet. Many people get to adulthood and still feel like they have no idea what to do with their lives. Don't worry if this is you; it's normal. You may not completely know how you will make money or how you will spend your adult days, but it's important to begin thinking about it now.

In this chapter, I cover how to discover a job path that matches your interests, the different types of skills needed for your career, and how to land the job.

Whatever You Are, Be a Great One

The world is a very productive place, with people learning, creating, problem-solving, and performing many types of jobs. Working gives you the opportunity to be productive with your time, which is valuable for your self-confidence. Working also offers many benefits, such as giving your life purpose and fulfillment.

There are different ways to classify work:

- **Job:** This means getting paid for your work.
- **Occupation:** This is a similar grouping of jobs.
- **Career:** This is a series of jobs or sometimes a progressive ladder of similar occupations over your lifetime. For example, you begin a job as a retail sales trainee, then progress to a sales specialist, then move on towards a sales rep, then maybe even the retail sales manager. Your job may begin in retail, and becomes a career when you stick with it and progress.

REMEMBER

The jobs you have and the career you choose will have a lasting impact on your adult life.

Someday is not a weekday

When you work, you help fulfill human needs by providing goods or services for other people to live on; you also generate income so you can buy goods and services for yourself. Being able to afford the items to live on gives you a sense of pride and accomplishment. When you work, you are not only helping yourself but also helping the community you live in.

Here are some reasons to work:

- **Money:** Let's face it; you need money for food, rent, and bills.
- **Independence:** Work helps you gain control over your own life.
- **Community:** For your well-being, live life with other people to gain a sense of belonging, and your place of work can be one place to find that community.
- **Purpose:** Work can provide a deeper meaning to life.
- **Enjoyment:** When your passions and skills collide, work can be enjoyable.

It's OK to put yourself out there, try new things, do great things, and work hard. Don't come up with excuses as to why you should work some other day. Do your part now. Waiting until "someday" to work or get your work done is a slippery slope. "Someday" is not a "weekday." If you consistently say, "I'll get to it someday," that day will likely never come. Do not wait until "someday" to pursue your passion; start now!

REMEMBER

Hard work requires commitment, even when you feel you'd rather be somewhere else. Also, most jobs require life-long learning, so be prepared to learn something new every day.

You do you

One of the best ways to figure out what interests you is to learn about yourself first. Check out Chapter 2 to really dive deep into discovering yourself and your values.

To understand the possibilities within the career world, you need to look inward as well. The more you understand your interests and skills, the easier it will be to pick your path.

Ask yourself, "What do I like to do?" (And I'm not talking about napping; we all know napping is amazing, but it doesn't really make for good full-time employment.) People who are the happiest in life choose jobs that they genuinely love; they may not even feel like they are working. I want you to be able to choose something you love to do and that mixes well with your abilities or natural talents. Some skills come naturally, but most of the time, a skill is something you need to learn and perfect.

Check out these online resources to help you determine your interests and how they could connect with your skills:

- **CareerOneStop:** `https://careeronestop.org/toolkit/careers/interest-assessment.aspx`
- **16personalities:** `https://16personalities.com/`

Keep in mind that your skills and interests are different. You may be interested in a specific career but not willing to put in the time and commitment it will take to learn the skills needed to be successful in the job. Here are a few questions for you to consider:

- What hobbies are your favorite?
- What activities do you enjoy doing?
- Can you see yourself participating in these hobbies or activities for 40 hours a week or more?

If the last question caught you off guard and had you rethinking your first two answers, you are not alone. Some hobbies and activities seem fun and exciting until you have to do them for extended amounts of time. Here's an example:

> Ethan loves playing basketball but does not want to put forth the time, commitment, and physical effort it would take to be an NBA athlete. He has decided to keep it a fun activity or hobby on the weekends to blow off some steam after his weekday job as a physical therapist.

REMEMBER

Keep in mind the difference between a hobby and a career. A *hobby* is something you like to do for enjoyment, usually during your leisure time. Sometimes I wish I could do a hobby for a career, but I don't think I could do crossword puzzles for 40 hours a week. Could you?

Aptitude versus attitude

An *aptitude* is a natural inclination you have toward certain types of tasks. If you have a high aptitude in a subject, you might find it easier to excel at it. You could be competent in math, science, athletics, writing, public speaking, empathy, music, dancing, art. . . the list goes on and on. Learning throughout your life can help you discover your aptitudes. You also can take aptitude tests to find out your strengths. In the case of Ethan from my earlier example, he chose physical therapy as a career because he realized he had a high aptitude for science, athletics, and interacting with others.

TIP

If you need to complete some research to determine what aptitudes *you* excel in, check out these online resources to help you along the way:

- **The Princeton Review career quiz:** `https://princetonreview.com/quiz/career-quiz`
- **O*NET Interest Profiler:** `https://mynextmove.org/explore/ip`
- **Truity career personality profiler:** `https://truity.com/test/career-personality-profiler-test`

Attitude is how you feel towards a certain subject, person, or situation. Your attitude can be positive, negative, or neutral. Having the right attitude when it comes to your aptitudes means that you know what you are capable of accomplishing. Ambition, dedication, and commitment describe a positive attitude. No matter how skilled you are at a subject, there will still be ups and downs. Your attitude is what helps you keep perspective when things get tough. If your *attitude* is not positive, or you are not motivated, then your *aptitudes* don't really amount to much within your career. Here are a few ways to help maintain a positive attitude (see Figure 8-1):

- List what you are thankful for each day.
- Stick to your routine each morning.
- Take a mental break every now and then.
- Listen to upbeat music.
- Interact with like-minded positive people.

- Be kind to yourself when you make mistakes.
- Set mini goals throughout the day and give yourself something to look forward to when you meet those goals.
- Stay in the "cup half full" frame of thought.

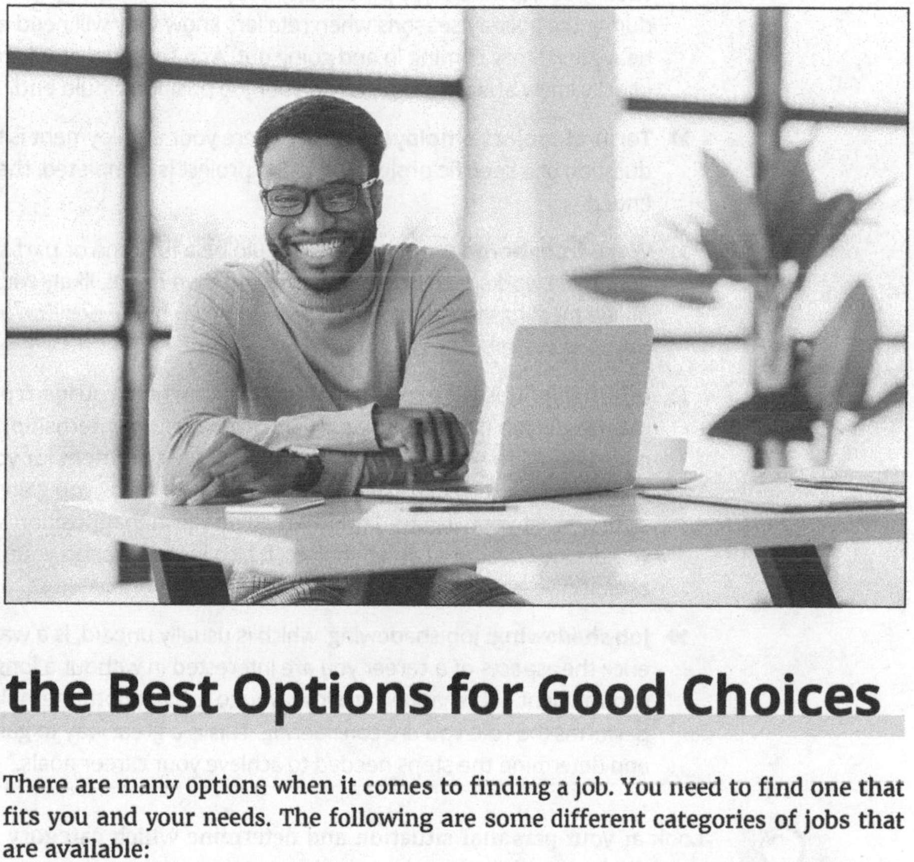

FIGURE 8-1: A positive attitude can help you use your aptitudes to be successful on the job.

Finding the Best Options for Good Choices

There are many options when it comes to finding a job. You need to find one that fits you and your needs. The following are some different categories of jobs that are available:

- **Full-time job:** This is a category of employment in which you must work a minimum number of days and hours determined by your employer. The most common is a 40-hour work week, usually 8 hours a day. Different employers can require varying hours.
- **Part-time job:** This is where you would work fewer than 35 hours per week. If you have a part-time position, you might not qualify for the medical insurance benefits a full-time employee might get, but it might fit better with your schedule.

» **Temporary employee:** Sometimes called a "temp," this could involve a full-time or part-time position. If you are a temporary employee, you rarely receive job benefits such as medical insurance, and your job assignment could end at any point, leaving you without job security. Temporary employees are treated like regular employees otherwise.

» **Seasonal employee:** This is similar to a temporary position, only you would usually be hired during a particularly busy season. You see this happen a lot during the holiday seasons when retailers know they will need extra help with heavy inventory coming in and going out. As a seasonal employee, you would usually know ahead of time when your job position would end.

» **Term-of-project employee:** This is where your employment is tied to the duration of a specific project. Once the project is completed, the position is ended.

» **Work-from-home employee:** This could be a full-time or part-time position. Your main workspace would be from your own home, likely with emails and online meetings to communicate. A work-from-home position might include traveling as well.

» **Internship:** This is a professional experience where you learn practical and meaningful job practices in your field of interest. An internship can either be paid, unpaid, full-time, part-time, or part of a requirement for your school or program. An internship likely has an end date. It helps you gain the experience of what your day-to-day life would be like in that position, and it helps you decide on future career choices. It also looks great on your resume for prospective employers or clients.

» **Job shadowing:** Job shadowing, which is usually unpaid, is a way to experience the aspects of a career you are interested in without a long-term commitment. Job shadowing allows you to follow another employee who performs the role you are considering. This is a great way to gain experience and determine the steps needed to achieve your career goals.

TIP

Look at your personal situation and determine which category of job would be a good fit for you right now in your life.

Investigating career clusters

As cool as it would be to learn about all career options through first-hand experiences, it's just not possible. A great way to look into career options is to research career clusters. Career clusters are large groupings of occupations that have many commonalities.

Clusters are useful in exploring your career choices. For example, you might be interested in human services. You could then narrow it down to counseling and mental health services and research job requirements and expectations within different types of counseling services. There are 16 common career clusters in Table 8-1. Do you see a couple that might interest you?

TABLE 8-1 Career Clusters

Career Cluster	Subgroups
Agriculture, food, and natural resources	Agribusiness systems
	Animal systems
	Environmental service systems
	Food products and processing systems
	Natural resources systems
	Plant systems
	Power, structural, and technical systems
Architecture and construction	Construction
	Design/preconstruction
	Maintenance/operations
Arts, A/V technology and communications	A/V technology and film
	Journalism and broadcasting
	Performing arts
	Printing technology
	Telecommunications
	Visual arts
Business management and administration	Administrative support
	Business information management
	General management
	Human resources management
	Operations management
Education and training	Administration and administrative support
	Professional support services
	Teaching/training

(continued)

TABLE 8-1 *(continued)*

Career Cluster	Subgroups
Finance	Accounting
	Banking services
	Business finance
	Insurance
	Securities and investments
Government and public administration	Foreign service
	Governance
	National security
	Planning
	Public management and administration
	Regulation
	Revenue and taxation
Health sciences	Biotechnology research and development
	Diagnostic services
	Health informatics
	Support services
	Therapeutic services
Hospitality and tourism	Lodging
	Recreation, amusements, and attractions
	Restaurants and food/beverage services
	Travel and tourism
Human services	Consumer services
	Counseling and mental health services
	Early childhood development and services
	Family and community services
	Personal care services
Information technology	Information support and services
	Network systems
	Programming and software development
	Web and digital communications

TABLE 8-1 ***(continued)***

Career Cluster	Subgroups
Law, public safety, corrections, and security	Correction services
	Emergency and fire management services
	Law enforcement services
	Legal services
	Security and protective services
Manufacturing	Health, safety, and environmental assurance
	Logistics and inventory control
	Maintenance, installation, and repair
	Manufacturing production process development
	Production
	Quality assurance
Marketing	Marketing communications
	Marketing management
	Marketing research
	Merchandising
	Professional sales
Science, technology, engineering, and mathematics	Engineering and technology
	Science and mathematics
Transportation, distribution, and logistics	Facility and mobile equipment maintenance
	Health, safety, and environmental management
	Logistics planning and management services
	Sales and service
	Transportation operations
	Transportation systems/infrastructure planning, management, and regulation
	Warehousing and distribution center operations

REMEMBER

If you choose a career cluster, research it, and then find that it doesn't fit, it's OK to change your mind and look into other options.

Pursuing the pathway to success

Everyone's path to success is different, and the definition of success is different for each individual. Once you decide what career path or cluster you might like to research and embark on, you may want to investigate the following categories of information:

- **Educational requirements:** Some jobs require a certain amount of education. They could require a high school diploma, a bachelor's degree, a master's degree, or even a doctoral degree. Some other requirements could be professional licenses that doctors, teachers, lawyers, counselors, electricians, building contractors, or financial advisors are required to have.
- **Wages or earnings:** Jobs vary greatly in pay. Some positions have higher pay than others, and some offer gradual pay increases the longer you have worked there. Different ways to get paid may include the following:
  - **Salary** is a fixed payment that is made monthly, every other week, or weekly. It's based on a yearly sum. It is important to note that if you are a salaried employee, you do not receive overtime pay.
  - **Wage** is a pay rate per hour multiplied by the number of hours you work. This is different from a salary because you are entitled to overtime if you work more than your standard week. On the other hand, if you do not work in a week, you receive no payment.
  - **Bonuses**, or extra money, are sometimes earned on top of your salary or wages, and they are assigned by the company. You might receive a bonus for years of experience, the highest in sales for the quarter, or overall good work.
- **Fringe benefits:** Extra benefits are important to keep in mind when researching a career or comparing different positions. Health insurance, sick leave, retirement, vacation days, company car, and the like are all fringe benefits. Selecting a lower-paying job with better fringe benefits might be something to consider depending on your situation.
- **Nature of the work:** This includes actual activities the job requires. Some questions to ask include

- Would you be working as part of a team or individually?
- Would you be doing some heavy lifting, both figuratively and literally?
- Would there be intense supervision or some autonomy?

» **Working conditions:** This refers to the environment you will be in day in and day out. For instance, a truck driver stays on the road traveling many hours a day and is away from home more often than not. A coding specialist might sit for hours a day behind a computer. Questions to ask would be:

- What is the work schedule like?
- Will I be working indoors or outdoors?
- What are the travel requirements?
- Will I be working days, nights, weekends, or holidays?

» **Job outlook:** This refers to the availability and opportunities of a certain job in the future. If the job outlook as a whole looks slim, it might not be a good idea to choose that career direction.

TIP

There are many online resources to help you research the career cluster and careers you are interested in. Some popular ones include

» **U.S. Bureau of Labor Statistics:** `https://www.bls.gov/ooh/`

» **Advance CTE:** `https://careertech.org/career-clusters`

» **CareerOneStop:** `https://careeronestop.org/`

REMEMBER

Do your research to determine what career could best match your skills, aptitudes, and interests. The job market is constantly changing, so try to avoid four years of training for a specific career only to get there and realize you hate it!

Now Hiring!

You found a career pathway to follow, but how do you go about finding a job? Searching for a job can be a scary and challenging process, but you got this! With advancing technology, finding jobs has never been easier. The internet has many platforms that list job openings from all over the world. If you are interested in a particular company or entity, more than likely you can go to the company's web page directly and apply there.

REMEMBER

Yes, you are looking for a job, but the company is also looking for an employee. You have all the right qualifications and skills, so the next step is to put yourself out there and apply. They need you!

Finding the right fit

To find the right job fit, you might need to search a little bit. One sure-fire way to secure a job opening is to interact with people. Networking involves surrounding yourself with and interacting with people who work in the industry you want to be a part of. Not only should you surround yourself with people who could potentially help you get a job, but you also need to impress them with your attitude, work ethic, and positive qualities. If you put in the hard work throughout your life, people will take notice and will gladly be personal or professional references for you.

Many people credit other individuals for helping them find a job. Think of the people you know and request information and advice from them. Word of mouth is sometimes the best way to hear about a job opening. Many times jobs are never listed, and you just might be the one who hears about them first.

Other places to search for job openings and even apply include

- LinkedIn: `https://linkedin.com`
- ZipRecruiter: `https://ziprecruiter.com`
- Indeed: `https://indeed.com/`
- Monster: `https://monster.com`
- CareerBuilder: `https://careerbuilder.com`

Dealing with the necessary evils: Applications and other paperwork

The way you present yourself when applying for a job can either make or break the opportunity. To be called upon for an interview, you must impress someone at the company with your paperwork; it's all they have to reference before they meet you in person. The formal application process usually goes like this:

» Complete a job application.

» Submit a résumé and cover letter.

» Interview.

TIP

Networking is very valuable when applying for a job. Having a contact at the company can help your paperwork stand out from all of the rest of the applicants who do not have an inside contact.

A résumé is a written document that includes a brief description of your skills, work experiences, and education. An employer might receive hundreds of résumés. To sort through them all, they will instantly throw out documents with misspelled words, poor grammar, and bad formatting. Even if you are fully qualified for the position, your résumé will most likely get thrown out if it is not professionally presented. See Figure 8-2 for an example of a presentable résumé. Be sure to include a cover letter with your résumé. A cover letter shows your enthusiasm and motivation for the position. Within the letter, you can strategically highlight your qualifications to match the job requirements, which means that you've spent some time looking inward and reflecting on your abilities, skills, and experiences so you can highlight the talents that are most applicable to the job you're applying for.

Most job applications are completed through a secure online portal. Filling in a job application can be a tedious process, but it is doable. Have your résumé on hand to refer to details about your previous work experience since the application will ask for some of the same information. The application will also ask you for your Social Security Number, desired salary, personal and professional references, and much more information. The application may also include information tailored to the specific job you are applying for. For instance, if you are applying to be an educator in a school, you need to include the correct teaching licenses, your philosophy of teaching, and possibly electronic aptitude surveys to show your skills in teaching and classroom management. Figure 8-3 shows a basic job application.

REMEMBER

Correct spelling and grammar are a must in your application, cover letter, and résumé. Employers will pull your name out of the job running if you cannot produce professional documents.

FIRST NAME **LAST NAME**

Address · Phone

Email · LinkedIn Profile · Twitter/Blog/Portfolio

Briefly state your career objective, or summarize what makes you stand out. Use language from the job description as keywords.

EXPERIENCE

DATES FROM – TO

JOB TITLE, COMPANY

Describe your responsibilities and achievements in terms of impact and results. Use examples, but keep it short.

DATES FROM – TO

JOB TITLE, COMPANY

Describe your responsibilities and achievements in terms of impact and results. Use examples, but keep it short.

EDUCATION

MONTH YEAR

DEGREE TITLE, SCHOOL

It's okay to brag about your GPA, awards, and honors. Feel free to summarize your coursework too.

MONTH YEAR

DEGREE TITLE, SCHOOL

It's okay to brag about your GPA, awards, and honors. Feel free to summarize your coursework too.

SKILLS

- **List your strengths relevant for the role you're applying for**
- **List one of your strengths**
- **List one of your strengths**
- **List one of your strengths**
- **List one of your strengths**

ACTIVITIES

Use this section to highlight your relevant passions, activities, and how you like to give back. It's good to include leadership and volunteer experiences here or show off important extras like publications, certifications, languages, and more.

FIGURE 8-2: An example résumé.

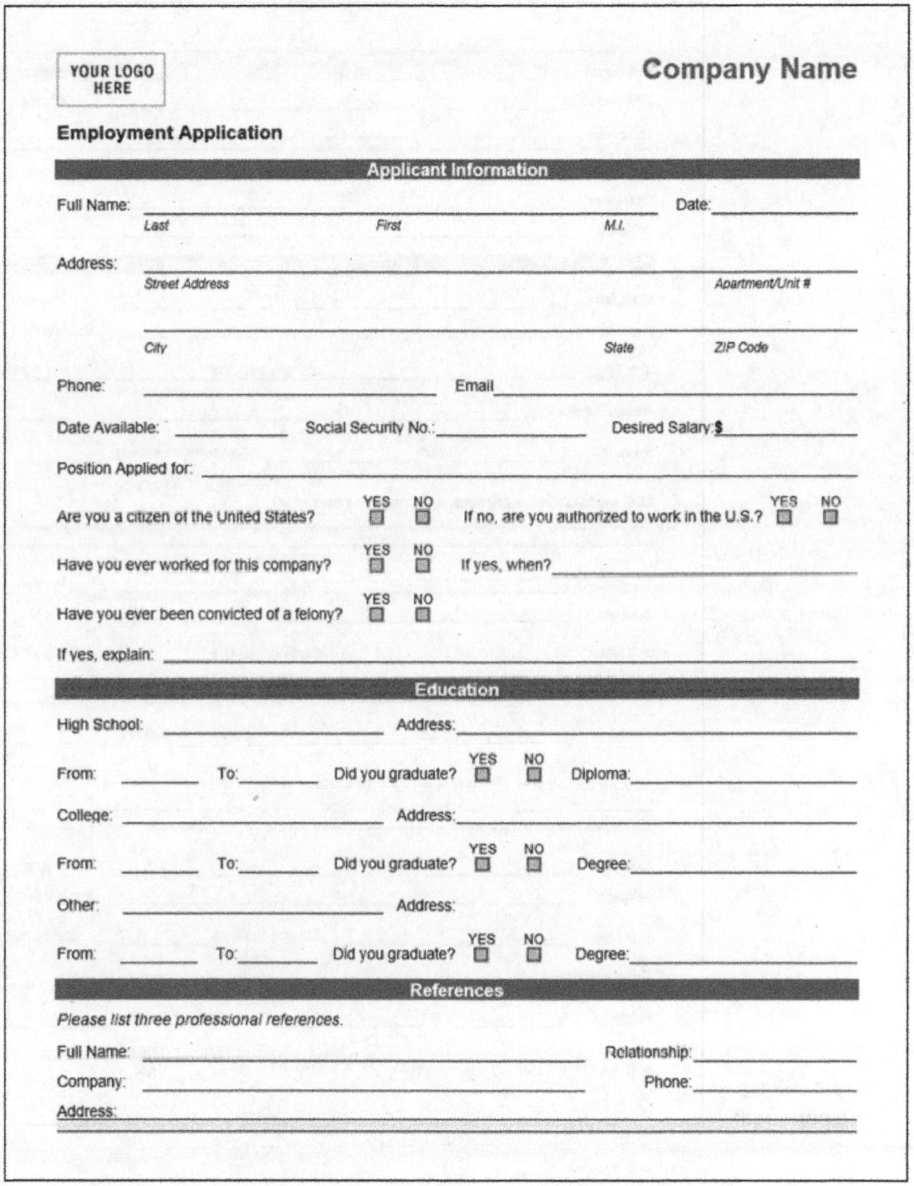
YOUR LOGO HERE

Company Name

Employment Application

Applicant Information

Full Name: ____________________ Date: ________
Last *First* *M.I.*

Address: ______________________________
Street Address *Apartment/Unit #*

____
City *State* *ZIP Code*

Phone: ____________ Email ____________

Date Available: ________ Social Security No.: ________ Desired Salary: $ ________

Position Applied for: ______________________________

Are you a citizen of the United States? YES ☐ NO ☐ If no, are you authorized to work in the U.S.? YES ☐ NO ☐

Have you ever worked for this company? YES ☐ NO ☐ If yes, when? ____________

Have you ever been convicted of a felony? YES ☐ NO ☐

If yes, explain: ______________________________

Education

High School: ____________ Address: ____________

From: ______ To: ______ Did you graduate? YES ☐ NO ☐ Diploma: ____________

College: ____________ Address: ____________

From: ______ To: ______ Did you graduate? YES ☐ NO ☐ Degree: ____________

Other: ____________ Address:

From: ______ To: ______ Did you graduate? YES ☐ NO ☐ Degree: ____________

References

Please list three professional references.

Full Name: ____________ Relationship: ____________

Company: ____________ Phone: ____________

Address: ______________________________

FIGURE 8-3: A basic job application.

Full Name: ______________ Relationship: ______________

Company: ______________ Phone: ______________

Address: ______________

Full Name: ______________ Relationship: ______________

Company: ______________ Phone: ______________

Address: ______________

Previous Employment

Company: ______________ Phone: ______________

Address: ______________ Supervisor: ______________

Job Title: ______________ Starting Salary: $ ______________ Ending Salary: $ ______________

Responsibilities: ______________

From: ______________ To: ______________ Reason for Leaving: ______________

May we contact your previous supervisor for a reference? YES ☐ NO ☐

Company: ______________ Phone: ______________

Address: ______________ Supervisor: ______________

Job Title: ______________ Starting Salary: $ ______________ Ending Salary: $ ______________

Responsibilities: ______________

From: ______________ To: ______________ Reason for Leaving: ______________

May we contact your previous supervisor for a reference? YES ☐ NO ☐

Company: ______________ Phone: ______________

Address: ______________ Supervisor: ______________

Job Title: ______________ Starting Salary: $ ______________ Ending Salary: $ ______________

Responsibilities: ______________

From: ______________ To: ______________ Reason for Leaving: ______________

May we contact your previous supervisor for a reference? YES ☐ NO ☐

FIGURE 8-3: (continued)

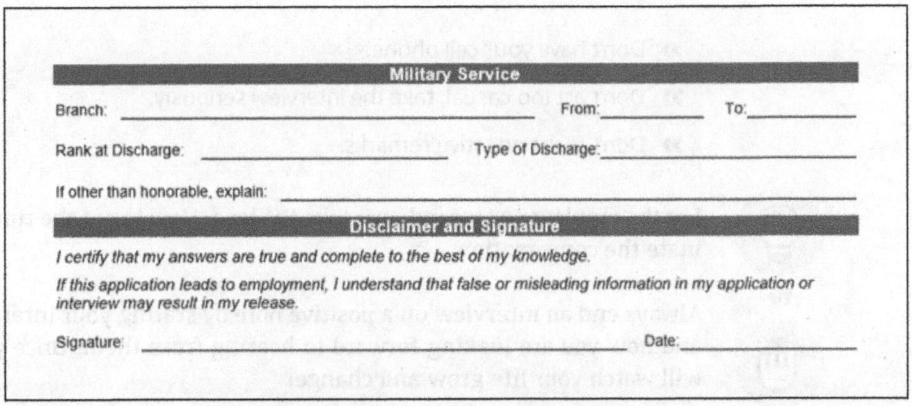
Military Service

Branch: ______ From: ______ To: ______

Rank at Discharge: ______ Type of Discharge: ______

If other than honorable, explain: ______

Disclaimer and Signature

I certify that my answers are true and complete to the best of my knowledge.

If this application leads to employment, I understand that false or misleading information in my application or interview may result in my release.

Signature: ______ Date: ______

FIGURE 8-3: (continued)

Making lasting first impressions

Congrats on getting an interview, but the process isn't over yet! Expect to be judged based on the first impression the employer forms during your interview. To get good marks, just be yourself. Be genuine, excited, professional, and dress to impress. Research the employer to determine their usual dress attire and then dress a step above that. Check out Chapter 9 for more information on what to wear on the job.

Here are some interview do's and don'ts:

- Do arrive 10 minutes early.
- Do make eye contact and shake hands.
- Do listen intently to the questions and remarks by the employer to respond appropriately.
- Do smile and show positivity.
- Do ask questions about the position.
- Do write a thank-you note after the interview.
- Don't be late.
- Don't fidget or show annoying mannerisms.
- Don't chew gum.

» Don't have your cell phone.
» Don't act too casual; take the interview seriously.
» Don't make negative remarks.

TIP

Let the employer or interviewer take the lead. Now is not the time to try and dominate the conversation.

REMEMBER

Always end an interview on a positive note by stating your interest in the position and how you are looking forward to hearing from them. Once you get hired, you will watch your life grow and change!

IN THIS CHAPTER

» Showing off your skills

» Dressing to impress

» Avoiding imposter syndrome

Chapter 9

Impressing the Boss and Succeeding on the Job

In this chapter, I cover how to be confident in your skills in the workforce, acquire some new skills along the way, succeed on the job, dress appropriately for your job, show professionalism through your attire, and overcome imposter syndrome. Let's dig in!

You've Got Skills

Throughout your life thus far, you have been working to build the foundation needed to be successful in the workforce. You have most likely received the training you need from your schooling, extra-curricular activities, volunteer work, work experiences, and guidance from parents, teachers, and mentors. Most careers require individuals to have a combination of many skills. You must have a strong work ethic, be trainable, and have basic problem-solving skills.

Skills that employers want vary from job to job, but they all include some form of soft skills and hard skills. Soft skills relate to *how you work*, and hard skills relate to *what you know*. Through a combination of soft skills and hard skills, you will find the right mix to be successful on the job!

Putting school smarts to use

Hard skills are technical skills that you learn in the classroom, in professional trainings, in online courses, in certification programs, or on the job. These skills are related to a particular field, and they require specific knowledge in that subject area. Hard skills are easier to define and evaluate than soft skills are. Hard skills are easily defined because they can be tested; you can either speak a second language fluently or you can't. Another example is if you want to be an architect, you must be able to understand and apply the technical skills of building and construction. You hope the bridge you drive across every day has been designed and built by an architect with the hard skills required to make the bridge safe and durable. Soft skills are more objective and vary by those evaluating them.

The following are some examples of hard skills:

- Computer skills
- Data analysis
- Scientific expertise
- Writing
- Geometry
- Photo editing
- Graphic design
- Social media management
- HTML, JavaScript, and other programming languages
- Software use, such as Microsoft Office, Google Office Suite, Salesforce
- Foreign languages
- Patient care
- Accounting
- Scheduling

All of these hard skills are pretty specific. In Figure 9-1, two people are putting their technical skills to use in the medical field. Some skills are transferrable to different careers, but to land the job you want, you need to know the specific hard skills required for that position.

Usually, you can find the degree requirements, licenses, and hard skills needed for a position listed in the job description. Check out Table 9-1 to see what level of higher education or training you need to meet your career goals.

FIGURE 9-1: Hard skills are technical skills that require training for a specific job.

TABLE 9-1 College Degree Levels

Degree Type	Years Required	Example
Associate Degree	2–3 years	Associate of Science (AS)
Bachelor's Degree	4 or more years	Bachelor of Arts (BA)
Master's Degree	Bachelor's degree plus 2–3 years	Master of Education (MEd)
Doctoral Degree	Master's degree plus 4 years or more	Doctor of Philosophy in Systems and Engineering Management (PhD)

TIP

Keep in mind that you do not have to attend college to have a successful career, but a high school diploma is a necessity. If college is not required, be ready for on-the-job training, apprenticeships, or program certifications for many job positions. For example, you do not need a college degree to become a certified electrician, but you must complete an apprenticeship that includes 8,000 to 10,000 hours (approximately 4 to 5 years) of on-the-job training plus testing to receive your license or certification.

TIP

If you do not have a certain hard skill, no worries; sign up for some college classes or community programs to perfect your skills. Also, many places provide on-the-job training to make sure you know the hard skills needed to be a part of their team.

Performing on the job

Job performance is a big deal. It's what employers use to gauge raises, bonuses, advancement, and job security. Soft skills are a large part of your performance. Soft skills are personality traits that affect how you interact with others and have their roots in your behavior, attitudes, and values. Soft skills are just as important, if not more so, as the hard skills or qualifications that you need for a job. Many people end up underperforming in a job not because they couldn't do the work but because they couldn't get along with others. Here are some valuable soft skills that can be helpful in any job:

- **Time management:** Can you consistently come to work, get there on time, and finish projects by the deadline?
- **Multitasking:** Can you handle multiple expectations and tasks at a time?
- **Attention to detail:** Can you pinpoint technical errors? Can you focus on the task at hand for hours at a time?
- **Innovation:** Can you come up with new ideas? Can you think outside the box? Are you proud of yourself and your ideas?
- **Problem-solving:** If you get in a bind, can you figure out a solution on your own?
- **Emotional maturity:** Can you control your emotions in stressful situations? Can you act appropriately and professionally in the workplace?
- **Dedication:** If you say you will do something, will you *actually* do it? Do you follow through on job assignments?
- **Duty:** Do you understand that you are required to meet the obligations of the job if you want to keep the job?
- **Enthusiasm:** Are you excited and positive in your approach to your work?
- **Honesty:** Can you be trusted with sensitive information and be honest about your mistakes?
- **Leadership:** Can you help set a direction and guide other people to the right place?
- **Collaboration:** Can you be respectful of others' opinions and ideas on your team? Do you work well with others?

Overall, employers are looking for good human beings. Are you reliable, can you be trusted, and can you communicate effectively? If you can show impressive soft skills, you will go far within an industry and could quite possibly move up the ranks.

TIP

While it's important to be qualified with the hard skills needed for a job, some employers might choose someone with more advanced soft skills because they can be trained in the hard skills.

REMEMBER

Soft skills can be sharpened by asking for feedback from others. From the list above, are there some soft skills you need to develop further?

WARNING

If you neglect your soft skills, you could be the cause of conflict in the workplace. Don't put your career at risk.

Dressing for Success

Style points matter! What this means is that the way you dress sets the stage for how people see you in the workplace, whether you like it or not. Different jobs have different dress requirements, but overall you must look "put together." The "I just rolled out of bed" look will not fly in most workplaces. The way you present yourself can be perceived as an extension of your work. It's human nature to lump the two together, and it's likely that this is what your boss will do.

Also, did you know the clothes you wear have a psychological effect on others and yourself? Your clothes send a message to friends and strangers alike about the image you want to portray. In addition, feeling like you look good contributes to your sense of well-being. I am not saying you need name-brand clothing, but to feel good, you need to look good. Your clothing can reflect:

- How you feel
- Your mood
- Your personality
- Your uniqueness

TIP

Dressing the part helps you set yourself up for success. When you first begin a new job, it is in your best interest to slightly overdress until you get a sense of the culture in the workplace. Do not assume Friday or any other day is a casual day; wait until you see how other employees dress. Sometimes there are some unspoken rules when it comes to dress in the workplace, so it is better to follow the lead of veteran employees.

Accepting uniformity

Looking put together on the job shows your readiness to work. It also shows your respect for the job opportunity. A workplace has expectations and requirements for clothing. Some places require employees to wear the same clothing items to portray professionalism and uniformity. For example, you may have noticed the individuals working in your favorite coffee shop are all wearing the same color shirt, pants, and apron. These employees are required to wear a uniform like those in Figure 9-2. Uniforms can provide cohesive energy among employees and also help customers know who the staff members are.

Uniforms are also used to help keep employees safe. Can you imagine a firefighter without their fireproof jacket and gloves, or a construction worker without their hardhat? Employers have good reasons to enforce uniforms. The required uniforms are usually practical for the job at hand. The use of uniforms is not an attempt to stifle your style or creativity; it is to promote teamwork with a sense of belonging and to keep employees safe.

FIGURE 9-2 Uniforms provide practical benefits as well as promoting a sense of belonging.

TIP

If a job requires you to wear a uniform, make sure you do your best to keep it clean. Wash it the day before you go to work so you look presentable in your uniform.

Demonstrating professionalism

Professionalism can be shown in many ways. It can be shown in what you wear, how you act, and what you look like. People can make a judgment about your professionalism in the workplace even before you open your mouth.

The following are some types of workplace dress codes and what is expected with each one:

- **Business professional:** This is the traditional attire used in places like banking, finance, law, or politics. Examples include well-tailored skirts, slacks, button-down shirts, blazers, dark-colored suits, ties, belts, and dress shoes. See Figure 9-3 for examples of what business professional looks like.
- **Business casual:** This is a common dress code in many offices. It blends traditional business style with a more relaxed look that still shows professionalism. Examples include khaki pants, slacks, blouses, sweaters, polo shirts, cardigans, blazers, sports coats, and optional ties.

FIGURE 9-3: Business professional includes items such as slacks, blazers, suits, and ties.

If you are still not clear on how your workplace is asking you to dress, use these tips:

- Look around the office and take note of what other people are wearing. Are people in leadership positions dressed more formally than people in other positions? If you hope someday to have a larger or more advanced role, it's perfectly acceptable to dress for the job you want, not the job you have.
- If you're unsure what to expect regarding the dress code for an interview, look at the company's social media page to get clues on what to wear.
- Avoid overly revealing clothing. Professionalism includes more conservative clothing choices.
- Be wary of distracting accessories or overly restrictive clothing. You must be able to properly perform your job functions.
- Wearing a tie is a common requirement in many industries. A tie universally portrays professionalism. Make sure you are tying your tie correctly by checking out Figure 9-4.

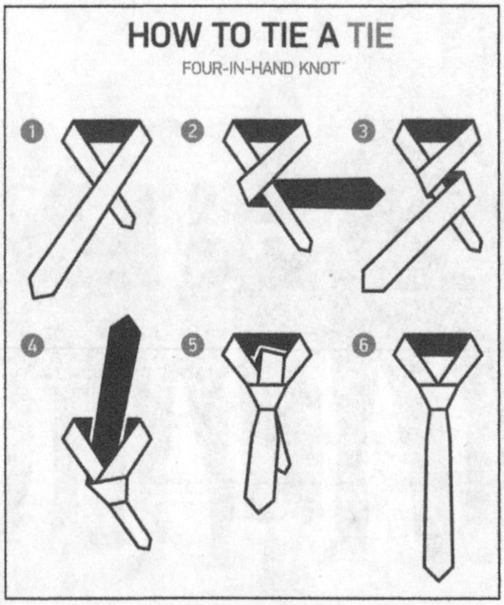

FIGURE 9-4: Instructions for tying a tie.

TIP

Your personality and uniqueness can still shine through in professional wear. You do not have to wear bizarre or silly clothing to stand out. Over time, through your work achievements and clothing combined, you could quite possibly develop your signature style.

REMEMBER

It's better to be overdressed rather than underdressed for any occasion, including the workplace!

Understanding casual day

Woohoo, it's casual Friday! Ripped jeans, t-shirt, and baseball cap, right? Wrong! Casual dress does not mean wearing the same clothing you wear in your leisure time. Some workplaces allow a casual dress code all the time, not just Fridays, and this dress code can get confusing. So what exactly are the expectations? Clothing that fits a day at the beach or a sporting event may not be appropriate to present a casual appearance at work.

In a more casual workplace, nice jeans are everyday attire. Men and women rarely wear suit coats or ties but instead opt for shirts with or without collars and casual blouses. Even in a *very* casual work environment, bosses still expect employees to adhere to high standards. For example, avoid clothing that

- Is dirty and wrinkled.
- Includes rips, holes, frays (even if it is the current style!).
- Includes lewd and offensive remarks or images.
- Shows your underwear.
- Shows your stomach.
- Shows too much of your back, chest, or legs.
- Shows too much cleavage.

TIP

To impress the boss and succeed on the job, make sure you read the employee handbook that explains policies, procedures, performance expectations, and dress code that every employee is required to abide by.

REMEMBER

Professionalism can help you be successful on the job by ensuring successful work relationships, a positive reputation, and great first impressions.

Overcoming Imposter Syndrome

Have you ever thought *There's a mistake. . . . I shouldn't have this job. You're trusting me with this sensitive information? What do you mean I'm in charge?*

Thoughts like these may run through your head when you feel you don't deserve the responsibility you've been given. If you've had these types of thoughts, you're not alone. *Imposter syndrome* is the feeling that sooner or later everyone will figure out you have no idea what you're doing. You might feel like a fraud and that people will soon find out about your fake abilities.

Imposter syndrome is a pretty common feeling, but there are ways to overcome those doubts:

- **Talk to people who have been in your shoes.** If you're just beginning in your career, talk to those colleagues who can edify you and lift you up.
- **Understand that you *are* an expert.** If you surround yourself with more experienced employees all the time, it might seem you could never fill their shoes, but someday you will have that same level of experience. Become a mentor for younger employees; it will help you realize how much you *do* know.
- **No one is perfect, not even your boss.** Don't focus on perfection, but rather on a job well done. Everyone makes mistakes. Instead of dwelling on them, learn from them.
- **Learn to celebrate.** When you meet a milestone, take a moment to breathe and celebrate your successes. Likely people will celebrate you as well; they are proud of you. I am proud of you!

REMEMBER

If you have been feeling like an imposter, remember that you earned your position fair and square. You set high goals for yourself, and you deserve everything you have achieved and more. Your employer chose you for the job, and they value your expertise. You got this! Now go impress the boss and earn those accolades!

IN THIS CHAPTER

- » Getting paid
- » Planning for the future
- » Keeping yourself on budget
- » Using credit cards responsibly

Chapter 10

Champagne Tastes, Beer Budget: Saving and Spending

One of the most adult-ish items you can receive is your very own paycheck. When you receive your first check, no matter your age, it marks your graduation into the working world, and you should be proud of your earnings. You are a successful, contributing citizen and have worked very hard for your first paycheck! Congratulations!

But not so fast — what you do next with your paycheck can either help you or hurt you. You might be saying, "It's my money; I earned it fair and square, and I can do whatever I want with it." That's correct; you *can* do whatever you want with your money, but I want to make sure you set yourself up for success in your daily living and long-term dealings.

Earning a paycheck brings new responsibilities and financial considerations. Wise money decisions do not necessarily come naturally, so it is important to do your research. Just by picking up this book, you have shown you are ready to get organized with your money. By digging into this chapter, you can learn what works and what doesn't without watching that first paycheck disappear too quickly! In this chapter, I cover different pay periods, taxes, bills, budgeting, giving, saving, investing, and the pros and cons of credit cards.

Getting Paid: Show Me the Money

Every job has its defined pay period when you will receive your paycheck. You should have a clear understanding of when you will get paid before you accept a position. Keep in mind that you have to work for an entire pay period before you receive your first paycheck, so don't expect any money upfront unless there is a sign-on bonus attached to the position.

Here are the most common types of pay period structures:

- **Weekly pay period:** If you get paid weekly, you receive a paycheck the same day each week — for example, every Friday could be payday. You receive 52 paychecks a year if you work all year long.
- **Bi-weekly pay period:** This pay period is the most common. You get paid every other week on the same day, such as every other Friday, and receive 26 paychecks a year. A few months out of the year, you would receive three paychecks in one month.
- **Semi-monthly pay period:** This pay period may seem the same as bi-weekly, but it differs because you get paid on an actual date twice a month. For example, your pay dates might be the 1st and the 15th of each month, with a total of 24 paychecks a year.
- **Monthly pay period:** If you get paid monthly, you get paid on the same date every month. The date is set by human resources and usually occurs at the end of each month, like the 27th or right at the beginning of the month, maybe the 1st, with a total of 12 paychecks a year.

Jamar's earns a salary of $52,000 per year. The amount he receives changes quite a bit for each pay period depending on which of the pay structures his company uses:

- Weekly he would earn $1,000 per paycheck.
- Bi-weekly he would earn $2,000 per paycheck.
- Semi-monthly he would earn $2,167 per paycheck.
- Monthly he would earn $4,334 per paycheck.

WARNING

Wow, this looks like a lot of money, and it is! But there is more to this story; these totals do not account for employment tax or benefit withholdings. Read more about taxes in the next section.

TIP

Your employer is likely to have you sign up for a direct deposit payment method. That means that you must have a bank account where your paycheck will deposit electronically on payday to your account. If you do not have a bank account, no worries. Just choose a bank and they will walk you through opening a new account.

TIP

Other ways of you might get paid include digital payments, paper checks, prepaid debt cards, and online money transfers such as PayPal, Venmo, Western Union, or TransferWise.

Wait, what!? Taxes?

It's time for your first payday! You have worked your heart out for the last month, anticipating how it would pay off. You log into your online banking and see the direct deposit amount. Do you scream for joy? Do a happy dance? Jump up and down in pure bliss? No? Wait. What happened!? You discover that you got paid a significantly smaller amount than you thought. *They took how much out for taxes?*

The federal government collects your income tax payments throughout the year by taking them directly from every paycheck. This may not seem fair, but it does keep you from having to pay a lump sum for federal taxes at the end of the year. Before you begin working for your employer, you are required to fill out a W-4 form. This form is also called an employee's withholding certificate, and it helps your employer figure out how much to withhold from your paycheck for federal income tax. It's your employer's responsibility to withhold this money based on the information you provide on your W-4. See Figure 10-1 for a W-4 form example.

TIP

When filling in your personal information on any government form, you must use your given legal name, no nicknames. And if you do not know your Social Security number, you'll find it written on your Social Security card, or you can go to `https://ssa.gov/` for more information.

Shalan earns $44,000 a year. She gets her first paycheck and pays close attention to the withholdings to double-check that everything is accurate to what she placed on her W-4 form. Figure 10-2 shows what her withholdings may look like. She will have to get used to the difference between her take-home pay and her gross income.

TIP

If you notice, Shalan's withholdings include medical insurance, dental coverage, and vision insurance. These items are usually a part of your compensation package, and they're considered very beneficial. If your company is able to offer different insurances and policies, your part of the payment will come out of your monthly pay, which affects your take-home salary.

REMEMBER

Your benefits and retirement deductions are specific to you depending on where you work and what your company offers.

Form **W-4**

Department of the Treasury
Internal Revenue Service

Employee's Withholding Certificate

► Complete Form W-4 so that your employer can withhold the correct federal income tax from your pay.
► Give Form W-4 to your employer.
► Your withholding is subject to review by the IRS.

OMB No. 1545-0074

2022

Step 1: Enter Personal Information

(a) First name and middle initial | Last name | (b) Social security number

Address

City or town, state, and ZIP code

► Does your name match the name on your social security card? If not, to ensure you get credit for your earnings, contact SSA at 800-772-1213 or go to www.ssa.gov.

(c) ☐ Single or Married filing separately
☐ Married filing jointly or Qualifying widow(er)
☐ Head of household (Check only if you're unmarried and pay more than half the costs of keeping up a home for yourself and a qualifying individual.)

Complete Steps 2–4 ONLY if they apply to you; otherwise, skip to Step 5. See page 2 for more information on each step, who can claim exemption from withholding, when to use the estimator at *www.irs.gov/W4App*, and privacy.

Step 2: Multiple Jobs or Spouse Works

Complete this step if you (1) hold more than one job at a time, or (2) are married filing jointly and your spouse also works. The correct amount of withholding depends on income earned from all of these jobs.

Do **only one** of the following.

(a) Use the estimator at *www.irs.gov/W4App* for most accurate withholding for this step (and Steps 3–4); **or**

(b) Use the Multiple Jobs Worksheet on page 3 and enter the result in Step 4(c) below for roughly accurate withholding; **or**

(c) If there are only two jobs total, you may check this box. Do the same on Form W-4 for the other job. This option is accurate for jobs with similar pay; otherwise, more tax than necessary may be withheld . . ► ☐

TIP: To be accurate, submit a 2022 Form W-4 for all other jobs. If you (or your spouse) have self-employment income, including as an independent contractor, use the estimator.

Complete Steps 3–4(b) on Form W-4 for only ONE of these jobs. Leave those steps blank for the other jobs. (Your withholding will be most accurate if you complete Steps 3–4(b) on the Form W-4 for the highest paying job.)

Step 3: Claim Dependents

If your total income will be $200,000 or less ($400,000 or less if married filing jointly):

Multiply the number of qualifying children under age 17 by $2,000 ► $

Multiply the number of other dependents by $500 . . . . ► $

Add the amounts above and enter the total here . . . . **3** $

Step 4 (optional): Other Adjustments

(a) Other income (not from jobs). If you want tax withheld for other income you expect this year that won't have withholding, enter the amount of other income here. This may include interest, dividends, and retirement income . . . . . . **4(a)** $

(b) Deductions. If you expect to claim deductions other than the standard deduction and want to reduce your withholding, use the Deductions Worksheet on page 3 and enter the result here . . . . **4(b)** $

(c) Extra withholding. Enter any additional tax you want withheld each **pay period** . . **4(c)** $

Step 5: Sign Here

Under penalties of perjury, I declare that this certificate, to the best of my knowledge and belief, is true, correct, and complete.

► **Employee's signature** (This form is not valid unless you sign it.) ► **Date**

Employers Only

Employer's name and address | First date of employment | Employer identification number (EIN)

For Privacy Act and Paperwork Reduction Act Notice, see page 3. Cat. No. 10220Q Form **W-4** (2022)

FIGURE 10-1: A W-4 form.

At the end of the year, your employer will send a W-2 form (see Figure 10-3). This is a report of what you have gotten paid throughout the entire year and what has been withheld from you for taxes. You use this form to complete your personal income tax filing. Filing your taxes is not as scary as it sounds! I recommend utilizing tax preparation software such as `https://turbotax.intuit.com`. For a small fee, this software walks you step by step through how to prepare your tax return. It asks you the right questions to help you discover what deductions you might qualify for; you might even qualify for a tax refund, meaning that you get money back! You can do some more research on taxes by reading *Taxes For Dummies, 2022 Edition.*

Gross Paycheck		$3,667
Taxes	8.75%	$321
DETAILS ^		
Federal Income	8.75%	$321
State Income	0.00%	$0
Local Income	0.00%	$0
FICA and State Insurance Taxes	6.97%	$256
DETAILS ^		
Social Security	5.65%	$207
Medicare	1.32%	$48
State Disability Insurance Tax	0.00%	$0
State Unemployment Insurance Tax	0.00%	$0
State Family Leave Insurance Tax	0.00%	$0
State Workers Compensation Insurance Tax	0.00%	$0
Pre-Tax Deductions	14.32%	$525
DETAILS ^		
Medical Insurance	5.45%	$200
Dental Coverage	1.36%	$50
Vision Insurance	0.68%	$25
401(k)	5.45%	$200
Long Term Disability Insurance	0.00%	$0
Life Insurance	1.36%	$50
Commuter Plan	0.00%	$0
FSA	0.00%	$0
HSA	0.00%	$0
Post-Tax Deductions	0.00%	$0
Take Home Salary	69.96%	$2,565

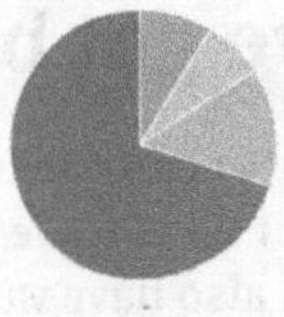

FIGURE 10-2: Tax withholdings

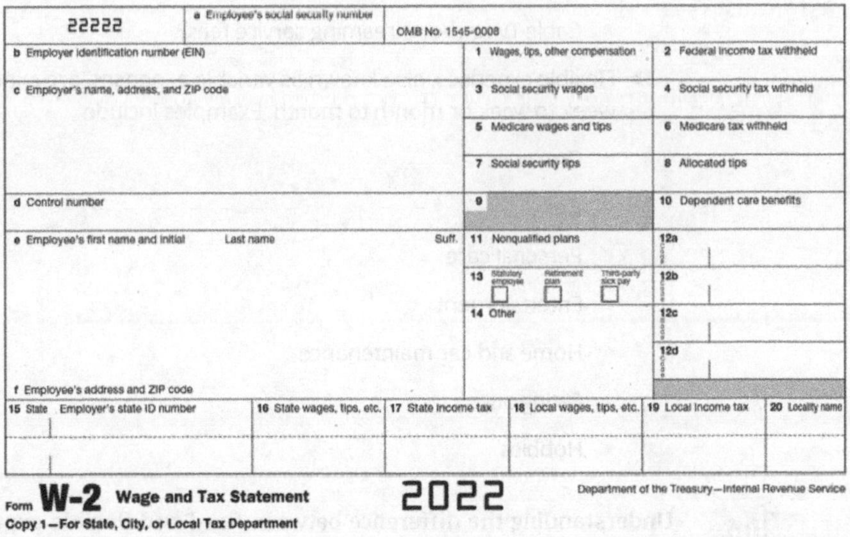

22222 | a Employee's social security number | OMB No. 1545-0008

b Employer identification number (EIN)

c Employer's name, address, and ZIP code

d Control number

e Employee's first name and initial | Last name | Suff.

f Employee's address and ZIP code

1 Wages, tips, other compensation | 2 Federal income tax withheld

3 Social security wages | 4 Social security tax withheld

5 Medicare wages and tips | 6 Medicare tax withheld

7 Social security tips | 8 Allocated tips

9 | 10 Dependent care benefits

11 Nonqualified plans | 12a

13 Statutory employee | Retirement plan | Third-party sick pay | 12b

14 Other | 12c

12d

15 State | Employer's state ID number | 16 State wages, tips, etc. | 17 State income tax | 18 Local wages, tips, etc. | 19 Local income tax | 20 Locality name

Form **W-2** Wage and Tax Statement **2022**

Copy 1—For State, City, or Local Tax Department

Department of the Treasury—Internal Revenue Service

FIGURE 10-3: A W-2 form.

TIP Depending on where you reside, you could see added state and county taxes listed in your withholdings. The taxes that are collected are used to support schools, road upkeep, emergency services, health services, and social service programs.

I've got bills: They're multiplying

You've come to terms with the fact that taxes must be taken out of your paycheck, but I have some more bad news. Taxes are not the only thing that must be paid. You also have various necessary expenses.

There are two types of expenses, fixed and flexible:

» Fixed expenses are expenses that are consistent in amounts each month. Examples include
  - Housing rent or mortgage
  - Insurance premiums
  - Car payment
  - Fixed loans
  - Tuition fees
  - Utility bills
  - Phone and internet bills
  - Gym membership
  - Cable TV and/or streaming service fees?

» Flexible expenses, also known as variable expenses, are expenses that change week to week or month to month. Examples include
  - Groceries
  - Gas
  - Personal care
  - Entertainment
  - Home and car maintenance
  - Eating out
  - Hobbies

REMEMBER

Understanding the difference between fixed and flexible expenses is a great start to managing your overall cash flow.

Managing your bills like a pro

If you think your money is a lot to keep track of, you are correct! It can seem very overwhelming to make sure all of your expenses and bills are paid on time. Here are some helpful tips to make timely bill payments so you can avoid late fees:

- » Create a list of all of your bills either electronically or in a notebook. Just having all the bills you owe written in one place can help you organize the payments. This list can also be the beginning steps of a budget.
- » Find a place to set all of your bills as they arrive in the mail. Throwing them on the dining room table in a scattered mess is sure to increase your anxiety. Try file folders to keep them organized.
- » Open your bills and read them when they come in the mail. Leaving them sealed up tight doesn't take away the reality that bills must be paid.
- » Check your due dates on each bill. Add the dates to your calendar if you need to. Most likely, you will get electronic and paper reminders to pay the bill, but find a system that works for you.
- » Determine a designated time once or twice a month to sit down and focus on paying your bills. This will ensure you do not miss any payments.
- » Set up automatic payments on a specified date close to your payday. This help you ensure you pay the bills on time. The billing company can set up automatic payments or your bank can help.
- » Stay alert. If you set your bills to automatic, it is still important to review the bills each month. Errors could be made, and you might be overcharged.

WARNING

Bad things can happen if you do not pay your bills on time. If you are paying for a service, they have the right to cancel that service if you don't pay. The electric company will not hesitate to shut off your electricity if they are not paid on time. Don't get left in the dark!

WARNING

Streaming services, apps, and electronic games are quick and easy to sign up for, sometimes on a free trial. But beware, you will be charged monthly for these services regardless of whether you continue to use them, and it can add up. Pay attention. If you aren't using them, call, click, and cancel!

Putting your paycheck to work

Before you decide to go on a shopping spree with your newly earned money, think twice. There are more important items and issues you may need to consider first. Here are some ways you can maximize your paycheck each pay period:

- » Pay your larger expenses first. Your rent, mortgage, electricity, water, and car payments take a large chunk of your paycheck, so pay them first when you have the money available. This keeps you from scrambling around when your money is running low.
- » Fill up your car with gas before paying for other nonessential items to ensure you have a full tank until the next payday.
- » Shop for your essential items and groceries close to payday. The more money you have left just sitting in your account, the more tempted you are to spend it on items you do not need.
- » Save a portion of your paycheck for unexpected things in life. Open up a savings account at your bank to transfer a portion of your earnings into each payday. You can save any amount, but a good place to start is 10 percent of your monthly income.
- » Time your hygiene purchases and necessities to be in different pay periods. For example, replace your shampoo and conditioner one pay period; then replace your toilet paper and paper towels in a different pay period. That way you don't spend hundreds of dollars on hygiene products with one paycheck.
- » Plan your meals for the pay period so you are not tempted to purchase extra food at the grocery store or eat out when you do not have the funds.
- » Keep track of holidays and birthdays so purchasing gifts is not a surprise expense. You don't have to wait until the last moment to purchase gifts for the people you love. Plan ahead by purchasing a little gift each pay period and hiding it for when the time is right. But beware, it will be easy to forget what you bought and where you hid it. Compile a list on your phone to keep track!
- » Live within your means. Do not use credit or loans to fund your lifestyle. (Read more about credit cards at the end of this chapter.)

TIP

Your employer may allow you to split your direct deposit among different accounts. This will allow you to put a portion of your paycheck directly into savings without having to transfer it over.

REMEMBER

Having a plan in place for maximizing your paycheck helps ensure you pay bills on time and have the necessities you need.

Securing Your Future

You are worth investing in, and one way to invest in yourself is to prepare for your future. Ten or twenty years from now, you will thank yourself for planning ahead. Your life today is very important, but it is also important to find a balance between today and being prepared for the future.

You cannot spend money like every day is your last. Finding a balance between what you spend today and what you need to save for tomorrow is an important step in securing your future.

Follow these tips to help find your balance:

- Track where you spend your money.
- Be realistic with what you can afford each month.
- Be patient when it comes to building up your savings; it takes time.
- Pay your bills on time.
- Cut out subscription expenses or other living costs that you do not use anymore.
- Start investing in your retirement as soon as possible.
- Set financial goals.

TIP

Not only can you invest in yourself financially, but you can also invest in yourself by continually upgrading your knowledge and skills within your industry. Who knows, this might lead to a better job with better pay!

Giving is better than receiving

"But it's my money! Why should I give it to someone else?"

Here's why: Money cannot buy happiness, but giving can. Research has proven that giving money to the less fortunate or a cause close to your heart has positive physiological effects on your health, happiness, and well-being. Living with a high income can give your life satisfaction, but not happiness. Spending money on others makes you happier than spending money on yourself.

Giving money to your religious institution or charity of choice matches the universal moral obligation we have to help others in need. Even if you are not megawealthy, you can help other people by giving a little bit every month. Start with giving 10 percent each month, and you will begin to notice a change in your life.

If you would like to begin giving to help others, here is a list of potential beneficiaries of your generosity:

- Your place of worship
- Local charities
- Compassion International (https://www.compassion.com/)
- Make-A-Wish Foundation (https://wish.org/)
- World Vision (https://worldvision.org/)
- Cancer Research Institute (https://cancerresearch.org/)
- Samaritan's Purse (https://samaritanspurse.org/)
- Hope for the Warriors (https://hopeforthewarriors.org/)
- Scholarship America (https://scholarshipamerica.org/)
- Charity Navigator (https://charitynavigator.org/)

REMEMBER

This is a short list, but there are thousands of other places or organizations that need donations to help people in need. Do your research to find one you can get on board with.

TIP

If you give locally, you are more likely to see first-hand the direct impact of your donation.

Saving more and spending less

The purpose of saving your money is to provide you with much-needed security in life. There are many reasons to save money. Most begin with a major goal, such as money to buy a car or for your college education. You may also want to save up for a vacation or an emergency fund. It is a good idea to have an emergency fund to fall back on when unexpected expenses, such as medical bills or car repairs, pop up. Trust me, you will thank yourself later for saving now.

Here are a few steps to help you create your own savings plan.

1. **Inventory your money.**

   It is important to know exactly how much money you have coming in and the different sources.

   - List your assets, such as cash, checking account, or savings account.
   - List your liabilities, such as credit card debt, student loans, car loans, rent, or mortgage.

- Calculate how much money you will have left over each month by subtracting your total liabilities from your total assets. This tells you what amount you have to work with.

2. **Set your savings goals.**

   Saving money is critical and will help benefit you in the future:

   - *Short-term savings goal:* This goal is for things you need to save for in the near future.
   - *Long-term savings goal:* This goal is for things you are saving money for within a much longer time frame.

3. **Decide on an amount to set aside each month.**

   The amount will vary depending on your end goal. Let's say you want to set up an emergency fund that totals $2,400 by the end of the year. If you divide $2,400 by 12 months, the total equals $200. This means that you need to set aside $200 per month to reach your emergency savings fund by the end of the year.

4. **Pick a spot to keep your savings.**

   Monitor your savings by selecting an account that will give you a good return on your money:

   - *Savings account:* The bank pays a small interest rate and usually has a low minimum balance requirement. You can withdraw your money from a typical savings account at any time.
   - *Money market account:* The bank pays interests on your balance periodically. You can deposit money at any time and have debit card access to the account.
   - *Certificate of deposit (CD):* This savings account is a fixed amount of money that is held for a fixed amount of time. This could be as short as five months or something longer like five years. The bank pays interest the entire time.

5. **Deposit your set amount and be patient.**

   Pretty soon you will have the savings you have wanted and will feel more financially secure.

TIP

Interest is the money the bank pays you at regular intervals for the use of your money. The interest is usually a certain percentage of the amount in your savings. Always compare interest rates before opening an account.

TIP

When saving for your retirement, which is a long-term goal, keep in mind there are many options for you. The most common type offered within your workplace is a 401(k) plan. For this plan, you will have a percent of each paycheck paid directly into a certain investment account. Your employer will match all or part of what you have contributed. That's a pretty sweet deal!

REMEMBER

The amount you spend is just as important as what you set aside to save. Think about the things you can and can't afford. If buying a pair of the newest, trendiest, and most expensive shoes will keep you from paying your rent that month, think twice. Be smart about how you spend your money. Are there coupons or discounts available for your purchases? Can you buy the generic brand instead of the name brand? Can you shop sales in your favorite stores? If you can answer yes to these questions, then you should make use of those options to spend much less money.

WARNING

Paying for convenience might be worth your money one day, but if you can do something yourself, it might lower your prices. Paying high delivery fees for fast food when you could grab it on the way home might be a good starting point to saving money. Paying a large number of fees on certain apps to do your grocery shopping for you and deliver it when you are fully capable of doing it yourself might be costing you more money than you think. Housecleaning services and laundry services are convenient and helpful if you can afford them, but if you need extra money in the bank, this is something you can do yourself.

Putting your money to work

You're working for your money, and it's time to make that money work for you! Investing your money is a must. When it comes to your retirement, long-term planning is key. You can plan for your retirement beginning now.

Experts say that you should invest 17 percent of your total yearly income in a retirement plan. For example, if you make $60,000 annually, you should set aside $10,200 each year. If you work for 35 years, you will have about $357,000 for your retirement. And this is all before any interest has been calculated!

If your retirement plan with your employer does not add up to at least 17 percent, open another retirement account in addition to the one you have to match the difference. This will ensure you are taken care of financially when you retire.

Here are some investment accounts that you can use to make your money earn more for you:

- General investment accounts such as stocks and bonds
- Individual Retirement Accounts (IRA), which can be Traditional or Roth IRAs
- Employer-sponsored retirement plans such as a 401(k)
- Education savings account

TIP

Consulting a financial advisor can help you organize your finances and find what accounts and investments will work best for you. You also can read more about retirement accounts in *401(k)s & IRAs For Dummies* (Wiley) by Ted Benna and Brenda Newmann.

Keeping Yourself out of the Red

You have probably heard the phrase *living paycheck to paycheck*. This means that as soon as you receive your income for the pay period, it is all gone due to your expenses. As soon as the money shows up in your account, you use it to pay your bills, and you are back to being broke until the next payday. Believe it or not, living paycheck to paycheck can occur at all different pay levels.

Living paycheck to paycheck occurs in many households because the cost of living increases over time but salaries sometimes remain the same. *Cost of living* refers to regular living expenses. These costs have consistently increased over the years, and changes in salaries have not moved in step with the increase. This is an issue because just buying food and gas takes a huge chunk out of your paycheck. Many times a person is more apt to have a "side hustle," or second job, to make up the difference. One way to avoid going broke each pay period is to create and utilize a budget.

Why do I need a budget?

Utilizing a budget is like creating your own instructional guide for your money. It is a place where you can set financial goals, set spending parameters, and ensure you are saving some money for a rainy day. One of the best features is that it can be personalized to your situation.

Here are some things a budget can do for you:

- It can help you reach your long-term and short-term savings goals.
- It can show you where you are overspending.
- It can help you map out your emergency fund.
- It can help you feel less anxious about your financial situation.

How do I stay on track?

Creating a budget is pretty simple, but following your budget is a different story. It requires that you have self-discipline. Sticking to your budget can ensure you are in a stronger financial situation for day-to-day living and long-term retirement.

There are five basic steps to creating your budget:

1. Identify all sources of your income.
2. Determine all of your expenses.
3. Choose a budget plan that works for you.
4. Adjust your spending to stay in line with your budget.
5. Follow your plan each month to ensure effectiveness.

List *all* sources of expected income, as in the example in Figure 10-4. Notice that the example in the figure shows that the expected income was higher than the actual income brought in that month.

PERSONAL MONTHLY BUDGET

PROJECTED MONTHLY INCOME	Income 1	$4,300.00
	Extra income	$300.00
	Total monthly income	**$4,600.00**
ACTUAL MONTHLY INCOME	Income 1	$4,000.00
	Extra income	$300.00
	Total monthly income	**$4,300.00**

FIGURE 10-4: An example of personal income breakdown.

Next, determine every expected expense, like the list in Figure 10-5. This includes everything like housing, utilities, food, charity, health, entertainment, and more. Your list may not look exactly like the figure; you may not have some of these categories, or you might have to add some of your own. Notice that in each category in Figure 10-5, some projected expenses were lower than the actual expenses. No worries if that happens; you will have to adjust another category. Adjusting your spending is not an easy task, but this is where your self-discipline is very important to continue for keeping you on track to your financial goals.

PERSONAL MONTHLY BUDGET

PROJECTED MONTHLY INCOME	Income 1	$4,300.00
	Extra income	$300.00
	Total monthly income	$4,600.00
ACTUAL MONTHLY INCOME	Income 1	$4,000.00
	Extra income	$300.00
	Total monthly income	$4,300.00

PROJECTED BALANCE (Projected income minus expenses)	$0.00
ACTUAL BALANCE (Actual income minus expenses)	$147.71
DIFFERENCE (Actual minus projected)	$147.71

HOUSING	Projected Cost	Actual Cost	Difference
Mortgage or rent	$2,000.00	$1,650.00	$350.00
Phone	$100.00	$97.00	$3.00
Electricity	$100.00	$115.00	-$15.00
Gas	$40.00	$28.00	$12.00
Water and sewer	$8.00	$8.00	$0.00
Cable	$0.00	$0.00	$0.00
Waste removal	$10.00	$10.00	$0.00
Maintenance or repairs	$23.00	$0.00	$23.00
Supplies	$0.00	$0.00	$0.00
Other	$0.00	$0.00	$0.00
Subtotal			$373.00

TRANSPORTATION	Projected Cost	Actual Cost	Difference
Vehicle payment	$500.00	$559.00	-$59.00
Bus/taxi fare	$0.00	$0.00	$0.00
Insurance	$100.00	$100.00	$0.00
Licensing	$0.00	$0.00	$0.00
Fuel	$200.00	$150.00	$50.00
Maintenance	$50.00	$20.00	$30.00
Other			$0.00
Subtotal			$21.00

INSURANCE	Projected Cost	Actual Cost	Difference
Home			$0.00
Health			$0.00
Life			$0.00
Other			$0.00
Subtotal			$0.00

FOOD	Projected Cost	Actual Cost	Difference
Groceries	$300.00	$245.00	$55.00
Dining out	$150.00	$120.00	$30.00
Other			$0.00
Subtotal			$85.00

PETS	Projected Cost	Actual Cost	Difference
Food	$50.00	$50.00	$0.00
Medical	$25.00	$0.00	$25.00
Grooming	$50.00	$50.00	$0.00
Toys	$10.00	$10.00	$0.00
Other			$0.00
Subtotal			$25.00

PERSONAL CARE	Projected Cost	Actual Cost	Difference
Medical	$80.00	$80.00	$0.00
Hair/nails	$50.00	$50.00	$0.00
Clothing	$100.00	$0.00	$100.00
Dry cleaning	$50.00	$20.00	$30.00
Health club	$49.00	$49.00	$0.00
Organization dues or fe	$60.00	$0.00	$60.00
Other			$0.00
Subtotal			$190.00

ENTERTAINMENT	Projected Cost	Actual Cost	Difference
Streaming Services	$45.00	$31.29	$13.71
Apps	$0.00	$0.00	$0.00
Movies	$0.00	$80.00	-$80.00
Concerts	$0.00	$0.00	$0.00
Sporting events	$0.00	$80.00	-$80.00
Live theater	$0.00	$0.00	$0.00
Other	$50.00	$150.00	-$100.00
Other	$0.00	$0.00	$0.00
Other	$0.00	$0.00	$0.00
Subtotal			-$246.29

LOANS	Projected Cost	Actual Cost	Difference
Personal			$0.00
Student			$0.00
Credit card			$0.00
Credit card			$0.00
Credit card			$0.00
Other			$0.00
Subtotal			$0.00

TAXES	Projected Cost	Actual Cost	Difference
Federal			$0.00
State			$0.00
Local			$0.00
Other			$0.00
Subtotal			$0.00

SAVINGS OR INVESTMENTS	Projected Cost	Actual Cost	Difference
Retirement account			$0.00
Investment account			$0.00
Other			$0.00
Subtotal			$0.00

GIFTS AND DONATIONS	Projected Cost	Actual Cost	Difference
Charity 1	$400.00	$400.00	$0.00
Charity 2			$0.00
Charity 3			$0.00
Subtotal			$0.00

LEGAL	Projected Cost	Actual Cost	Difference
Attorney			$0.00
Alimony			$0.00
Payments on lien or judgment			$0.00
Other			$0.00
Subtotal			$0.00

TOTAL PROJECTED COST	$4,600.00
TOTAL ACTUAL COST	$4,152.29
TOTAL DIFFERENCE	$447.71

FIGURE 10-5: An example of a personal budget.

Figure 10-5 isn't the only kind of budget sheets you could use. Figure 10-6 shows an example of a college budget.

College Monthly Budget

Monthly Budget	Actual Spent	Money Spent: 81%
$2,430	$1,960	

Academic Expenses

Items	Budget	Actual Spent	Notes
Tuition & Fees	$ 800.00	$ 800.00	
Books & School Supplies	$ 300.00	$ 300.00	
Miscellaneous	$ 150.00	$ 150.00	
Total	**$ 1,250.00**	**$ 1,250.00**	

Living Expenses

Items	Budget	Actual Spent	Notes
Rent	$ 280.00	$ 280.00	
Food - Meal Plan	$ 200.00	$ 100.00	
Food - Others	$ 50.00	$ 50.00	
Groceries	$ 110.00	$ 50.00	
Utilities (gas, electricity)	$ 35.00	$ 35.00	
Phone	$ 40.00	$ 40.00	
Insurance	$ 55.00	$ 55.00	
Transportation	$ 300.00	$ 20.00	
Total	**$ 1,070.00**	**$ 630.00**	

Personal Expenses

Items	Budget	Actual Spent	Notes
Entertainment	$ 30.00	$ 10.00	
Clothing	$ 30.00	$ 20.00	
Savings	$ 50.00	$ 50.00	
Others	$ -		
Total	**$ 110.00**	**$ 80.00**	

FIGURE 10-6: An example college budget.

You can also create a budget for events, holidays, trips, or vacations. Figure 10-7 shows an example for a family who is trying to stay within an allotted amount for the holidays, which can get expensive!

Holiday budget planner

HOLIDAY BUDGET	$1,315.00
ACTUAL SPENT	$1,060.00
DIFFERENCE (over/under budget)	$255.00

GIFTS

Item	Budget	Actual	Difference
Family	$500.00	$350.00 ✓	$150.00
Friends	$250.00	$100.00 ✓	$150.00
Co-workers	$0.00	$0.00 ✕	$0.00
Teachers, nannies, babysitters, etc.	$0.00	$0.00 ✕	$0.00
Charitable donations	$0.00	$0.00 ✕	$0.00
Other (tab in last column of this row to add row)	$0.00	$0.00 ✕	$0.00
Total	$750.00	$450.00 ✓	$300.00

HOLIDAY MEALS

Item	Budget	Actual	Difference
Groceries	$200.00	$200.00 ✓	$0.00
Libations	$0.00	$0.00 ●	$0.00
Decorations	$50.00	$50.00 ●	$0.00
Other (tab in last column of this row to add row)		●	$0.00
		●	$0.00
Total	$250.00	$250.00 ●	$0.00

PACKAGING

Item	Budget	Actual	Difference
Gift wrap	$15.00	$10.00 ✕	$5.00
Tags	$0.00	$0.00 ✕	$0.00
Supplies (ribbon, tape, etc.)	$0.00	$0.00 ✕	$0.00
Boxes	$0.00	$0.00 ✕	$0.00
Postage	$10.00	$10.00 ✕	$0.00
Other (tab in last column of this row to add row)		✕	$0.00
Total	$25.00	$20.00 ✕	$5.00

ENTERTAINMENT

Item	Budget	Actual	Difference
Party help (bartender, caterer, cleaners, etc.)	$0.00	$0.00 ●	$0.00
Decorations	$0.00	$0.00 ●	$0.00
Food and beverages	$0.00	$0.00 ●	$0.00
Clothing	$0.00	$0.00 ●	$0.00
Tickets	$0.00	$0.00 ●	$0.00
Dinners out	$100.00	$150.00 ◆	-$50.00
Other (tab in last column of this row to add row)		●	$0.00
Total	$100.00	$150.00 ◆	-$50.00

TRAVEL

Item	Budget	Actual	Difference
Airfare	$0.00	✕	$0.00
Lodging	$0.00	✕	$0.00
Transportation	$50.00	$50.00 ✕	$0.00
Other (tab in last column of this row to add row)		✕	$0.00
Total	$50.00	$50.00 ✕	$0.00

MISCELLANEOUS

Item	Budget	Actual	Difference
Holiday photos	$60.00	$60.00 ●	$0.00
Gas	$80.00	$80.00 ●	$0.00
Other (tab in last column of this row to add row)		●	$0.00
Total	$140.00	$140.00 ●	$0.00

FIGURE 10-7: An example holiday budget.

One of the biggest and most special events of your life could be a wedding! Have you ever thought about how much it would cost? Check out the example in Figure 10-8 and see how difficult it might be to stay within the budget.

REMEMBER

A budget is a tool that can help you reach your financial goals. Getting out of debt, saving more, or just having better control of how much you spend are all great reasons to begin using a budget. Give it a try! I bet you will begin to feel more confident about your financial abilities and soon you'll become a budgeting wizard! You can also check out *Managing Your Money All-In-One For Dummies* for more information.

Wedding Budget

Summary	Estimated	Actual	Over/Under
Reception	$5,500.00	$5,300.00	▲
Apparel	$5,000.00	$5,000.00	▲
Photography	$2,950.00	$2,950.00	▲
Decorations	$2,300.00	$2,300.00	▲
Transportation	$1,450.00	$1,400.00	▲
Gifts	$1,400.00	$1,300.00	▲
Music	$1,200.00	$1,250.00	▼
Flowers	$800.00	$800.00	▲
Stationery / Printing	$400.00	$400.00	▲
Other Expenses	$300.00	$300.00	▲
Total Budget	$21,300.00	$21,000.00	▲

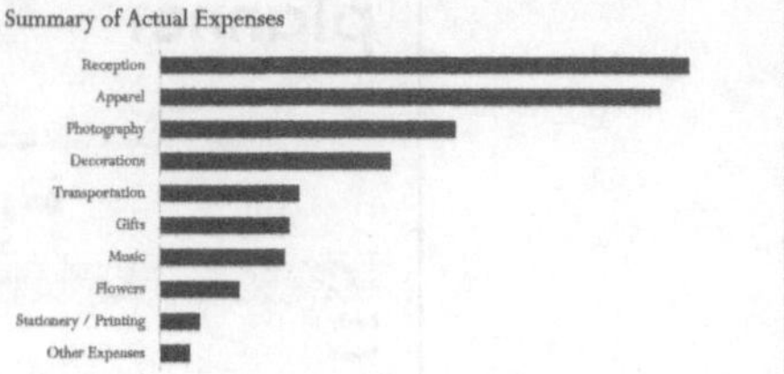

Apparel	Estimated	Actual	Over/Under
Engagement ring	$5,000.00	$5,000.00	▲
Wedding rings	$0.00	$0.00	▲
Tux, suit, and/or dresses	$0.00	$0.00	▲
Veil/headpiece	$0.00	$0.00	▲
Shoes	$0.00	$0.00	▲
Jewelry	$0.00	$0.00	▲
Accessories	$0.00	$0.00	▲
Others	$0.00	$0.00	▲
Total for Apparel	$5,000.00	$5,000.00	▲

Gifts	Estimated	Actual	Over/Under
Attendants	$1,200.00	$1,100.00	▲
Parents	$200.00	$200.00	▲
Readers/other participants	$0.00	$0.00	▲
Others	$0.00	$0.00	▲
Total for Gifts	$1,400.00	$1,300.00	▲

Music	Estimated	Actual	Over/Under
Musicians for ceremony	$1,200.00	$1,250.00	▼
Band/DJ for reception	$0.00	$0.00	▲
Others	$0.00	$0.00	▲
Total for Music	$1,200.00	$1,250.00	▼

Reception	Estimated	Actual	Over/Under
Room/hall fees	$5,500.00	$5,300.00	▲
Tables and chairs	$0.00	$0.00	▲
Food	$0.00	$0.00	▲
Drinks	$0.00	$0.00	▲
Linens	$0.00	$0.00	▲
Cake	$0.00	$0.00	▲
Favors	$0.00	$0.00	▲
Staff and gratuities	$0.00	$0.00	▲
Others	$0.00	$0.00	▲
Total for Reception	$5,500.00	$5,300.00	▲

Other Expenses	Estimated	Actual	Over/Under
Officiant	$300.00	$300.00	▲
Church/ceremony site fee	$0.00	$0.00	▲
Wedding coordinator	$0.00	$0.00	▲
Rehearsal dinner	$0.00	$0.00	▲
Engagement party	$0.00	$0.00	▲
Showers	$0.00	$0.00	▲
Bachelor/ette parties	$0.00	$0.00	▲
Hotel rooms	$0.00	$0.00	▲
Total for Other Expenses	$300.00	$300.00	▲

Decorations	Estimated	Actual	Over/Under
Bows for church pews	$1,800.00	$1,800.00	▲
Table centerpieces	$500.00	$500.00	▲
Candles	$0.00	$0.00	▲
Lighting	$0.00	$0.00	▲
Balloons	$0.00	$0.00	▲
Others	$0.00	$0.00	▲
Total for Decorations	$2,300.00	$2,300.00	▲

Flowers	Estimated	Actual	Over/Under
Bouquets	$800.00	$800.00	▲
Boutonnières	$0.00	$0.00	▲
Corsages	$0.00	$0.00	▲
Ceremony	$0.00	$0.00	▲
Reception	$0.00	$0.00	▲
Others	$0.00	$0.00	▲
Total for Flowers	$800.00	$800.00	▲

Photography	Estimated	Actual	Over/Under
Formals	$1,200.00	$1,200.00	▲
Candids	$800.00	$800.00	▲
Extra prints	$0.00	$0.00	▲
Photo albums	$0.00	$0.00	▲
Videography	$950.00	$950.00	▲
Others	$0.00	$0.00	▲
Total for Photography	$2,950.00	$2,950.00	▲

Stationery / Printing	Estimated	Actual	Over/Under
Invitations	$400.00	$400.00	▲
Announcements	$0.00	$0.00	▲
Thank-You cards	$0.00	$0.00	▲
Personal stationery	$0.00	$0.00	▲
Guest book	$0.00	$0.00	▲
Programs	$0.00	$0.00	▲
Reception napkins	$0.00	$0.00	▲
Matchbooks	$0.00	$0.00	▲
Calligraphy	$0.00	$0.00	▲
Others	$0.00	$0.00	▲
Total for Stationery / Printing	$400.00	$400.00	▲

Transportation	Estimated	Actual	Over/Under
Limousines/trolleys	$900.00	$900.00	▲
Parking	$200.00	$200.00	▲
Taxis	$350.00	$300.00	▲
Others	$0.00	$0.00	▲
Total for Transportation	$1,450.00	$1,400.00	▲

FIGURE 10-8: An example wedding budget.

Managing Credit Cards

When shopping, you might see people use many forms of payment. To make a purchase you have several options:

- Paper and coin currency is cash money in hand.
- A debit card is tied to your bank account, and the money is immediately deducted when you pay.
- A credit card is tied to a line of credit, which means you are essentially borrowing from a creditor.
- A phone app is most likely tied to a debit card, credit card, or bank account.

A debit card enables you to access money that you put into your bank account to obtain it quite easily for purchases. A credit card is different. You know you must *apply* for a credit card, and you must disclose your Social Security number, your income, employer information, loans, debt, and housing situation on the application. Figure 10-9 shows what a generic credit application looks like. With the information from the form, the creditor looks up your credit score and compares it to the other info you have provided to decide if you are a good candidate for the creditor to loan money.

REMEMBER

If you are approved for a credit card, you then obtain a card with a line of credit and the terms of the agreement. But there's a catch! If you use the card, you must pay back the money!

CREDIT APPLICATION		
APPLICANT INFORMATION		
Name:		
Date of birth:	SSN:	Phone:
Current address:		
City:	State:	ZIP Code:
Own Rent (Please circle)	Monthly payment or rent:	How long?
Previous address:		
City:	State:	ZIP Code:
Owned Rented (Please circle)	Monthly payment or rent:	How long?
EMPLOYMENT INFORMATION		
Current employer:		
Employer address:		How long?
Phone:	E-mail:	Fax:
City:	State:	ZIP Code:
Position:	Hourly Salary (Please circle)	Annual income:
Previous employer:		
Address:		How long?
Phone:	E-mail:	Fax:
City:	State:	ZIP Code:
Position:	Hourly Salary (Please circle)	Annual income:
Name of a relative not residing with you:		
Address:		Phone:
City:	State:	ZIP Code:
Relationship:		
CO-APPLICANT INFORMATION, IF FOR A JOINT ACCOUNT		
Name:		
Date of birth:	SSN:	Phone:
Current address:		
City:	State:	ZIP Code:
Own Rent (Please circle)	Monthly payment or rent:	How long?
Previous address:		
City:	State:	ZIP Code:
Owned Rented (Please circle)	Monthly payment or rent:	How long?
EMPLOYMENT INFORMATION		
Current employer:		
Employer address:		How long?
Phone:	E-mail:	Fax:
City:	State:	ZIP Code:
Position:	Hourly Salary (Please circle)	Annual income:
Previous employer:		
Address:		
Phone:	E-mail:	Fax:
City:	State:	ZIP Code:
Position:	Hourly Salary (Please circle)	Annual income:

FIGURE 10-9: A credit application

CREDIT APPLICATION

APPLICATION INFORMATION CONTINUED		
Name of a relative not residing with you:		
Address:		Phone:
City:	State:	ZIP Code:
Relationship:		

CREDIT CARDS			
Name	Account no.	Current balance	Monthly payment

MORTGAGE COMPANY	
Account no.:	Address:

AUTO LOANS			
Auto loans	Account no.	Balance	Monthly payment

OTHER LOANS, DEBTS, OR OBLIGATIONS		
Description	Account no.	Amount

OTHER ASSETS OR SOURCES OF INCOME	
Description	Amount per month or value

I authorize Contoso, Ltd. to verify the information provided on this form as to my credit and employment history.	
Signature of applicant	Date
Signature of co-applicant, if for joint account	Date

FIGURE 10-9: (continued)

Giving credit where credit is due

There are many different types of credit cards to obtain and many different creditors. A creditor wants you to apply for its card because the company makes money from the fees they apply. Many companies offer some pretty cool plans and features:

» A **reward credit card** gives you points for a percentage of what you spend on the card. Rewards could include airline points, travel, gift cards, merchandise, groceries, gas, and much more.

- A **cashback credit card** allows you a reward in the form of cash that you can use to pay off the card or use for whatever you would like.
- A **travel credit card** takes a percentage of what you spend and gives you points toward an airline or hotel.
- A **store credit card** offers you a line of credit to a specific store. For example, if you apply for a credit card at Target Stores, the only place you can use that card is at Target.

Applying for a credit card is not for everyone. Some people want to steer clear of credit cards, whereas others use them responsibly to earn rewards. Let's take a look at some advantages and disadvantages of credit cards.

- Advantages of having a credit card:
  - You can build a better credit score if you pay back on time. (Read more about credit scores in the next section.)
  - It is convenient and easy to use.
  - You can earn various rewards.
  - Online shopping is easy.
  - You can pay off large purchases over time.
- Disadvantages of having a credit card:
  - It is very tempting to overspend.
  - You can create debt for yourself.
  - There are fees for using the card such as a late fee, annual fee, over-limit fee, returned payment fee, and more.
  - Misuse of the card can hurt your credit score.
  - When you initially apply for a credit card, your credit score will take a hit.

TIP

To avoid any credit card fees, follow the cardholder agreement completely, pay off the amount each month, and check your statements regularly.

REMEMBER

Having a credit card is convenient and useful, as long as you do not overspend. Be smart about your finances to avoid unnecessary costs and fees. Most creditors are banking on the fact that you will not pay your balance in full each month. That way they can charge you interest and other fees.

Making the grade: Credit scores and reports

Something that will follow you around your entire life is your credit report. You must pay bills on time to ensure you make a good score on your report. A credit report includes all of your current and historical credit activity. It includes credit card reports, loan reports, mortgage reports, and more. The name of each creditor is listed as well as the current balances, credit limits, payment history, and if the account is open or closed. All of these put together make up your credit score.

If you do not pay bills on time, or if you have a large amount of debt, your score may be low. If you cannot take care of a small credit card, it will show on your report. When it comes time for a larger purchase, such as a car or home that you would like to borrow to purchase, you'll find it harder to get a decent loan. You will end up paying higher interest and fees because the credit companies and lenders see you as a larger risk. If your credit score is sufficiently bad, you will most likely be rejected for a loan or credit line. Also, if you are fresh out of high school, you might not have any credit to score high on a report. This is when you could get a small credit card that you can easily make monthly payments on in full to show that you can pay back what you borrow. This will likely give you a high credit score for those other purchases you would like to help meet your financial goals. Here's a breakdown of the credit score categories:

- 300–629: Bad
- 630–689: Fair
- 690–719: Good
- 720–850: Excellent

TIP

There are many sites and apps where you can track your credit report for free. Do some research and find a spot where you can access your report and check your score. One place to start your research is `https://usa.gov/credit-reports`. It is also a good idea to check your credit report regularly to ensure there aren't errors on it.

Buying now and paying later

A loan is different than credit because you receive a lump sum upfront and then pay the loan back through scheduled monthly payments. A loan is used for larger purchases such as paying college tuition, purchasing a car, purchasing a house, making home improvements, and much more. Loans are not designed to be taken out frequently. You may have one or two loans at a time (for example, a loan for a house and a second one for a car).

There are different types of loans. Maybe you are at a place in your life where a loan is a good option for you. Here are a few of the different types available:

- **Personal loan:** Used for vacations, events, weddings, emergencies, medical treatments, home renovations, and more.
- **Auto loan:** Used to buy a vehicle with terms to pay back the loan in a certain number of years.
- **Mortgage loan:** This helps you finance the purchase of a home. There are many types of mortgage loans.
- **Student loan:** Used to pay for tuition, living expenses, and fees at accredited schools. In other words, this one is not even an option if you aren't a student.
- **Home-equity loan:** Also known as a second mortgage. You take the equity you have on your home already and typically borrow up to 85% of what your home is worth in equity.
- **Debt-consolidation loan:** Used to pay off other debts you might have incurred. So instead of paying many different creditors each month, the debt is paid off with the lump sum you have borrowed, and you make one payment each month toward the debt-consolidation loan.
- **Buy now, pay later loan:** This is a point-of-sale installment loan where you might pay a little bit at the time of purchase but then settle on an agreement to pay the rest over the course of several months, usually without paying any interest. This is popular through online services and apps such as Affirm, Sezzle, Afterpay, PayPal, or Klarna.
- **Payday loan:** A short-term loan that you must pay back with your next paycheck. This type of loan isn't credit-based; instead, it's based on your paycheck. But beware, if you cannot pay the loan back by the next payday, many fees are added and this could put you further in debt.

WARNING

Only take out a loan if you know you will have the ability to pay it back over time. An unpaid loan can devastate your credit score and report.

REMEMBER

Purchasing large items is a part of your life, but having the most expensive, nicest house and a luxury car doesn't make you more of an adult. Just because you *can* borrow money, doesn't mean you *should*. Living within your means and being financially responsible shows the true maturity of an adult!

IN THIS CHAPTER

» Knowing when it's time to live on your own

» Organizing your space

» Buying a car

Chapter 11
How Much?! Paying for Housing and Buying a Car

In this chapter, I cover the ins and outs of living on your own for the first time, how to make the most of the space you have, and how to sort out your transportation needs. Deciding to be on your own is an exciting time, but you need to make sure you're ready. I'm here to help!

Moving Out . . . It May Be Time

Home sweet home — the home you have grown up in. We all remember our childhood home. Whether you still live at home with your parents, live away from home but with roommates, or live on your own, there are a couple of things to think about when it comes to your home. The ultimate goal of a home is to provide these three things.

» A home provides for you physically, such as protection against weather, outside elements, a place to sleep, to eat, and to be safe.

- A home provides emotional security. You can find a place to relax in privacy and comfort. Your decor might even reflect your taste.
- A home provides you with a social atmosphere that gives you a sense of belonging and love. Your home might serve as a gathering place for family and friends to live, work, and play together.

Some of the basic needs from Maslow's hierarchy of human needs (which I mention in Chapter 2) can be met just by having a home. When your housing serves an emotional and social need, it's more than just a roof over your head. It becomes a home. How can you determine when it is time to move out and get a place on your own? When is it time to create that sense of belonging and security in your own home? The time is different for each individual. The following are some indicators that it may be time to move out of your parents' house, family members' house, or other current living situation:

- You begin to feel like you do not have ownership over your personal items, even if you purchased them.
- You have an emergency fund in savings.
- Your schedule is the opposite of those you live with and you begin to feel uneasy coming home at crazy hours.
- You want a pet, but they are not allowed in your current living situation.
- You want more privacy.
- You cannot decorate your space to express your creativity.
- You already pay most of your own bills.
- Your mental health is affected negatively by your living situation.

REMEMBER

Living in a place of your own brings a sense of accomplishment but also much more responsibility.

Honey, I'm home

When it comes to housing, people have different needs and wants. You may think something is necessary for a home, but others may see it as a drawback. Here are some questions to consider when thinking about housing:

- **Size**
  - How many people will be living in the space?
  - Will you need room for regular guests and visitors?

- What will the space be used for? For example, will you need a work space or home office?

- **Stage of life**
  - Is this your first time living on your own?
  - Are you married with children?
  - Do you need space to take care of your extended family?
- **Special considerations**
  - Do you or a family member have a special need regarding mobility?
  - Do you need to be close to public transportation or a safe area to walk for a person with vision impairment?
  - Will elderly individuals be living with you?
- **Location**
  - Is it important to live close to your school, job, or place of worship?
  - Would you rather live in a busy city neighborhood, a quiet part of town, or in the country?
  - Do you want quick access to stores, restaurants, or public transportation?
  - Is the size of the city important to you?
- **Lifestyle**
  - What type of day-to-day living is important?
  - Do you want to be close to friends and places for an active nightlife?
  - Will you be working from home?
- **Financial considerations**
  - Is there a high cost of living in the area?
  - Does the neighborhood require a home owners association (HOA) fee?
  - Does the house require extra maintenance, such as caring for a pool or large landscapes?

TIP

Believe it or not, location should be at the top of your list when deciding on a home. Do you really want to live in a property where you will need to commute hours a day to your workplace or school? Do you want to settle down in a neighborhood with a high crime rate? Location may not be in the forefront of your mind when looking at some eye-catching housing options, but trust me, you will thank yourself later if you focus on *where* your house is located.

Different types of housing

After you have decided what type of location you want to live in, you have to consider the types of housing available. Depending on the location, you might have many options available to you, or you might be limited. The two most common types of housing are stand-alone housing and multi-dwelling units:

- Stand-alone housing has the following characteristics:
  - Built to house one individual or a family.
  - Is freestanding — not sharing any walls with another unit.
  - Can be large, small, or multiple stories tall.
  - Offers more privacy than multi-dwelling units.
  - Is usually a more expensive option than other types.
- Multi-dwelling units have the following characteristics:
  - Contain several housing units in one structure.
  - Can be a duplex, which is one building with two separate units that share one wall. One person usually owns both units and either rents both or lives in one and rents out the other.
  - Can be multiplex housing, which is where three or more units share the same building, such as a condo, which can be rented or owned.
  - Can be considered a townhome, where the single-family home is at least two floors and shares one wall with another house. Each townhome is individually owned.
  - Can be apartments. An apartment building is a structure that has multiple rental units. Apartments range from three or four units to high-rise apartments that have hundreds of units. An apartment complex has separate buildings with units grouped together for rent.
  - Include student housing such as dorm units.
  - Often are more affordable than stand-alone housing.
  - Are readily available and can be used for a short or long amount of time.
  - May include shared laundry facilities, pool area, workout area, or other special features.
  - Are usually less private than a stand-alone dwelling.
  - Have limited storage, yard area, and parking.
  - May not allow pets.

TIP

When attending a college or university, many students choose to live in student housing. A dorm room is a small, shared space that consists of one room for sleeping, eating, entertainment, and studying. Many students feel that living in student housing allows them to meet new people and experience everything college life has to offer.

REMEMBER

Throughout your life, you will likely live in different types of housing. Depending on your stage of life, it might be time to downsize or upsize. You may find yourself taking care of your parents, much like a role reversal. They might need to live with you or consider other options such as retirement homes with senior living care. Taking care of your aging family members is a large responsibility that should be done with the upmost dignity and respect. After all, they did raise you into the amazing human you are today!

Renting versus buying

When you're looking at places to live, you must consider whether you will rent or buy. Renting means you will pay money to live in housing that is owned by someone else. The proprietor is your go-to person if there are problems or issues with the unit. Here are some pros and cons of renting a place to live.

Pros:

- It is not a long-term commitment. A lease is a written rental agreement. Leases are available in different durations: month-long leases, 12-month leases, or 24-month leases, for example. At the end of the lease term, you can decide whether to renew your lease if you would like to live there longer.
- You have very little maintenance responsibility. For example, if you walk into your apartment and realize the plumbing has flooded your bathroom, it is not your responsibility to pay for the repairs. The property manager or building owner will take care of that.
- There is no large down payment, only a security deposit. When you first move in, you deposit an equivalent of a month's rent to cover any damages that occur while you live there. It is important to take care of the apartment so you can get this deposit back if you move out.
- Renting can help you decide what neighborhood you might want to buy a home in.

Cons:

- Your rent price could go up when it comes time to renew your lease.

- Pets are usually not allowed. If they are, the property owner likely requires a pet deposit.
- You may not have to pay for maintenance and repairs, but you are still at the mercy of the owner for how quickly they decide to repair items.

Buying a home also can be a good option. The following are some of the pros and cons of purchasing a home of your own.

Pros:

- Buying a home can help you build equity, or the difference between what your home is worth and how much you still owe. If you can pay off your mortgage in 15 to 30 years, you can enjoy retirement with much lower monthly expenses.
- You may have more privacy if you buy a stand-alone house rather than a unit in a multi-dwelling structure.
- It is a more permanent option for long-term stability.
- You have more control to make any changes or renovations that you would like since your home is yours.
- You can have pets!

Cons:

- It can be very expensive. You need some sort of a down payment — usually between 3 percent and 20 percent of the total purchase — although there are some types of loans that require no down payment.
- You have to pay all the maintenance, repair costs, and labor costs out of your own pocket.
- You have less flexibility after purchasing because you have "put down your roots." It is a much more complicated process to move elsewhere when you own your home.

REMEMBER

Only you can decide if renting or buying is right for you. Take comfort in knowing that you have options when it comes to housing and then make an educated decision from there.

Moving day

So you have decided on the perfect house to move into. It's the right location, the right size, the right style, and, most important, the right price! Congrats, that is awesome! But the work is just beginning. How in the world do you prepare to move? Here are a few pointers:

- Have a garage sale! What I mean is, get rid of the "stuff" you have accumulated throughout the years that you don't really need. If you haven't used something in six months to a year, it just might be time to get rid of it by selling or donating it. You can sell used items online at eBay, Mercari, Poshmark, or similar websites. Other items can be donated to Goodwill, Salvation Army, or other donation sites in your community. Don't move anything extra just to put it in storage at your new place.
- As you are collecting items to sell or donate, go ahead and begin packing to move. You can pack up items that you don't expect to use before you move. For example, if you are moving in the winter, you can pack up your summer clothes.
- You may pack for yourself, pay for a service to pack for you, rent a U-Haul or trailer, or pay for movers. Whatever you choose, decide early so that you can make arrangements early enough to stay organized and make the move less stressful.
- Schedule the electricity, water, and gas for your new place in advance. The last thing you want is to get all moved in and have no utilities for the first 24–48 hours.
- Pack a weekend suitcase with all your usual necessities. Having a change of clothes, toothbrush, and toiletries on hand where you can easily find them in the midst of moving chaos can be helpful. There will most likely be unexpected delays!
- If you are moving on your own, stock up on boxes, tape, trash bags, and paper towels. Check with grocery stores or convenience stores to see if they have boxes you can use have free instead of purchasing new ones. Also, if you are renting a moving truck for your large furniture, make sure it has a loading ramp.

TIP

When packing boxes, place the heavy items on the bottom and lighter items on the top. Use a smaller box for books and other heavy items to avoid creating a box that's too heavy to lift. Items from the same room should be in the same boxes and labeled with the room it is from. Don't mix items from different rooms in the same box; you will thank yourself later when unpacking. Wrap your large electronics and furniture in a protective cloth to keep them from being damaged.

Better Living by Design

You finally have your own space! It might be your first apartment or condo, your own room, or a house you just bought. One of the first things on the agenda is deciding how you want to set up your space. Designing a living space might seem daunting to some, but exciting to others. No worries — anyone, including you, can design a pleasing, safe, and functional living space. Whether you are just planning to brighten a room or redesign the room entirely, you should have a plan and vision should be in place.

Here are some questions to ask yourself:

- What is your goal for the space?
- What activities will take place in the space?
- What type of storage do you need?
- What do you want your space to look like?
- What current parts of the space work well?
- What needs improvement?
- What is your budget?

REMEMBER

Having a plan in place, or more importantly, a budget, is crucial to redesign success. If you have limited resources, there is no point in planning expensive changes.

TIP

Even small, inexpensive touches, like painting, can drastically change the appearance and feel of a room.

Designing for your best life

Most of us spend at least half of our lives indoors. The space we stay in has a large influence on how we feel and how we act. Our interior spaces can be a big influence our mental health.

The following are some things you may want to consider when you're planning a design for your living space:

- Did you know sunlight can lighten your mood and raise your spirits? If your space has windows, get window covers you can open to let in the sunlight.

» Having limited clutter can increase the illusion of space, which can contribute to positive mental well-being. Openness in a home can keep things brighter and happier.

» Your decor can include plants and flowers, which serve as natural air filters to literally help you breathe easier.

» Color has a major impact on the mood and feel of a room. Lighter colors may make the room feel more spacious and darker colors may make the room feel smaller.

- Red can spice up a space, but it is also considered the color of aggression and power, which could make you feel anxious at times. Use red sparingly.
- Green is soothing and calm. Balance, nature, harmony, and growth are promoted by the color green. Although green can create a soothing feeling, a little may go a long way. Do not use too much green because it could darken or take over the room.
- Orange is an energetic color. It is a warm tone and can make your space feel cozy. Orange is usually used in energetic places to get you moving. If you want to promote a calming atmosphere, orange is not the best color for the job.
- Blue is a calming color that can be used to create a serene environment. If an ocean or water design are your goals, choose blue. Keep in mind that blue can also be associated with sadness. The color blue might leave you "feeling blue," so if you want to kick depression out, the color blue is not for you.
- Purple is luxurious and is associated with creativity and individuality. However, too much purple can create a feeling of irritability in some people.
- Yellow is a warm color that is associated with happiness and creativity. Yellow is often used in children's rooms. A light yellow can even serve as a neutral color.
- Brown is a color in nature and can make a home feel safe and secure. Brown kitchen cabinets or brown wooden floors are just the right touches. Too much brown can feel dull.
- Gray can create a neutral balance in a space. Too much gray can make a room feel cold and uninviting.
- White is very common in homes. White ceilings, white walls, white trim, or white built-ins are popular because white goes with anything. White promotes a feeling of brightness, spaciousness, cleanliness, and purity.

- Technically, black is the absence of color, and it is often linked with the feeling of sorrow, death, or depression. If used subtly; however, black can be sophisticated and dramatic.

REMEMBER

Having a good design plan that suits your style and promotes positive mental health is important for your livelihood. Here are a few more principles and elements to consider when designing your personal space:

- Space
- Line
- Shape
- Texture
- Color
- Balance
- Emphasis
- Harmony
- Proportion
- Rhythm
- Scale

Check out Figure 11-1 to see if you can identify these principles and elements applied to the room in the image.

TIP

To learn more about how to put the principles and elements of design to work in a space, check out `https://sketchup.com/` for a free tutorial.

Designing for safety and security

Keep in mind that your safety and others' safety is a priority when designing a space. You wouldn't take the handrail off of your staircase or leave a glass mirror unsecured just because you think it would look better. That is not responsible, especially since someone could get hurt. Creating a safe environment is crucial to your feelings of security and belonging.

You can never feel fully at rest if you are anxious about getting hurt in your own home. Think about who will be living in the space with you. Is it someone with a special need or mobility issue or an elderly individual? If so, you need to make accommodations for that person to help everyone feel safe and functional in their own home.

FIGURE 11-1: A living room space.

Here are ways you can keep your home safe on the inside and out:

- Install a smart doorbell.

  A smart doorbell includes a camera on the doorbell for you to access from your phone or other device. You can see who is at the door *before* you open it. It may also have a speaker where you can talk and hear a response from the person ringing the bell. The camera is recording at all times, so if you have a package go missing from your porch, you can see the culprit.

- Include a deadbolt on your doors.
- Use motion-activated outdoor lights.
- Install security cameras.
- Install an entire home security system (see Figure 11-2).

TIP

Thanks to technology, there are some very inexpensive security systems you can install yourself.

- Keep smoke alarms and carbon monoxide detectors up to date by testing them on a monthly basis.
- Install a locked fence around a swimming pool.
- Do not keep a spare key under your welcome mat.

- Do not allow your mail to pile up outside your door or in your mailbox. Someone might think you are away.
- Keep a fire extinguisher in your house and be sure it is up to date.
- Keep cabinets that contain cleaning supplies or chemicals locked at all times.
- Close your garage door.
- Have a home emergency plan for fires, weather, and other emergencies.
- Join the neighborhood watch group.
- Turn off all small appliances when you are not using them and blow out any candles before you leave the house.
- If you smell gas, leave the house and call your gas company as soon as possible.
- Keep hallways and other areas well-lit and clear of clutter to prevent falls.

TIP

You can refer to the ADA standards, `www.ada.gov`, for accessible design regulations to remain in compliance with your design features and new construction.

FIGURE 11-2: Home security system.

Sitting in the Driver's Seat

You need to get from here. . . to there. . . to everywhere. . . every day! You have to get yourself to work, places of entertainment, places to eat, and home, and then do it all over again the next day. Sometimes it might feel like you spend half your day riding in some form of transportation. Owning a car might be necessary for some people, whereas public transportation might work just fine for others.

How do you decide whether you need a car of your own? Do you get tired of waiting on a ride-sharing service or a friend to pick you up? Do you wish you could determine your schedule and leave from events or work when you want? If you answered yes to these questions, a car might be the right investment for you.

Here are a few benefits to having a car:

- **Independence and freedom:** You have full control of where you go and when you arrive and depart from places.
- **Privacy:** If you are feeling overwhelmed at school, work, or home, you can sit alone in your car for a few minutes to regroup. You can also crank up the stereo and sing karaoke without anyone judging you.
- **Safety:** Always riding with others puts you at their mercy. If you have a car, you can be smart about your driving safety.
- **Time savings:** Owning a car will inevitably help you save time. You will not have to wait on a bus or subway. If your daily schedule changes, you are free to move about when you would like. You can also steer clear of traffic and take a different route home if needed. (On the downside, parking can be a pain in many places.)
- **Vacation:** Driving to a vacation destination can often be more economical than taking other forms of transportation.
- **Flexibility:** If you need some milk to go with your cereal, you have the flexibility to hop in the car and head to the market.

TIP

When deciding what form of transportation would be right for you and your daily lifestyle, make a pros and cons list. Every form of transportation has its advantages and drawbacks. Depending on where you live, one form of transportation may be better than the other.

Needs versus wants: Affording a car

Maybe you have decided that purchasing a car is worth the investment for you. Automobiles come in all shapes and sizes, and making a choice can be overwhelming. Before you choose, you need to keep in mind the difference between what you need and what you want:

- **Need:** requiring something essential or very important
- **Want:** having a desire or wish to possess something

You might be asking why I'm clarifying the difference between a need and a want. The reason is that it's very easy to get caught up in all the bells and whistles available on various models of cars and commit yourself to more than you can reasonably afford.

When it comes to cars, keep in mind that the primary purpose is to get you from point A to point B. Do you really *need* your back massaged and heated by your seats on the way? Do you *need* all the fancy features the salesperson is sweet-talking you into? While those things may be nice, they're considered wants and could end up costing you a pretty penny. All you truly need in a car is safety and room for your passengers or cargo. So research the automobile that will get you to and from your destination safely. Only you can decide if your budget can withstand the extra expense for leather seats, sunroof, navigation system, and in-car entertainment.

Here are some advantages and disadvantages to buying a new car or a used car:

- Benefits of buying a new car:
  - Since you are the first driver, the vehicle is considered much more reliable.
  - You will get the most advanced technology.
  - You will have a complete warranty, which means if something breaks down, the warranty pays to have it repaired.
  - You can customize it to your liking.
- Downfalls of buying a new car:
  - New cars are typically much more expensive than used cars.
  - Once you drive the car off the lot, it loses a significant amount of value.
  - Your sales tax will most likely be higher.
- Benefits of buying a used car:
  - You can get premium features that you want at a lower cost.
  - It holds its value longer; it won't depreciate as quickly.

    - You can get it at a much lower cost.
    - Tax and insurance premiums will be lower.

- Downfalls of buying a used car:
    - It is not seen as reliable or as high quality as a new car, even though it has made it through inspections.
    - It may not come with a warranty. In other words, after you drive it off the lot, you are responsible for any repair costs.
    - You do not get to customize it and do not have as many purchasing options.

WARNING

Determining the better deal on buying new or used also depends on the automobile market supply and demand.

WARNING

Don't make an impulse purchase when it comes to a car. It is a major decision that needs to be thought through completely. Buying a car on a whim can leave you with buyer's remorse.

You gotta pay for that

"I found the perfect car! Let me test-drive it! Hurry up, let's make a deal!"

Slow down a minute. . .. I'm glad you found the perfect car, but keep in mind that you have to pay for it.

The following steps outline the general process for purchasing a car.

1. Do your research on available automobiles.
2. Find the right loan for you or access the cash you have been saving.
3. Determine if you have a car to trade in. A trade-in is a vehicle that you allow the dealership to buy in exchange for credit toward the car you are purchasing. Before you head to the dealership, check out `https://consumerreports.org/cars/car-value-estimator/` to get an estimate of your trade-in value.
4. Double-and triple-check the fine print in the sales price and warranties so you fully understand what you are receiving.
5. Once you have a deal presented, research other places to ensure it is in fact a quality deal.
6. Purchase and enjoy.

But wait, there's more.

Now that you have your car, it is a huge responsibility to care for. Ongoing maintenance is the best way to ensure you will be safe and ready for the miles you drive. Check out some important "must-dos" for car maintenance:

- Keep your car clean, especially the windshield. Replace your windshield wiper blades once a year. If you cannot see to drive, how can you be safe?
- Check your tire pressure every month. Many cars have technology that will tell you if your pressure is low. If your car has low tire pressure, you may not be able to handle or stop the car as well. Take off the tire cap and use a pressure gauge to check your tires. If your tires need air, you don't have to go to a professional to have it done. You can fill them yourself. Many gas stations and travel stops have air pumps (sometimes free, sometimes paid) that you can use to fill up your tires.
- Check your car's oil level. The motor oil is used to lubricate all the moving parts in the engine.

TIP

You can take care of your car and make minor adjustments on your own for the most part. YouTube (`https://youtube.com/`) is a great place to search and find video tutorials to help troubleshoot car issues you might be having and help perform some of the essential tasks such as checking the oil, airing up your tires, and replacing your windshield wiper blades.

- Every 3,000–5,000 miles you drive, you should take the car to a quick lube place or a car dealership for an oil change.
- Get your brake pads replaced approximately every 24,000 miles, or sooner if you can tell they are wearing down.
- Keep the interior of your car clean and tidy. The first reason is to keep it safe and less distracting for you; the second reason is to retain a higher resale value.
- If a headlight or taillight goes out, change it ASAP. If you drive with a blown light, the police can pull you over and give you a ticket. Plus you can't see where you are heading!
- Change the air filter every year.
- Keep gas in your car; don't let the gas gauge reach empty.
- If you receive notification that there is a recall on the model of your vehicle, get it fixed soon to avoid any damage.
- Invest in good car insurance; in fact, it is illegal not to have car insurance. Accidents happen, and you want to be prepared when they do.

- Park your car in a garage, under a structure, or use a car shade. This will keep your car from getting extra hot in the summer months and possibly help you avoid car damage due to inclement weather.
- Keep your insurance and important car papers in the glove compartment for safekeeping.
- Keep your car locked and remove any valuables.
- Keep an emergency kit in your car that includes jumper cables, an ice scraper, a car cell phone charger, first aid supplies, and a blanket.
- Always drive the speed limit and abide by driving laws. If you do end up with a ticket, follow the instructions precisely and pay it immediately. The last thing you want is to have a warrant out for your arrest because you failed to take care of your tickets.

  Speeding is tempting but not worth it in the long run. Speeding barely saves you any time — usually only a few minutes. For example, on a 60-mile trip, driving 90 miles an hour instead of 70 miles an hour will only save you 11 minutes. On a 10-mile drive, it will save you less than 2 minutes. You are dramatically increasing the possibility of causing harm to yourself or others, plus the legal consequences can get expensive.
- Changing a tire (see Figure 11-3) is not as hard as it may seem. Knowing how to change a tire can help you in the future with unexpected flats. Here are the general steps for changing a tire:
  1. Pull over to a safe spot.
  2. Place the car jack (usually stored with your spare tire) under the car frame and use it to raise the tire high enough that it is not bearing the weight of the car.
  3. Remove the hubcap.
  4. Use the wrench to loosen the tire bolts, use the car jack to lift the car a little more, then take off the damaged tire.
  5. Place your spare tire on the car and tighten the bolts by hand.
  6. Lower the car jack until the tire touches the ground.
  7. Finish tightening the bolts with the wrench.
  8. Remove the car jack from under the car.

REMEMBER

Your spare tire is not meant to travel miles upon miles. It will get you safely where you need to go, but head to a maintenance center to purchase a new tire soon.

FIGURE 11-3: Changing your tire is not as scary as it might seem.

REMEMBER

Always ask an expert when you are not sure about a vehicle problem. Sometimes attempting to fix a problem yourself can lead to a whole slew of other problems.

REMEMBER

Having a car is considered a privilege. Own up to the responsibility to drive safely and conduct routine checkups to make sure your car is working and in tip-top shape. You got this!

4 Maintaining a Healthy Mind in a Healthy Body

IN THIS PART . . .

Gain knowledge about nutrients, food labels, healthy eating, and how your body works to ensure you remain healthy throughout adulthood.

Figure out the right exercise plan for you and your lifestyle.

Protect yourself from various health hazards by planning a good sleep, hygiene, and health-care routine.

Take care of your mental health with tips to remain calm in difficult situations, handle your stress, spot the signs of illness and addiction, and ask people for help to maintain a healthy mind.

IN THIS CHAPTER

» Understanding the basics of nutrition

» Feeding body and soul

» Forming healthy food habits

Chapter 12 Eating for Fun and Fuel

I don't know about you, but I love food! I love the smell of food, I love the taste of food, I love preparing food, and I have come to love the benefits food provides for me. Did you know that good nutrition is vital to your well-being — not just physically, but mentally? Eating food nourishes your body and mind and helps you to be happy.

In this chapter, I cover essential knowledge regarding nutrition, how to make smart choices about the food you put in your body, and how to turn those healthy choices into healthy habits.

Nutrition: More Than Taking Your Vitamins

Have you ever been so super hungry that it turns into irritability, then turns into anger? You may know the word for that: *hangry*! You only feel happy again once you have your next meal or snack.

Not nourishing your body or listening to the way your body talks to you contributes to stress, tiredness, and the inability to focus.

If you're not consuming the right types of foods, you may experience issues like the following:

- Developing illnesses
- Becoming overweight
- Developing high blood pressure
- Having tooth decay
- Developing high cholesterol
- Being at higher risk for heart disease
- Developing type 2 diabetes
- Becoming depressed
- Developing an eating disorder

You may never have been taught the importance of proper nutrition, or it may not have been a priority in your life until now. Just by picking up this book, you have shown the initiative to invest in yourself and your future, which includes caring for your health.

Proper nutrition is at the foundation of good health. Let's dig into some steps to begin your journey to good nutrition.

- Consume a variety of foods every day. Fruits, veggies, grains, dairy, and proteins are a few of the types of foods you need each day.
- Consume sugary, fatty, and salty foods occasionally in limited amounts.
- Choose water instead of sugary soft drinks.
- Opt for healthier alternatives in your meals. For example, bake those potatoes instead of frying them!
- Create a meal plan each week to avoid tempting fast food.
- Don't eat while you're watching TV or playing on your phone. You are likely to eat more if you're distracted.

TIP

The best way to get the proper nutrients each day is through food. Your body processes the nutrients in food more efficiently than through nutritional supplements.

Introducing the team of nutrients

Nutrients are the good things in our food that fuels our bodies and keeps them in good working order. That is why you need to choose healthy foods regularly. Nutrients do amazing things in your body, like maintain basic bodily functions and help the body to repair itself.

Six major groups of nutrients work together as a team to help your body and mind be the best they can be. Let's take a look at the nutrients that can help you!

» **Carbohydrates**

- Carbs give you energy.
- They consist of the sugars and starches within your foods.
- They are separated into two categories: simple and complex carbohydrates. Simple carbs are the sugars in your food. Simple carbohydrates are broken down quickly for short term energy. Complex carbs are the starches. They take longer to be broken down and give more sustained energy for longer periods of time.
- Fruits, veggies, and milk provide natural sugars along with other nutrients.
- Cereal, bread, pasta, rice, and dry beans contain starch and are rich in other nutrients.
- Carbohydrates also include fiber within starchy foods. Fiber is very important to help your digestive system function properly and remain healthy.
- Carbs keep your brain, heart, muscles, kidneys, and overall nervous system in good working order.

» **Fats**

- Fats make your food taste good, but more importantly, give your body the energy it needs for normal growth and healthy skin.
- Other nutrients rely on fat to carry them where they need to go.
- Without a little bit of fat in your diet, the other nutrients wouldn't make it to their designated locations.

» **Proteins**

- Proteins are another source of energy in your food and are made up of chemical compounds (amino acids) that build, maintain, and rebuild body tissues.

- Each type of food that contains protein contains a different combination of amino acids that provide a specific vital function to your body.
- Your body naturally makes most amino acids but some can only come from your food.
- A complete protein includes the amino acids your body cannot make. Complete proteins are found in meat, poultry (chicken, turkey, and so on), fish, milk products, and eggs.
- If you do not eat or like meat, you can get your protein from items like grains, dry beans, peas, nuts, and veggies. Just know that you must eat different combinations of these items to get all the nutrients that are in a complete protein.
- The best way to ensure you are getting the protein you need is to eat a variety of different foods each day.

» **Vitamins**

- Thirteen vitamins are essential to your day-to-day intake.
- The job each vitamin has is so unique that other vitamins cannot take their place. If you're eating a variety of healthy foods, you're already getting the daily needed vitamins.
- There are two groups of vitamins: fat-soluble and water-soluble.
- Fat-soluble vitamins consist of vitamins A, D, E, and K. These vitamins are present in foods that contain fats and are absorbed along with the fats in your diet.
- **Vitamin A** is found in green leafy veggies, carrots, and oranges, and it contributes to healthy skin, healthy hair, strong bones, strong teeth, and contribute to healthy eyes.
- **Vitamin D** is found in milk, eggs, salmon, and liver. The D vitamin builds strong bones and teeth and aids in utilizing calcium in the body.
- **Vitamin E** is found in whole grains, green leafy vegetables, beans, and peas that contribute to your muscles and the formation of your red blood cells.
- **Vitamin K** is in dark green leafy veggies and cabbage. Vitamin K is what helps your blood clot when you have a cut or scrape.
- Water-soluble vitamins include the B-complex vitamins and vitamin C. The water in your body helps these vitamins dissolve and get to work.
- The **vitamin B-complex** include (but aren't limited to) riboflavin, niacin, B6, B12, and thiamine. You can find B-complex vitamins in many foods such as whole grains, peanut butter, meat, poultry, fish, milk, and eggs. These

vitamins are very important because they make sure your entire nervous system is healthy along with your muscles and other tissues.

- **Vitamin C** is found in citrus fruits such as oranges and grapefruits. It's also in strawberries, bell peppers, broccoli, and tomatoes. The C vitamin helps with strong bones and teeth as well as with healing wounds.

» **Minerals**

- To work properly, your body needs 16 minerals a day: calcium, phosphorus, sodium, potassium, magnesium, manganese, sulfur, chloride, iron, iodine, fluoride, zinc, copper, selenium, chromium, and cobalt.
- You are most likely getting the bulk of these minerals if you eat different types of foods daily.
- Minerals have certain jobs to perform and are essential to your internal organs and bones.
- Getting the minerals you need now will prepare you for strong bones later in life. For example, calcium is vital to strong bones!

» **Water**

- In addition to the liquids you drink, such as milk, juice, and water (obviously), soups, fruits, and vegetables provide a high water content.
- You need around 4–6 cups of water each day. For a more personalized approach, divide your body weight by two, and that number is how many ounces of water you should have in a day.
- The benefits of water include carrying nutrients where they need to go, controlling your calories, promoting healthy skin, contributing to increased energy, promoting better concentration, regulating body temperature, lubricating joints, flushing toxins from the body, and much more.
- Try to drink fluids throughout the day to keep from getting dehydrated, which can cause medical complications.

TIP

To make sure you get enough nutrients each day, eat with an emphasis on fruits, whole grains, beans, low-fat protein, and dairy. Check out Figure 12-1 to see a variety of nutritious foods.

TIP

If you're not sure how to start maintaining a healthy diet, pick one thing to focus on. Maybe just begin by getting enough water to drink each day or try whole-grain bread instead of white bread with your sandwich. Small changes like this will go a long way.

FIGURE 12-1: Foods like these contain the nutrients you need each day.

Running on empty

Having an overall feeling of "blah" has happened to all of us at one point or another. But having that feeling all the time might be evidence that something more is happening within your body. When your body doesn't receive the nutrients it needs over a period of time, you will begin to notice symptoms of a nutritional deficiency.

Some symptoms, like being tired, lack of focus, not sleeping, frequent colds, and weight fluctuations, may not seem serious at first. Other symptoms could affect certain body parts like skin, tongue, eyes, or bones. You can address many deficiencies just by adding more nutrients to your diet. Your doctor may also recommend supplements.

Here are a few common nutritional deficiencies.

- **Iron:** The most common consequence of a lack of iron is anemia. Symptoms include tiredness, weakened immune system, and impaired brain function. Eat more red meat or beans if you have an iron deficiency.
- **Iodine:** Iodine is essential in your thyroid function. Your thyroid either controls or is involved in many bodily functions, such as brain development, bone support, and growth. Eat more fish, dairy, and eggs to combat this deficiency.

- **Vitamin D:** Almost every cell in your body requires vitamin D, so it's not surprising that most people do not have enough of this vitamin. Muscle weakness, bone loss, and easily fractured bones can occur with little to no vitamin D. The best dietary supplement for vitamin D is fatty fish and egg yolks. Increasing your exposure to the sun (with proper protection from the sun's harmful rays) can help because the UVB rays in the sun help your body make vitamin D!
- **Calcium:** Calcium is needed in every cell in your body. It's what makes strong bones and teeth. Osteoporosis, or soft and fragile bones, occurs in many individuals with a calcium deficiency. Drinking your milk and consuming green leafy vegetables will help you get enough calcium.

TIP

It's possible to be deficient in any nutrient. The preceding list includes only the most common deficiencies. Treat your body nicely now to ensure you stay healthy later in life.

REMEMBER

You might be running on empty if you:

- Are easily upset or irritable
- Cannot concentrate
- Feel like you're in a fog
- Are very tense
- Cannot sleep well

Visiting with your doctor and sharing your symptoms and concerns may help you determine whether you need a nutrient supplement if your body cannot obtain enough through your diet alone.

TIP

Lack of water is usually the culprit if you are getting headaches, are constipated, are constantly tired, and have dry skin that won't seem to clear up. You can start a water regimen by setting an alarm on your watch or phone to remind you to drink throughout the day.

Fueling thought

Contrary to what you might have seen or been taught, calories are not bad for you. You need calories for energy! A calorie is a unit of measurement. The calories in food give you fuel and energy for all of your physical activities. Technically, when you work out or exercise, you burn off the calories you have eaten. However, if you consume large numbers of calories and do not burn them off with physical activity, then calories can become a problem and lead to weight gain. On the other hand, if you do not get enough calories, you might lack the energy to be successful in your physical activities, which also leads to weight loss. Furthermore, you might lack the energy to maintain focus in your mental activities.

The number of calories you need depends on your age, gender, and activity level. The following are the generally accepted ranges for different age groups:

- Males ages 14–25 need approximately 2,800 calories a day.
- Males ages 26–40 need approximately 2,600 calories a day.
- Females ages 14–18 need approximately 2,000 calories a day.
- Females ages 19–25 need approximately 2,200 calories a day.
- Females ages 26–40 need approximately 2,000 calories a day.

Keep in mind that these are approximate numbers and recommendations. If you're very active, you need more calories a day. If you live a mostly sedentary lifestyle, then you do not need to consume as much.

TIP

The source of your calories is very important. You can get energy from fats, carbohydrates, or proteins. Fats have the highest concentration of calories per gram, whereas carbohydrates and proteins have about half of that.

TIP

Nutrient-dense foods (foods that are high in nutrients related to the number of calories) are a must-have! Reach for foods like fruits, vegetables, whole grains, and lean meats. These foods provide more than just the calories you need for your physical activity; they are also high in nutrients like vitamins, minerals, and fibers. Candy, sugar-filled drinks, and junk food add to your calorie intake but are considered empty. Empty calories mean that you just get the fat or carbohydrate energy without other nutritional benefits. So although candy, chips, and junk food taste amazing, beware! Consuming too many empty calories can lead to health issues as well as obesity. Consume these types of foods in moderation.

What Goes in Must Come Out

When you gotta go, you gotta go! OK, but for real, proper digestion is a huge part of a healthy body. To make use of the nutrients in the food you eat, you must first digest it. Digestion takes place when your body uses the nutrients from everything you consume.

The chemicals in your saliva and the chewing of your food begin the digestion process. After you've chewed your food, it moves through your mouth to the esophagus and then to the stomach. Your stomach has digestive juices that break down your food even more for the next three to five hours. The next stop for your food is the small intestine, where the nutrients are absorbed into your bloodstream. It continues through your body until the unneeded nutrients and undigested food become body waste.

Figure 12-2 shows a detailed diagram of how your food works for you through digestion.

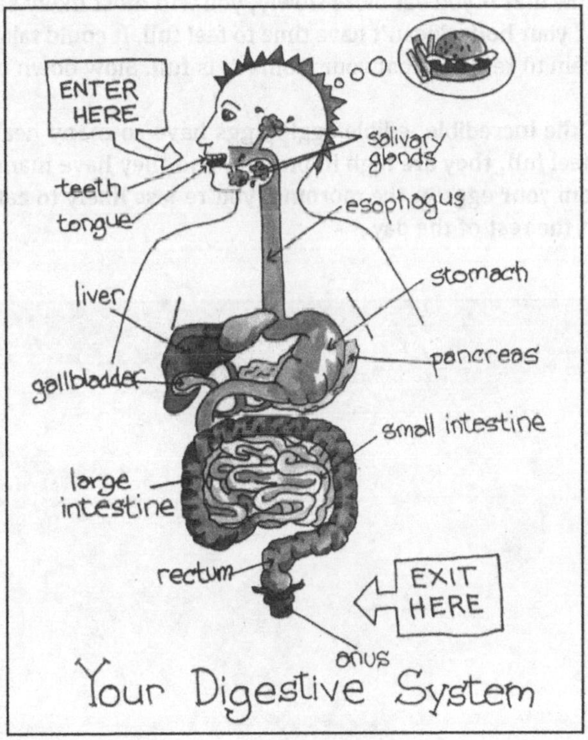

FIGURE 12-2: The digestive system.

TIP To maintain a healthy gut and good digestion, drink plenty of water, get enough fiber, and try incorporating a probiotic that is usually in yogurts with live cultures.

Soul Food

The way that you eat and your overall body, mind, and soul health have a direct relationship. Bad eating habits can lead to serious health issues such as heart disease, high blood pressure, diabetes, and even cancer. But no fear, you can develop good eating habits at any time in your life to reduce risk of these diseases.

Healthy eating is about finding the right balance. You *can* enjoy your favorite foods that might be high in empty calories, fat, or sugar. The secret is eating them only once in a while instead of daily. Balance your favorite comfort foods with healthier choices and physical activity. Figure 12-3 illustrates what a healthy balanced diet looks like.

TIP

Did you know that if you eat more slowly, you will most likely eat less food? If you "speed eat" your body doesn't have time to feel full. It could take up to 20 minutes for your brain to register that your stomach is full. Slow down to eat less.

TIP

Eat eggs, "the incredible, edible egg!" Eggs have so many health benefits. They make you feel full, they are high in protein, and they have many nutrients. If you feel full from your eggs in the morning, you're less likely to eat as many calories throughout the rest of the day.

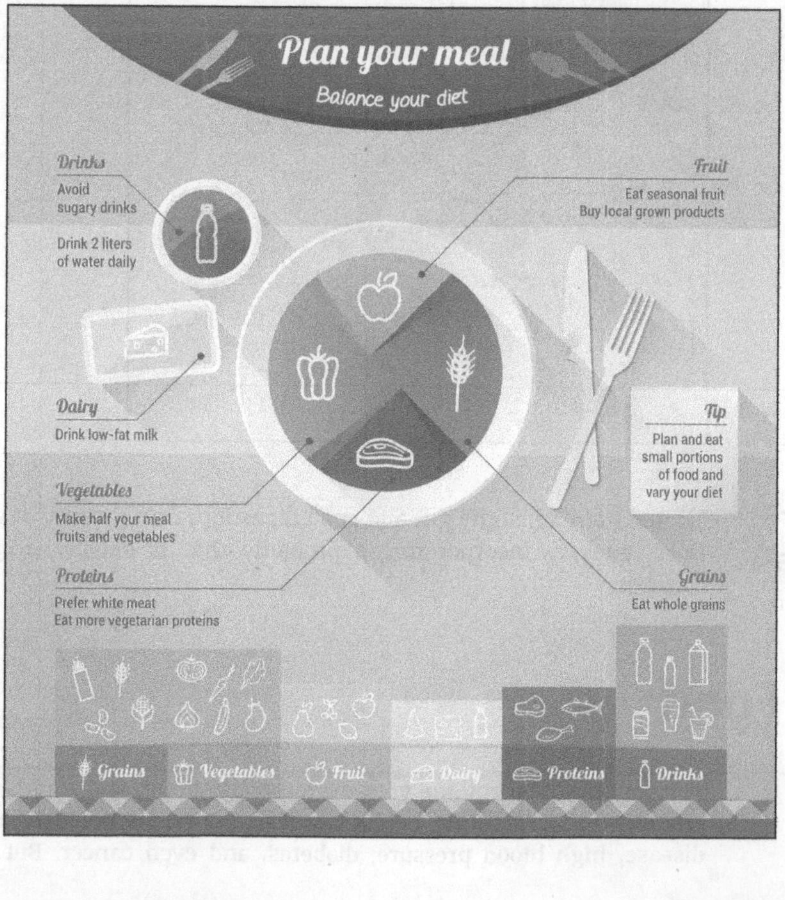

FIGURE 12-3: A balanced diet.

All-you-can-eat buffet

Imagine something with me for a second. You have just walked into the largest buffet you have ever seen in your life. There is a salad buffet with green lettuce, beautifully colored veggies, bacon bits, cheese, croutons, and so many dressings to choose from you might actually veer from your usual ranch dressing. Next, you see a fruit tower with a chocolate fountain, then you see a soup station with your favorite loaded baked potato soup. Over to the left is the meat carving station, choose-your-own pasta station, and build-your-own-burger station. To the right you see tortilla chips and french fries with endless salsa and queso, then you spot it. . . the dessert buffet: chocolate cakes, cookies, cheesecake, pies, homemade ice cream, and so much more! How will you ever decide what to eat?

There is something that can help narrow your choices. `www.Myplate.gov` **is a great place to find a guide to making healthy food choices. Foods are divided into five groups. Check out Figure 12-4 for a detailed look at how much of each food group you need daily and what items you should reach for on the buffet!**

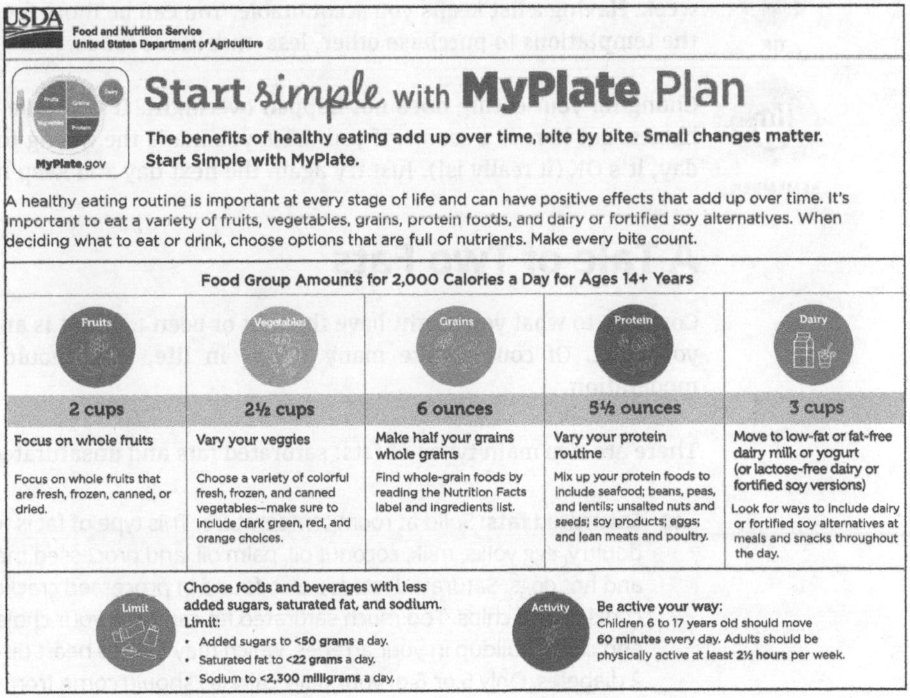

FIGURE 12-4: Food groups.

TIP

Try writing down everything you eat for a week or keep track of your food choices in an app such as MyFitnessPal or MyPlate Calorie Counter. Keep it available where you can later reflect on your choices. When reflecting, ask the following questions:

- Did I eat something from every food group each day? If not, what am I missing?
- Why am I not eating a variety of foods? Do I need to make different choices at the grocery store? At restaurants?
- Am I eating too many empty-calorie foods? What could I eat instead?

After reflecting, make changes a little at a time. Maybe try to make a goal to eat vegetables or fruit each day. Avoid aisles in the store that might tempt you with fatty and sugary foods.

TIP

Always do your grocery shopping with a list. Use Figures 12-3 and 12-4 to see what types of foods you should be buying and then make a meal plan or menu for the week. Having a list keeps you accountable. You can be more focused and can fight the temptations to purchase other, less-nutritious foods.

REMEMBER

Changing your eating does not happen overnight. It will take time to form new habits. But here is a secret: If you think you made the wrong food choices on one day, it's OK (it really is!). Just try again the next day and keep moving forward.

A Tale of Two Fats

Contrary to what you might have thought or been told, fat is an important part of your diet. Of course, like many things in life, fats should be consumed in moderation.

There are two main types of fats: saturated fats and unsaturated fats.

- **Saturated fats:** Solid at room temperature. This type of fat is found in beef, poultry, egg yolks, milk, coconut oil, palm oil, and processed meats like bacon and hot dogs. Saturated fats are also found in processed crackers, pastries, cookies, and chips. Too much saturated fat can raise your cholesterol total and cause buildup in your arteries, which may lead to heart disease and type 2 diabetes. Only 5 or 6 of your daily calories should come from saturated fats each day.

» **Unsaturated fats:** Liquid at room temperature. This type of fat is found in vegetable oils, salmon, avocados, olives, nuts, and seeds. Unsaturated fats are much healthier for you than saturated fats because they benefit your heart and can *reduce* your cholesterol total. About 200–400 of your daily calories should come from unsaturated fats.

REMEMBER

Cholesterol is a fat-like substance that is in every cell in your body. Your body makes all the cholesterol it needs, so many people end up with high cholesterol levels because they eat foods with too much saturated fat. You have a greater risk for heart disease if your cholesterol levels are high. So make a plan today to choose unsaturated fats!

TIP

If you want to lower your cholesterol, eat foods like apples, oatmeal, beans, and prunes. These foods are high in fiber and can keep your body from absorbing excess cholesterol.

The fine print

Nutrients like minerals, vitamins, fats, protein, and carbs are great and all, but how do you know what type and how much of is in the food you like? I'm glad you asked!

In 1973, it became law to have nutrition labels applied to all foods. The law has understandably gotten more detailed since then, but the premise remains that food manufacturers must tell you, the consumer, what is being put in your food. I'm hoping you have noticed a food label on the back of your favorite granola bar, but it's pretty easy to ignore if you don't know what you're looking at. The required food label — the Nutrition Facts (see Figure 12-5) — must include the following:

» Servings per container

» Serving size

» Calories per serving

» Total fat

» Cholesterol

» Sodium

» Carbohydrates

» Fiber

- Sugars
- Vitamins
- Minerals

When taking a first glance at a food label, a product may seem like a good nutritious food choice. Only 250 calories per serving. Awesome. But then you read further and notice that it defines the serving size as only 1 cup! Yeah, I don't know about you, but I know I will probably eat way more than 1 cup in one sitting. It's important to pay close attention to the label and read carefully.

Answer these questions while you're studying the food label in Figure 12-5:

- How many servings are in the container?
- If you ate the whole container, how many calories would you consume?
- How many grams of saturated fat are in this food?
- How much sodium (salt) is in the container?
- What vitamin or mineral has the highest daily value percentage on the label?
- How many calories is the percent daily value based on?

Nutrition Facts

Servings Per Container 2

Serving Size 1 cup (228g)

Amount Per Serving	
Calories 250	
	% Daily Value*
Total Fat 12g	**18%**
Saturated Fat 3g	**15%**
Trans Fat 3g	
Cholesterol 30mg	**10%**
Sodium 470mg	**20%**
Total Carbohydrate 31g	**10%**
Dietary Fiber 0g	**0%**
Sugars 5g	
Protein 5g	
Vitamin A	4%
Vitamin C	2%
Calcium	20%
Iron	4%

* Percent Daily Values are based on a 2,000 calorie diet. Your Daily Values may be higher or lower depending on your calorie needs.

	Calories	2,000	2,500
Total Fat	Less than	65g	80g
Sat Fat	Less than	20g	25g
Cholesterol	Less than	300mg	300mg
Sodium	Less than	2,400mg	2,400mg
Total Carbohydrate		300g	375g
Dietary Fiber		25g	30g

FIGURE 12-5: Nutrition Facts food label.

TIP

Restaurants also have the nutrition facts breakdown of their dishes. Some have it on the menu; in other places you must ask for it or find it online. Pay attention to the nutrition facts the next time you eat at a fast-food restaurant. You might be surprised how many calories are in your favorite food!

Relating to food

Let me tell you something you need to hear. Your body is perfect just the way it is; the scale does not measure your worth! Society may be telling you one thing, but it's wrong. Social media, manipulated supermodel photos, and filtered celebrities images show an unachievable body and face because the images are curated not to show what people really look like. Just by reading this book, you're showing the initiative to take control of your eating habits and become a healthier, safer you. I am proud of you for that! It shows that you truly care about yourself and want to improve for the better.

Many people have unhealthy relationships with food because of a negative body image, among other reasons. Think about your relationship with food as you read over the following signs of disordered eating:

- You feel guilty or shameful when you eat certain foods.
- You consider certain foods as off-limits.
- You eat when you're bored or not hungry.
- you "stress eat" or eat because you're emotional.
- Your food choices determine how successful you think your day was.
- You do not like to eat around others.
- You have tried every popular diet with no success.

If some of these apply to you, the following strategies may help improve your relationship with food:

- Your body talks. Listen to it. Your body will tell you if it's hungry, full, thirsty, and so on. If you have been in a habit of ignoring what your body is saying, it might be hard to begin listening to your body, but give it a try. You might have been taught to clear your plate, but it's OK to stop when your body says it's full.

- There is no such thing as "bad" food. Yes, there are foods you should enjoy in moderation, but feeling guilty because you have labeled a food bad should not be a thing.
- Learn to enjoy your food with family and friends. Take your time to eat, converse, and relax. Make some new positive memories that include food.
- Don't punish yourself if you feel you indulged a little too much. Think about your overall week of food choices instead of your hour-by-hour choices.

REMEMBER

A positive body image and a positive relationship with food are vital to your health and happiness. You do not have to do it alone. Surround yourself with family and friends to help you achieve your food goals.

WARNING

Some relationships with food can lead to an eating disorder. Anorexia disorder (avoiding food), bulimia disorder (vomiting after meals or abusing laxatives), and binge-eating disorder (losing control over your eating) affect many people. Seek medical attention immediately if you think you might have an eating disorder. If you are not sure where to turn, check out the information at the National Eating Disorder Association: `https://nationaleatingdisorders.org/help-support/contact-helpline`.

The latest fads

Don't be fooled. The only way to lose weight is to lower your caloric intake and move more. There is no magic pill that will shed 20 pounds in a week. Fad diets claim to give you fast, dramatic results. It's very tempting to fall victim to the "too good to be true" claims. These fad diets or pills are relying on you to take the easy way out. Good nutrition and physical activity take hard work. However, fad diets insist that you cut out certain types of foods completely, which is not a good idea since those vital nutrients in that food will also be cut out. Fad diets have also been known to extremely restrict your calorie intake. Eating less than 800 calories a day is not enough to sustain your body's essential functions. Even if you see success with a fad diet, it's not sustainable.

Proper nutrition includes eating a variety of foods, unsaturated fats, limiting sugar, eating smaller portions, and engaging in physical activity. If you need to lose weight or want to lose a few pounds, the science is simple: eat less, move more!

TIP

Healthy weight loss is losing 1–2 pounds a week; it takes time. If someone is claiming otherwise, it can lead you to an unhealthy method of weight loss. Unfortunately, after the constraints of a fad diet are lifted, weight gain can happen.

Hydration station

Your body consists of mostly water. Every organ, tissue, and cell in your body needs water to function properly. You need water to digest your food and prevent dehydration. The benefits of water are endless, but what about other types of drinks? Do they help you or harm you? You decide.

- High-sugar carbonated sodas consumed regularly can cause
  - Tooth decay
  - Heartburn
  - Risk of obesity
  - Reduced bone strength
  - Heart disease
  - Kidney disease
- Sugary energy drinks consumed on a regular basis can cause
  - Irregular heartbeats
  - Dehydration
  - Restlessness and inability to sleep
  - Anxiety

If you need a boost of energy, tea or coffee with no added creamer or sugar can help you with that. Soft drinks and sugary energy drinks will give you an immediate high, but the downfall or crash will hit you hard.

TIP

All beverages that contain water contribute to your daily water needs. Juicy fruits and vegetables also contain water that your body can utilize.

IN THIS CHAPTER

» Understanding the benefits of exercise

» Maintaining heart health

» Finding your fit

Chapter 13
Exercise: Good for You in the Long Run

How long have you been reading this book? I know it's a thrilling page-turner, but how long have you been *sitting still* reading it? Maybe you just picked it up, or maybe you have been reading for a couple of hours. Either way, can we conduct an experiment? Do you think you could put the book down for 10 minutes to take a short walk? Maybe around your block, your office building, or your house? Give it a try. Go ahead, set the book down, and I'll see you back here in 10!

Assessment time!

» How do you feel? Does your brain feel a little less foggy?

» Are you in a better mood?

» Do you have a little extra pep in your step?

» Do you feel some tension relief?

I hope you were able to answer yes to at least some of these questions. Walking, even for a short 10 minutes "resets" your body to focus, reduces stress, and helps to energize your body, mind, and soul. And here's a bonus — walking *outdoors* adds an extra layer of stress relief. If you're feeling up to it, try the experiment again to gain even more positive results!

This chapter covers the many benefits of exercise, heart health, and the different ways you can get the physical activity you need. Let's get started!

"Good Good" Feelings

Physical activity has many rewards and benefits. Figure 13-1 illustrates some of the ways physical activity is good for you. The great thing about being physically active is that it's something you can begin right now.

Exercise gives you those "good good" feelings, also known as endorphins. Endorphins are chemicals that your body naturally produces. They help you to cope with stress and make you happier. When you exercise, your endorphins soar, making you happier and less stressed!

Following are some other reasons that being physically active is so important for your health:

- Leads to better quality of sleep
- Combats anxiety
- Helps keep your brain healthy and feeling less depressed
- Lowers your risk of heart disease, stroke, and type 2 diabetes
- Reduces your blood pressure
- Prevents some forms of cancer
- Helps you maintain a healthy weight
- Allows you to practice your coordination skills
- Keeps your bones strong
- Helps you stay alert
- Improves your posture
- Improves your blood circulation
- Increases your lung capacity, allowing you to breathe easier

TIP

Physical activity does not always have to be a strenuous exercise program. In fact, it can be fun, especially if you do it with friends. You can add exercise into your day by walking, bicycling, skateboarding, cleaning the house, raking leaves, or even doing the laundry.

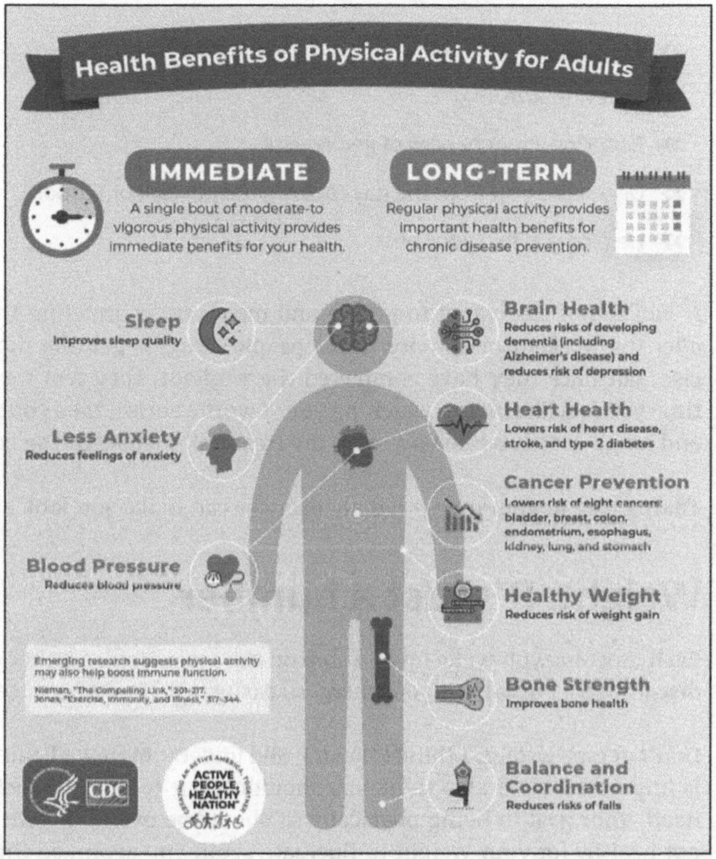

FIGURE 13-1: Health benefits of exercise.

REMEMBER

If your job requires intense physical labor, it's especially important to keep your body in shape to be able to do your job safely and well.

Anti-aging: More than a cream

Physical activity and exercise can make you feel and look younger. It can also make your body stay healthy as you age.

Exercise helps keep you youthful by

- Increasing your energy
- Increasing blood flow to make your skin look brighter and younger
- Increasing your ability to learn new things
- Keeping your memory sharp

- Keeping your metabolism high to burn fat quicker
- Relieving stress
- Reducing your chances of getting sick
- Distracting you from the day-to-day grind of work or school
- Helping you feel your best

TIP

If you're not motivated to get up and move, try channeling the energy you feel *after* the workout or activity. Some people struggle gaining motivation for exercise, but once they have completed the workout, they feel the benefits. So next time you feel like binge-watching your favorite series, take your device to the gym and binge-watch while you're on the treadmill instead of the couch.

REMEMBER

Taking care of yourself with daily exercise can make you look and feel younger.

Weight: It's just a number

Each morning you wake up and step on the scale. You're either elated, content, or discouraged. But why is your mood so easily influenced because of a number?

Don't get me wrong, I think knowing and understanding a healthy weight number is important, but I also think you shouldn't put too much stock into the number itself. Your goal in being physically fit should be overall health and wellness. It's not healthy for your weight to fluctuate again and again, so finding a happy balance is important.

Here are some factors that affect your weight:

- The rate at which your body uses energy when you're inactive is called your basal metabolic rate (BMR). Your body is always working for you, doing things like keeping your heart beating, your breathing going, and your body heating and cooling itself. Your BMR uses about 60% of your body's energy needs.
- Your genetic makeup, or what you inherited from your family, accounts for your height, size, and body structure.
- How much you move your body contributes to how much energy is consumed. If you're very active, you use more energy than a sedentary or inactive person. If you're physically active, you increase your BMR, which means you'll still be burning fat long after your workout.
- Your body composition includes your lean tissue and body fat. When you exercise, you produce more muscle. This can improve your body and appearance.

- The nutrients in your food supply the energy your body needs to be healthy.

Here are some tips and tricks for maintaining a healthy weight:

- Work on positive eating habits, as discussed in Chapter 12.
- Keep your eating habits realistic and consistent.
- Eat breakfast every day to get your metabolism moving.
- Get physically active. Strive for at least 30 minutes of physical activity each day. Remember, it doesn't have to be all at once.
- Keep a food and activity journal. This will help you see first-hand what you're eating and how active you are. There are some helpful apps such as MyFitnessPal, Ate Food Journal, Sworkit, or MyNet Diary Calorie Counter to use to keep track right on your phone.
- Keep track of your weight. But instead of weighing yourself every day, I recommend you weigh yourself once a week or every other week. Weighing yourself everyday provides a less accurate representation of your average weight than weighing weekly because you will likely see shifts due to how much you ate or drank that day. Be consistent with when and how you are weighing. Determine if you will weigh morning, afternoon, or night and with or without clothes and shoes. It's important to keep track of your weight every so often so you can adjust your activity and diet if needed. If you have recently started a weight-lifting regime, don't get too concerned if you do gain a few pounds. Muscle weighs more than fat!
- Hang out with people who have the same health goals as you. Find someone who can keep you motivated on your health journey.

REMEMBER

The number on the scale does not define you. It can't tell you how much you worked out that day, it can't tell you about the increased self-esteem you gained by meeting an activity goal, and it can't tell you about your worth!

TIP

If you are interested in learning how to calculate your Body Mass Index (BMI) check out: `https://cdc.gov/healthyweight/assessing/bmi/index.html`.

A dumbbell a day keeps the doctor away

Did you know that being physically active reduces your risk of getting illnesses and helps prevent other health conditions? When you work on making your body stronger and healthier in the present, it helps keep you healthier in the future!

Some of the conditions or illnesses that physical activity can help you avoid include

- Heart disease and stroke: Working out makes your heart muscle stronger, lowers your cholesterol, and improves your blood flow.
- High blood pressure: Exercise strengthens your heart, which enables your heart to pump more blood with less effort. The result is a lower blood pressure.
- Type 2 diabetes: By working out, you reduce your body fat, which can help control type 2 diabetes.
- Obesity: Physical activity can reduce body fat, build muscle mass, and help your body use calories more efficiently to avoid obesity.
- Osteoporosis: Lifting weights promotes bone formation, which helps prevent osteoporosis.
- Depression and anxiety: Working out regularly can help improve your mood and self-esteem and it can lessen the symptoms of depression and anxiety by providing an outlet to relieve your stress.
- Immune system compromises: Your immune system is your body's natural defense against infections. Working out reduces your stress, allowing your immune system to work more efficiently.

The Heart of the Matter

Your heart is the lifeline of your body. It's the most important muscle you have. Taking care of your heart now can help you maintain a healthy heart as you age. You're twice as likely to get heart disease if you do not strengthen your heart with exercise. Just like you work out to get that six-pack of abs, you can work out to make your heart stronger. All exercise benefits your heart, but here are a few that target your heart muscle:

- **Walking:** Get that heart rate up.
- **Lifting weights:** Build those muscles.
- **Swimming:** A full-body workout!
- **Yoga:** Gain calmness while you exercise.
- **Cycling:** Use those leg muscles to get your heart rate up.
- **Cardio:** Any exercise that raises your heart rate.

REMEMBER

Exercise reduces your risk of heart disease, heart conditions, and stroke. Start your workout today to show love to your heart (see Figure 13-2)!

FIGURE 13-2: Exercise reduces your risk of heart disease and stroke.

Exercises That Are Right for You

A great starting place for increasing your activity is to just get up and move. A good starting point is to take on short, productive activities such as sweeping, vacuuming, or gardening. As you continue to move, you might begin to think about the different types of exercise and their benefits. Understanding the different exercises will allow you to develop an exercise regimen that is right for you!

You need a variety of activities to benefit your body in different ways. A complete exercise program works on three elements. Combining these three elements provides your body with overall health and wellness:

- Aerobic endurance
- Muscular strength
- Flexibility

TIP

To take full advantage of any exercise, you must find a way to make it a habit. You do not have to work on each element every day, so having a plan is a must! Here's one way you can incorporate all three elements into a workout routine:

- Conduct some type of aerobic exercise at least three times a week for at least 30 minutes each time.
- Include a strength-building session or weight-lifting program two times a week. You should aim to work all of the major muscle groups, such as your arms, legs, back, abs, and chest. Allow yourself around 48 hours between strength workouts to rest those muscles and build new tissue.
- The easiest way to include your stretches for improved flexibility in your plan is to stretch before and after any workout, which helps prepare your body for the different types of exercise. You might also consider stretching each night before bed.

REMEMBER

It's much easier to stick to an exercise plan if you can have fun at the same time. Participating in more physical activities with your friends can help with your motivation. Maybe you and your friends could play tennis, basketball, go hiking, or go for a run together. This allows for two important parts of your life — physical fitness and socializing — to be combined.

Walking it out

Your heart, lungs, and blood vessels have the job of delivering oxygen to every part of your body. They work most effectively if you train them with regular aerobic exercise. The goal of aerobic exercise is to raise your heart rate for a sustained amount of time. You can find your estimated target heart rate at `https://heart.org/en/healthy-living/fitness/fitness-basics/target-heart-rates`.

Aerobic exercise usually includes a warm-up, exercise for at least 20 minutes, and a cooldown. Examples include

- A brisk walk
- Running
- Cycling
- Swimming
- Dancing

TIP

Obtaining a gym membership usually gives you access to organized aerobic classes, such as dance aerobics, cycling, and swimming. So go ahead, grab some friends and try out some aerobic exercise together, just like in Figure 13-3.

FIGURE 13-3: Aerobic exercise with your friends can be fun and beneficial!

Getting swole

Building and maintaining muscle is vital to your health and well-being. Having strength allows you to push or pull with force. You know how frustrating it is not to be able to open the pickle jar or to have difficulty opening a heavy door! Weight-bearing exercises can help the strength of your muscles, bones, and joints. A weight-training program can also help improve your balance and boost your energy levels.

Lifting weights at the gym is a great place to begin your weight training. You can find weight-lifting equipment specially designed for each part of your body. You can even find free-weight equipment like dumbbells, weighted medicine balls, and barbells to incorporate into your training. If you're lifting weights at a gym, be sure to consult a personal trainer or instructor to ensure you're using the equipment safely and correctly.

Of course, you can also gain muscular strength without lifting weights at all. You can use your own body as weight resistance. Check out Figure 13-4 for some muscle-building exercises that you can do in the comfort of your own home.

FIGURE 13-4: Body-weight exercises for building muscle.

Getting flexible

You should be able to move your joints and muscles fairly easily with little to no pain or stiffness. Good flexibility will allow you to move more comfortably when you do anything from walking to bending over to reaching up high for something on the top shelf. Flexibility exercises can help you with your posture as well as ease your stress.

Some popular flexibility workouts include yoga, Pilates, or tai chi. These workouts not only benefit your body but also incorporate your mind and spirituality. You can create your own workout by combining different types of stretches each morning and evening. Stretching can also be done at any time of the day. Take a break from class or the office to stretch the muscles that often get cramped at a desk or in front of a computer. Figure 13-5 shows examples of stretching you can do right from your desk.

WARNING

Keeping your workouts safe is a must! If you overdo it, you could develop an injury. Be sure to stay hydrated before, during, and after working out. Give yourself a warm-up period to prepare yourself for vigorous activity by stretching and walking for a few minutes. Once you have done your exercise, have a cooldown period to allow your heart rate to return to normal. Stretch one more time to avoid muscle tightness and soreness. Jogging or running outdoors is great, but always let someone know when you're heading out alone. A running buddy is best!

FIGURE 13-5: Office stretches at your seat.

Taking it one day at a time

Your fitness journey is possible when you take it one day at a time. Making healthy choices can be a struggle sometimes, but in each new day, there is a chance for a fresh start! You can even increase activity in your day-to-day life. Here are some sneaky ways to add physical activity to your day:

- Skip parking in the closest spot. Parking further away enables you to get in a brisk walk.
- Take the stairs!
- Take a dance break.
- Walk your dog daily.
- Join a fun group such as dance, yoga, running club, or sports group.
- Pick an activity such as laser tag, mini-golf, or bowling for date night.

- Go shopping — actual in-person shopping rather than online shopping. Get out and about to browse around.
- Walk or ride a bike to school or work.

TIP

If you don't exercise regularly, think about some exercises you could begin with a friend. Having an accountability partner will help keep you motivated to reach your fitness goals for health and well-being.

IN THIS CHAPTER

» Getting your shut-eye

» Maintaining good hygiene

» Protecting yourself

» Maintaining good health

Chapter 14
Loving Yourself with Healthy Habits

In this chapter, I let you in on some healthy habits that will allow for you to become a healthier and happier you. I cover the importance of a good night's rest, the ins and outs of hygiene, how to keep safe inside your home and outside of it, and how to maintain overall wellness. After you read this chapter, you will be on your way to loving yourself with healthy habits!

Getting Some ZZZs

It's 10:00 p.m. You should probably go to bed because you have to be somewhere at 8:00 a.m., but the next episode in your favorite series is calling your name. Now it's 11:00 p.m., but your social media begins to ding, so you scroll for a while. Soon it's midnight, and you really begin to think about heading to bed, but one game on your game system wouldn't hurt. Before you know it, it's the wee hours of the morning and you still haven't gone to sleep. You begin to panic about your 8:00 a.m. appointment!! Sound all too familiar? If it does, you're not alone.

You may think you can get more done if you sleep less, but the opposite is true. When your body does not get enough sleep, everything you try to do feels like double the effort. You cannot concentrate and you end up making mistakes. Sleep is your body's way of rejuvenating itself and rebuilding energy for the next day. A full night's sleep helps you feel well-rested and makes you more likely to be able to check your chores for the day off your list. If you continually do not get enough sleep, it can lead to health problems.

TIP

Aim for at least seven hours of sleep each night to ensure your body is rested and rejuvenated to help you with the next day's tasks.

Lying in the bed you made

You've heard the saying "Get a good night's rest." There is more to that idea than just falling asleep. Your body goes through various stages while you're sleeping to ensure you get a "good night's rest." The stages include non-REM (rapid eye movement) and REM sleep:

- Stage 1 is non-REM sleep where your body is transitioning from being awake to asleep. This is like if you doze off and then quickly wake up and adamantly deny falling asleep at your desk! This stage lasts only a few minutes before you move to the next stage. In this stage
  - Eye movement slows down.
  - Breathing and heart rate slow.
  - Your muscles relax.
- Stage 2 is non-REM sleep that comes before your deep sleep. This is where you're sleeping pretty lightly and can easily be woken up. In this stage
  - Your breathing and heart rate slow down even more.
  - Your body temperature drops.
- Stage 3 is the final stage of non-REM sleep and is where you're gaining your deepest sleep. This is when good things begin to happen; your body begins working for you as you rest. During this stage
  - Your breathing and heart rate are at their slowest.
  - Someone would have difficulty waking you, or you might not hear your alarm.
  - Your eyes are completely motionless.
  - Your body is completely relaxed.
  - Your immune system gains strength.
  - Cell regeneration, or replacing damaged cells, occurs.
  - You repair and grow tissue.

» Stage 4 is REM sleep. This is the stage where you get to live out all of your wacky, awesome fantasies while dreaming. In this stage
  - Your eyes rapidly move.
  - Your breathing and heart rate increase slightly.
  - Your brain is very active.

TIP

Your body goes through each of these stages over and over again as you sleep at night. One full cycle of all the stages usually equals about an hour and a half. Getting at least seven hours ensures your body has time to repair itself.

Dreaming big

So you want to start dreaming, but you seem to toss and turn all night. The following suggestions may help you get better-quality sleep:

» Stay off your devices at least 30 minutes before bedtime. I know it's convenient to scroll through social media or even read a book from your phone to make yourself sleepy, but the blue light emitted by devices interrupts your ability to fall asleep easily, and honestly, your device is addicting. You will probably end up staring at your phone way longer than you anticipated. When you finally do put it away, you could end up staring at the ceiling for another hour to recover from the blue light.

» Kick the caffeine before bedtime. Your body may feel tired, but your brain will not relax if you have given it a stimulant. Try to avoid caffeine anywhere from three to seven hours before bedtime. Each body is different, so stay in tune with yours. Maybe your last caffeine kick needs to be at lunch!

» Go outside during the day. Increased natural light during the day allows for a better night's sleep.

» Get up and move. Exercise more.

» Do not take excessively long naps. A short nap is great and has some benefits, but if you sleep for hours during the day, you might be left wide awake at bedtime.

» Let your bed be where you sleep. In other words, don't bring your laptop to your bed to finish off your report or meet a work deadline. Create a sanctuary with a soft pillow and blanket to make you feel comfortable to sleep better.

WARNING

There are many sleep disorders, including insomnia, sleep apnea, restless leg syndrome, narcolepsy, and more that can harm your sleep quality, leading to other health problems. Be sure to visit your doctor if you have difficulty sleeping at night.

Having Some Good Clean Fun

Personal hygiene is one of the best and most effective ways of protecting yourself from diseases and illnesses. Plus it helps you look clean and attractive. Important hygiene skills you need to incorporate into your everyday life include handwashing, bathing, combing your hair, and brushing your teeth.

Your hygiene can also affect the way people see you. An employer may see bad hygiene as a risk factor if you work in a kitchen. You may come off as lazy and unprepared if your appearance looks like you rolled out of bed five minutes before you had to be at work. Even more important is that good hygiene can contribute to your mental well-being. If you're clean and put together, your self-confidence will increase!

Lookin' fresh

Your skin is a very important organ in your body. It protects you and warns you about extreme temperatures and pain. It produces sweat and oils for moisture and to maintain your body temperature. Taking care of your skin is a must. Cleaning yourself in the shower or bath should be a daily occurrence. The soap and water remove dry skin and bacteria that can cause body odor or certain infections. Clean skin leads to healthy skin. There are many different skincare products and soaps on the market. It's up to you to find what works best for you. The same can be said for washing your hair. Clean, brushed, and styled hair can give you self-confidence and also helps others feel confident that you're prepared to step up to challenges!

Acne is a skin problem that 80 percent of individuals develop. The best treatment for mild acne is to wash your face and affected areas at least twice a day. There are many acne cream treatments you can get without a doctor's prescription that might work for you. Don't pop your pimples because doing so can spread the bacteria and further damage your skin; it could even leave scars. If your acne is severe, consider seeing a dermatologist who specializes in skin issues.

REMEMBER

Sweating or perspiring is a natural process to regulate your body temperature. There are many sweat glands under your arms; therefore, there's a lot of sweat under there! When your sweat and skin bacteria meet, it produces an odor. To keep others from smelling your body odor, wear a deodorant or antiperspirant every day.

TIP

Some individuals shower every day, but if you begin detecting overly dry skin, showering every two to three days should be enough. Your hands need to be washed much more frequently. Most infections begin when a person puts unwashed hands close to their mouth or nose. Figure 14-1 illustrates step-by-step instructions for handwashing.

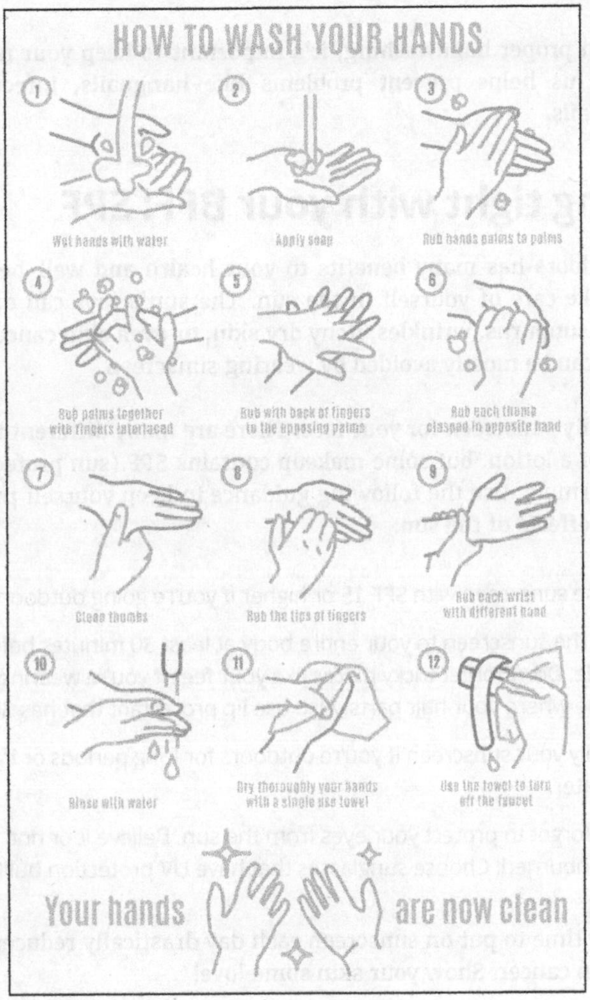
HOW TO WASH YOUR HANDS
1 Wet hands with water
2 Apply soap
3 Rub hands palms to palms
4 Rub palms together with fingers interlaced
5 Rub with back of fingers to the opposing palms
6 Rub each thumb clasped in opposite hand
7 Clean thumbs
8 Rub the tips of fingers
9 Rub each wrist with different hand
10 Rinse with water
11 Dry thoroughly your hands with a single use towel
12 Use the towel to turn off the faucet
Your hands are now clean

FIGURE 14-1: Proper handwashing technique.

Always wash your hands

- After you use the bathroom
- Before you handle food
- After you've touched animals
- While you care for someone who is sick
- After you treat a wound
- After you've blown your nose, coughed, or sneezed
- After you've touched trash

TIP

Along with proper handwashing, it's important to keep your nails trimmed and healthy. This helps prevent problems like hangnails, infected cuticles, and ingrown nails.

Staying tight with your BFF: SPF

Being outdoors has many benefits to your health and well-being, but you still need to take care of yourself in the sun. The sun's rays can damage your skin, leading to sunburns, wrinkles, itchy dry skin, or even skin cancer. The damage to your skin can be mostly avoided by wearing sunscreen.

Select a daily sunscreen for your face. There are many different types. Most are in the form of a lotion, but some makeup contains SPF (sun protection factor) built into the formula. Use the following guidance to keep yourself protected from the damaging effects of the sun:

- Choose sunscreen with SPF 15 or higher if you're going outdoors.
- Apply the sunscreen to your entire body at least 30 minutes before you go outside. Don't forget tricky places like your feet if you're wearing sandals and the line where your hair parts. Also use lip protectant that has SPF.
- Reapply your sunscreen if you're outdoors for long periods or if you go into the water.
- Don't forget to protect your eyes from the sun. Believe it or not, your eyes can get sunburned! Choose sunglasses that have UV protection built into them.

REMEMBER

Taking the time to put on sunscreen each day drastically reduces your chances of getting skin cancer. Show your skin some love!

WARNING

I get it — you want a bright summer glow, but please avoid tanning beds! Artificial rays can cause premature aging, immune suppression, allergic reactions, eye damage, and skin cancer.

Getting some breathing room

Good dental hygiene is important for any adult. Brushing your teeth when you wake up and before you go to bed at night helps remove bacteria that can cause decay and bad breath. You know that sticky feeling you have on your teeth when you wake up in the morning? That's plaque. If left on your teeth and mixed with sugar or starches, it forms an acid that eats away at your teeth. This combination creates cavities. If cavities are left untreated by a dentist, they can cause further tooth decay, root infections, gum disease, and discolored teeth.

The following are some guidelines for taking good care of your teeth:

- See a dentist every 6 months to get your teeth professionally cleaned and inspected for problems. The sooner decay is found, the simpler the procedure to get it fixed. Call a dentist to schedule a check today!
- Brush your teeth after eating and every morning and night.
- Floss between your teeth regularly.
- Drink plenty of water during the day to cleanse your teeth from the sugary and starchy foods you eat.
- Replace your toothbrush often — about every three to four months.

TIP

Coffee breath doesn't smell good on anyone. Cleanse your teeth after drinking or eating foods with a strong aroma. Maybe even pop in some sugar-free gum!

REMEMBER

Your smile can make other people see you as an amicable person. It can also give you a self-confidence booster when you look in the mirror. Your teeth must last a lifetime, so give them the care and attention they deserve.

Coughing and sneezing spread diseases

Coughing and sneezing — whether as a result of allergies or a common cold — are your body's mechanisms for protecting your airway from unwanted particles. The air you expel when you cough or sneeze also happens to include *a lot* of germs that can spread the flu, RSV, COVID-19, whooping cough, and more.

Let's look a little bit at some hygiene etiquette:

- Cover your mouth with a tissue if you cough or sneeze. If you don't have a tissue, cough into your elbow or wash your hands immediately. An alcohol-based hand sanitizer also works.
- Throw your used tissues in the trash. The bacteria can still live in the tissue.
- If you need to blow your nose, head to a private place or the restroom. It's extremely rude to blow your nose right in front of someone, especially at the dining room table.
- It's also rude and just gross to continue to sniff your mucus up your nose over and over again. Blow your nose in a private place, dispose of the tissue, then wash your hands.
- Coughing or sneezing without covering your mouth is rude and disrespectful. If you do have a virus, keep it to yourself, and don't spread your germs!

WARNING

If you continue to cough, sneeze, and sniff for an extended amount of time, you might have an infection. It's always a good idea to be seen by your doctor. If an infection is left untreated, it could move to your lungs and become much more serious.

Protecting Yourself

Have you ever had a gut feeling? You know, one that you feel deep down inside that something isn't quite right? This feeling might even trigger adrenaline in your body for a flight or fight response, which puts you in the position of deciding whether to run away or protect yourself. This feeling can happen at any moment in your life. Maybe you're hiking and are surprised by seeing a bear! Maybe you find yourself on an empty street at night with the feeling someone is following you. Don't ignore your gut feeling in any situation.

Instinct (that gut feeling) is innate in all human beings, and it's meant to guide your choices and keep you protected. Here are some general safety tips to practice daily:

- Be alert to possible dangers.
- Be aware of your surroundings.
- Avoid people and places where you do not feel safe.
- Anticipate possible problems.
- Trust your instincts.
- Act confident.

WARNING

There are people in this world who will treat you respectfully, but there are also people who will treat you the opposite. Be aware of who you are around because some individuals might perform criminal acts and try to hurt you. Take action to report criminal activity you see and always trust your instinct about the people you're with and the places you end up.

The best defense is a good offense

Practicing safety at home and while you're away from home is the best way to prevent possible dangers.

For home-based safety, do the following:

- Do not give your address or location to strangers, either in person or online.
- Double-check identification for individuals who might be hired for work at your house before you let them inside. Examples are a plumber, electrician, or repair worker.
- Keep your house locked while you're away *and* while you're home. Use deadbolt locks where applicable.
- Secure windows so that they cannot be opened from the outside.
- Do not leave items lying around outside that could be used to aid in a break-in. For example, do not leave a spare key under the mat and do not have tools or large rocks lying around that could easily shatter a window.
- Keep the area around your house well lit at night.
- Create a safety plan with the other people in your house in the event of an emergency, such as a weather emergency or break-in.

When you're out and about, keep yourself safe by doing the following:

- Let someone know where you're going. I don't mean announce on social media where you will be traveling and that you will be away, a simple text to a friend will suffice.
- Carry your identification with you, such as a driver's license.
- Learn how to make an emergency call on your phone. Some phones have shortcuts for emergency calls, but when in doubt, dial 9-1-1!
- Always wear your seatbelt.
- Do not text or scroll through social media on your phone while driving (see Figure 14-2). No text or post is worth someone's life. Always avoid distracted driving.
- Use common sense when you're with your friends.

TIP

Having a plan in case of an emergency and practicing your plan is a way to be prepared. Knowing what to do in emergencies to protect yourself and others can help ease your anxiety while at home or out and about.

REMEMBER

Maslow's hierarchy (see Chapter 2) includes feeling safe as a basic human need. Practice safe habits to feel confident and secure in your own home and surroundings.

FIGURE 14-2: Avoid distracted driving to prevent accidents.

After dark

So you enjoy the nightlife! You're not alone. Going out with your friends for food and entertainment is a great addition to your social life. Get out there and experience life, but remember some important safety tips to ensure everyone has a safe, good time!

- If you arrive at your destination with your friends, leave with your friends. Stay together. Establish a meeting spot if you're attending a crowded event. If you decide to leave, make sure it's not with a stranger and that your friends are made aware you're heading out.
- Have a fully charged phone before you go out for the night.
- Keep your valuables hidden in your car or close to your body.
- Stay in well-lit areas.
- If you're within the legal age to consume alcohol, avoid getting drunk or using drugs. Staying fully aware of your surroundings is the best way to stay safe. Also, mixing drugs and alcohol can have many devastating consequences.
- Always have a designated driver; plan for your ride home *before* you go out. Utilizing a rideshare such as an Uber or Lyft may be an option for you.
- Avoid drinking and driving at all costs.

- Do not take drinks from strangers or leave your drink unattended.
- Avoid situations that could get dangerous or hostile.

TIP

If you're traveling to a new destination, look up the directions ahead of time to avoid getting lost. Do not act frazzled or stressed when entering a new place; act confidently. You don't want people to assume it's your first time anywhere, because that could make you look like an easy target.

TIP

Consider learning various self-defense techniques. Organized classes can teach you how to protect yourself from a physical attack as well as how to exude confidence.

Safe travels

Whether you take a road trip or jet-set around the world, vacation is a must. It provides you with a much-needed getaway from the daily grind. Traveling to unfamiliar places can be exciting but can also bring about challenges. Being prepared is key. Here are some tips for traveling effectively and safely:

- Do advance research about the places you will be traveling to know what to expect when you arrive.
- If traveling by plane, pay close attention to the departure times, arrival times, and gate locations shown on your purchased tickets. Get to the airport a few hours early to ensure you get through security and baggage check-in with time to spare to catch your flight. Keep your identification, passport, and personal belongings close to you at all times to avoid misplacing them or theft.
- If traveling by car, get a quick tune-up to confirm everything is working properly before you leave for your destination. Plan the best route that includes pit stops to fill up with gas and to get out and stretch every few hours.
- Bring more than one credit or debit card with you. Yours could easily go missing or be stolen while traveling.
- Travel with a small first-aid kit.
- Try not to look like you're from out of town. Tourists are vulnerable to crime, so try your best to fit in.
- Keep your friends and family updated with your travel plans.

- Keep your hotel room locked with the deadbolt and windows closed. Put away your valuables when you leave the room.
- Don't let your guard down. If you stop to take in the sights or snap a picture or two, remain aware of the things and people around you.

TIP

A "stay-cation" instead of a vacation might be an option for you. If you do not have the time or funds to travel, plan a stay-cation to visit all of those places you wish you had time for right in your own hometown.

Painting a Picture of Health

If you haven't figured it out yet, being healthy is not just one simple notion. It's many different aspects combined to form your health and wellness. One aspect of maintaining good health is being seen by medical professionals. Adulting means no one is going to call and make appointments for you, no one will keep track of when you're due for a checkup, and no one will make you go to a doctor — no one, except you!

You are responsible for your well-being, and it's up to you to take the steps you need to stay healthy. With a little bit of knowledge of the medical industry, you can be prepared to take control of your health journey.

Following is a list of some of the different types of doctors, medical professionals, and medical facilities, when you should see them, and where they practice:

- **Primary care physician (PCP):** This doctor is the one you see for your general checkups. An annual checkup is vital to health, even if you feel fine. Your general checkup could lead to early discovery of health conditions, which helps you get the proper treatment quickly. Your PCP is the first point of contact if you're not feeling 100%. This doctor will refer you for testing, bloodwork, or other procedures as they see fit. They might also refer you to a specialist if needed.
- **Physician specialist:** This type of doctor focuses on a certain area of medicine or group of patients. Examples of specialists include cardiologists, allergists, endocrinologists, psychiatrists, urologists, optometrists, pediatricians, and gastroenterologists.
- **Obstetrician/gynecologists (OBGYN):** This is a doctor who specializes in preventative care and treatment for female health conditions. Yearly checkups and tests such as a Pap test and breast exams should be a

priority. If you're pregnant, you will see your OBGYN throughout your entire pregnancy as well as during labor and delivery.

- **Medical clinic:** This is a place where your PCP usually practices and is separate from the hospital. At a clinic, your doctor provides preventative care, routine checkups, and medical treatment when you're sick.
- **Emergency room:** This is a department located inside a hospital. In an emergency room, immediate treatment is administered for those with severe illnesses and trauma. You should head to the emergency room if you have trouble breathing, heart attack or stroke symptoms, deep wounds, serious burns, severe pain in your body, or any other dangerous conditions.
- **Emergency medical technician (EMT):** Calling 9-1-1 is the quickest way to get immediate medical care from an EMT who can transport individuals to the hospital in an ambulance.
- **Urgent care clinic:** If you're feeling sick with common illnesses such as the cold or flu or minor injuries like sprains, minor cuts, and burns, you can go to an urgent care clinic. You can be seen quickly if you think you cannot get in to see your PCP soon enough.

Setting a time and date

Being in charge of your medical care may be overwhelming at first, but I promise, you can do it! The paperwork that comes along with medical insurance and medical care can seem daunting, but it just needs to be read with a careful eye. Figure 14-3 shows what new patient paperwork may look like so you can familiarize yourself with what information you may need to provide when you go to a new doctor. Be sure to research the needed information on this form before you arrive at the doctor's office.

If you have medical insurance, your provider will most likely refer to doctors and hospitals as "in-network" and "out-of-network." All that means is that in-network doctors take your insurance, and out-of-network doctors do not. If you're looking for a PCP or specialist, it's probably in your best interest to choose a doctor who is in the network. This means your care will be covered by your insurance plan. All you might pay out of pocket during your visit is your co-pay, which is much less than an out-of-network provider would cost.

NAME: ____________ GENDER: ____________ DOB: ____________ DATE: ____________

ALLERGIES: ____________

List ALL MEDICATIONS you take, including over-the-counter (OTC) medications and vitamins. Include specific doses and when taken. If you don't know, please call your pharmacist to confirm.

____

____

____

PERSONAL MEDICAL HISTORY: (Please circle all that apply)

ADHD	COPD/ Emphysema	High Cholesterol	Rheumatoid Arthritis
Alcoholism	Dementia	HIV	Seizure Disorder
Allergies, Seasonal	Depression	Hepatitis	Sleep Apnea
Anemia	Diabetes: 1 or 2	Irritable Bowel Syndrome	Stroke
Anxiety	Diverticulitis	Lupus	Thyroid Disorder
Arrhythmia (irregular heart beat)	DVT (Blood Clot)	Liver Disease	Ulcerative Colitis
Arthritis	GERD (Acid Reflux)	Macular Degeneration	
Asthma	Glaucoma	Neuropathy	
Bipolar	Heart Disease	Osteopenia/Osteoporosis	
Bladder Problems / Incontinence	Heart Attack (MI)	Parkinson's Disease	
Bleeding Problems	Hiatal Hernia	Peripheral Vascular Disease	
Cancer:	High Blood Pressure	Peptic Ulcer	
Headaches	Kidney Stones	Psoriasis	
Crohn's Disease	Kidney Disease	Pulmonary Embolism (PE)	

Last Menstrual Period	Date:	Normal Abnormal
Colonoscopy	Yes/No Date:____	Normal Abnormal
Mammogram	Yes/No Date:____	Normal Abnormal
Dexa (Bone Density)	Yes/No Date:____	Normal Abnormal
Pap	Yes/No Date:____	Normal Abnormal

Other medical problems not listed above:

____

Surgical History: Please list all prior surgeries and approximate dates performed.

____

____

SOCIAL / CULTURAL HISTORY:

Education Level: ☐ Elementary ☐ High School ☐ Vocational ☐ College ☐ Graduate / Professional

Are there any vision problems that affect your communication? ☐Yes ☐ No

Are there any hearing problems that affect your communication? ☐Yes ☐ No

Are there any limitations to understanding or following instructions (either written or verbal)? ☐Yes ☐ No

Current Living Situation (Check all that apply):

☐ Single Family Household ☐ Multi-generational Household ☐ Homeless ☐ Shelter ☐ Skilled Nursing Facility ☐ Other: ____________

FIGURE 14-3: Patient history form.

Smoking/ Tobacco Use: ☐ Current ☐ Past ☐ Never **Type:** ________ **Amount/day:** ________ **Number of Years:** ______

Alcohol: ☐ Current ☐ Past ☐ Never **Drinks/week:** ________

Recreational Drug Use: ☐ Current ☐ Past ☐ Never **Type:** ________________________________

Are you sexually active? ☐Yes ☐ No

Are there any personal problems or concerns at home, work, or school you would like to discuss? ☐Yes ☐ No

Are there any cultural or religious concerns you have related to our delivery of care? ☐Yes ☐ No

Are there any financial issues that directly impact your ability to manage your health? ☐Yes ☐ No

How often do you get the social and emotional support you need?

☐ Always ☐ Usually ☐ Sometimes ☐ Rarely ☐ Never

Comments (Please feel free to comment on any answers marked "yes" above):

____

____

FAMILY HISTORY:

FATHER: Living: Age ________ Deceased: Age ________

Alcoholism	Bipolar Disorder	Depression	High Cholesterol	Osteoporosis
Anemia	Cancer: ________	Diabetes 1 or 2	High Blood Pressure	Stroke
Asthma	COPD/Emphysema	DVT (Blood Clot)	Kidney Disease	Thyroid Disorder
Arthritis	Dementia	Heart Disease	Migraines	

Other: ____

MOTHER: Living: Age ________ Deceased: Age ________

Alcoholism	Bipolar Disorder	Depression	High Cholesterol	Osteoporosis
Anemia	Cancer: ________	Diabetes 1 or 2	High Blood Pressure	Stroke
Asthma	COPD/Emphysema	DVT (Blood Clot)	Kidney Disease	Thyroid Disorder
Arthritis	Dementia	Heart Disease	Migraines	

Other: ____

SIBLINGS:

____

____

List other medical providers you see on a regular basis (i.e. Cardiologist, Mental Health Provider, Kidney Doctor, Dentist, etc.)

____

____

Patient Signature: ________________________ Date: ________________

FIGURE 14-3: (continued)

Here are a few tips for scheduling medical appointments:

- When making an appointment, let the office staff know you're a new patient and explain the reason for the visit. You may have to wait a few weeks to be seen if it isn't an emergency.
- Have your health insurance card out and ready. They will ask you for the policy number and/or group number, which are clearly labeled on the card for you. If you do not have a card, contact your insurance provider to obtain this information. Your doctor needs this information to research what your policy does and doesn't cover within their scope of care.
- Ask questions if you have any. Ask if you need to bring any previous medical records or medication lists.
- Pay attention to PCP recommendations from friends and family. If they have had positive experiences with certain doctors, it's likely that you will, too.

REMEMBER

Once you choose a PCP or specialist, you don't have to keep seeing them if you feel uncomfortable with their care or recommendations for treatment. Your doctor should be knowledgeable, compassionate, confident, trustworthy, and attentive.

WARNING

If your doctor's office has recommendations for you, it's up to you to follow those. If they request lab work, follow through by making an appointment at the lab and getting blood drawn. If your doctor prescribes you medication, pick it up from the pharmacy and take it as directed. If they need to see you again in 3 months for a follow-up, make the appointment as soon as possible. Adulting means taking care of yourself. Ignoring doctor recommendations or avoiding the doctor's office completely is not responsible or reasonable. I hope you have a long successful life, and your health and wellness contribute to that success. Take it seriously.

Handling an emergency

Unexpected events are bound to happen in your life. You might find yourself in need of emergency care or you might be the one who witnesses an event where emergency care is needed. Either way, emergency situations are serious and sometimes a matter of life or death.

If you find yourself in an emergency, stay calm. If you panic, you could make the situation worse and injure more individuals. In certain situations, you may need to take one of the following actions:

- » Calling 9-1-1. If you're not sure if an emergency call is warranted, call anyway! It's better to be safe than sorry.
- » Begin CPR. If someone is nonresponsive, is not breathing, and does not have a pulse, begin CPR until help arrives. If you're not familiar with CPR, the 9-1-1 dispatcher will walk you through it.

The following are some common emergencies and practices that may be appropriate if they happen.

REMEMBER

Always call 9-1-1 before beginning any type of emergency care.

- » **Fainting:** Get the person to a safe and comfortable place. Fainting and dizziness can be a sign of many serious medical conditions.
- » **Chest pain:** This should be taken very seriously. Check for signs of a heart attack or stroke, which include arm weakness, slurred speech, confusion, jaw, neck, or back pain.
- » **Seizure:** Clear the area around the person displaying symptoms of a seizure. Do not restrain the person. Turn the individual to their side if possible. Keep track of how long the seizure lasts to inform EMTs.
- » **Bleeding:** Apply direct pressure to the bleeding wound until help comes.
- » **Choking:** If the person makes a choking motion around their neck, encourage them to continue coughing. If they cannot cough anymore, perform the Heimlich maneuver, as shown in Figure 14-4.

TIP

A Good Samaritan law encourages bystanders to provide immediate aid. If you act in good faith to help another person when they are in distress, a Good Samaritan law offers legal protection against being held civilly liable for their injuries.

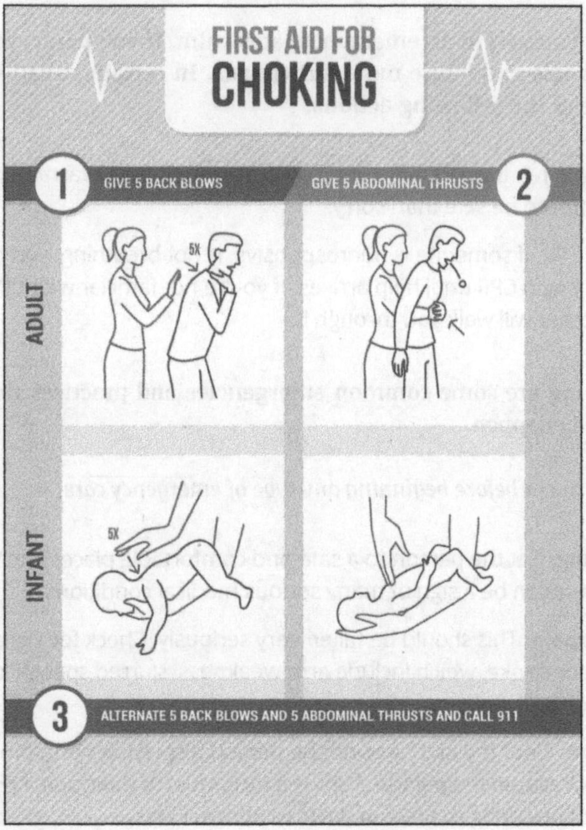

FIGURE 14-4 Heimlich maneuver.

IN THIS CHAPTER

» Keeping mental health on your mind

» Surviving the storm

» Addressing substance abuse disorder

Chapter 15

Minding Your Mental Health

Your mental health affects how you think, act, and feel. Mental health includes your emotional, physiological, and social well-being. In your everyday activities, finding a balance between your emotional, physical, and social health is vital. If one area is off course, it will most likely contribute to difficulties in the other areas. When you can find a balance in your life regarding your mental health, you can better get along with others, manage your problems, and cope with stress.

In this chapter, I discuss the importance of mental health and how to prioritize caring for yourself.

What Is Mental Health?

Mental health and physical health are closely related. For example, if you live with depression, you may be at increased risk of physical problems, such as diabetes, heart disease, and stroke. On the other hand, if you live with a chronic illness or health issue, you may also experience anxiety or depression.

Your mental health can change over time and can be affected by a variety of situations. Here are a few instances when your mental health might be impacted, but remember, each person may be impacted differently by the same issues:

- You find yourself in a demanding job that stretches your abilities and coping skills.
- You begin working nights or longer hours than usual.
- You begin experiencing economic hardship.
- You are a care partner for an ill or aging loved one.
- You are grieving a loss.
- You are experiencing challenging family changes and dynamics.

REMEMBER

Finding a balance in your life can help you maintain a healthy mental state and outlook. If your mental health is suffering, know that you are not alone. Asking for help doesn't make you any less of an adult; in fact, it can make you stronger. A doctor can help you find ways to get back to a healthy mental space.

Stressing out

Stress is the emotional or physical strain or tension that is your body's natural response to pressure. Every person deals with stress. You may always experience some form of stress in your life, but there are ways to manage it.

Stress is not entirely negative. Before a big game, a new job, or an important exam, you are likely to feel some stress. Sometimes this stress can compel you to work harder and focus more. However, too much stress can contribute to emotional and physical problems. Table 15-1 lists a few of the possible emotional and physical indicators of stress.

Following are some ways that you may be able to relieve some symptoms of feeling stressed:

- Taking a walk or run
- Soaking in a bath
- Reading a book
- Watching a movie
- Playing a sport
- Journaling

» Praying or meditating

» Talking to a trusted friend

» Listening to music

» Practicing deep breathing

TABLE 15-1 **Signs of Stress**

Emotional	Physical
Irritability	Headache
Anger	Teeth grinding or jaw clenching
Fear	Feeling of exhaustion
Sleeplessness	Tight muscles
Inability to concentrate	Should or neck pain
Feeling of overwhelm	Upset stomach, irritable bowel, or other digestive issues
Lack of motivation or increased apathy	Weight gain or loss
Constant worry	High blood pressure
Memory issues	

I want to you to know that you are not alone. If you are feeling stress in any way, shape, or form, it is important to seek professional assistance. Counselors, therapists, and psychologists can provide the support you need to stabilize challenging mental health situations. Your primary care physician or another certified doctor can prescribe medication that can help you to feel better. Here are a few resources for you to investigate if you feel you've reached a point of needing professional support.

» Substance Abuse and Mental Health Services Administration: `https://samhsa.gov/find-help/national-helpline`

» U.S. Department of Health & Human Services: `https://mentalhealth.gov/get-help`

» Mental Health America: `https://mhanational.org/`

TIP

Try completing the following statements. If you feel like writing your answers right here on the page, go ahead! Sometimes writing down how you feel is liberating.

- I feel most stressed when . . .
- My symptoms of stress are . . .
- Sources of my stress include . . .
- I cope with my stress by . . .
- Things I do to handle my stress in a positive way are . . .

REMEMBER

Your attitude in situations can determine how stressful they will be. For example, waiting in a long line can be stressful if you become frustrated and angry over the delay, or you could choose to use the time to relax.

- Try and see the positive side to situations.
- You cannot solve the world's problems in a day, so pick and choose the ones you can take head-on.
- Have an open mind.

WARNING

If you experience emotional stress and are having trouble finding a way to cope for yourself, seek professional health. Counselors and mental health professionals can show you ways to deal with your stress and help you feel better so you can function in your day-to-day activities.

Finding your happy place

No two people deal with stress in exactly the same way. I'm using the phrase *finding your happy place* to mean finding something that brings you joy, peacefulness, and clarity (see Figure 15-1). Your happy place can be an actual place, a make-believe place, an activity, or a hobby. When you have a location or an activity that brings you a sense of calm, creating images of yourself in your "happy place" can boost your mood no matter where you are.

One way you may create your happy place is by determining your goals and dreams in life. Maybe it is to own an oceanfront property one day, maybe it is to land your dream job, or maybe it is to graduate with honors. Whatever it is, dream big and envision it happening whenever you feel stressed. Another way to find your happy place is to remember or relive a pleasant past experience that made you feel happy or tranquil. This place or activity you create can bring a sense of happiness in your mind, thus helping you cope with your stress in any situation. Remember, you can choose how you personally define "happy place." After all, it is your private place!

FIGURE 15-1: Your "happy place" may bring you joy, peacefulness, or clarity.

TIP

Being present and giving individuals your full attention is respectful and enjoyable. Stressing over deadlines or family issues creates a fog in your life because you tend to feel the weight of the world on your shoulders. If you feel that you're distracted by your thoughts when you're spending time with others, taking a few minutes to reset by envisioning your happy place can help you focus more and give the people you love your full attention.

In the Eye of the Storm

Have you ever received some very sad news that hit you like a ton of bricks? You can't breathe, think, or respond. Sadness is a human emotion that we all feel at different times in our lives. Losing a championship game, enduring a breakup, getting let go from a job, or experiencing the loss of a loved one may all create feelings of disappointment and sadness.

Some signs of sadness include crying more often, sleeplessness, loss of interest in usual activities, and appetite changes. Each person is different, but sadness is usually a temporary feeling that fades over time. That doesn't mean that you don't feel sad again when you recall that memory in the future, but usually after a period of healing, you move on with your life and with a revised sense of "normal."

When you are sad and upset, it can feel like you are in the eye of the storm. Here are some ways to positively work through your sadness:

- Prioritize caring for yourself.
- Validate your emotions rather than trying to suppress them. It is okay not to be okay.
- Go to work or do something to keep you distracted for the time being.
- Take it one day at a time.
- Have a good cry if you need to. You will probably feel better because crying can stimulate the production of endorphins, or your "feel good" hormones.
- Reach out to others for help. Often, other people in your life have gone through a similar situation and can help comfort you.
- Stay in the present and allow each day to bring forth a new beginning. Take it easy on yourself and allow yourself time to heal.

WARNING

Depression is a clinically diagnosed condition that affects how you feel, think, and act. Depression affects all aspects of your life, and for some people it means not being able to find enjoyment in anything. Sadness is an emotion; depression is a mental illness. Here are some symptoms of depression:

- A feeling of sadness that does not go away
- Exhaustion that is persistent
- Feeling irritable all of the time
- Headaches and body aches that do not go away
- Feelings of worthlessness or guilt that seem to always linger
- Constant appetite changes
- Lack of focus and loss of interest in things that used to make you happy
- Changes in your sleeping habits, continually sleeping more or less than usual
- Thoughts of harming yourself or ending your life

If you show any of these symptoms, visit your doctor as soon as possible to determine a treatment plan.

The calming effect

It might be a challenge to remain calm in society's hectic hustle and bustle of day-to-day life, but you need to find ways to cope with daily challenges like anxiety, stress, and pressure. Here are some tips for adding a little more calmness to your life:

- » Turn to worship or meditation (see Figure 15-2) for hope and prayer.
- » Go outside more.
- » Make your bed, pick up your clothes off the floor, and clean your house. Having a put-together environment welcomes calmness into your mind.
- » Get a massage, take a hot shower, or take a nap.
- » Slow down the pace at which you are living life and don't overextend yourself with too many commitments.
- » Plan on arriving early everywhere. This will lessen your stress and emotions related to always being late.
- » Assume nothing. This can lead to unneeded chaos. If you are not sure about something, ask about it.
- » Do not procrastinate any longer. Get that task that is weighing you down done! You will immediately feel a sense of calm and relief when you are finished.
- » Turn off your work email on the weekend or on your days off.
- » Remember to breathe. There are apps for your phone to help you take deep breaths to remain calm.
- » Take life one day at a time and remember that you always have tomorrow to try it again!

People need people

No one likes feeling lonely. Without other people in your life, you cannot commiserate with those who have gone through similar trials as you have, and you cannot feel the positive effects of their support (see Figure 15-3). Your mental health relies on socializing with the people around you — real people, not online acquaintances, "friends" you interact with through video games or social media. Real-life people.

FIGURE 15-2: Take time to find what works to keep you calm.

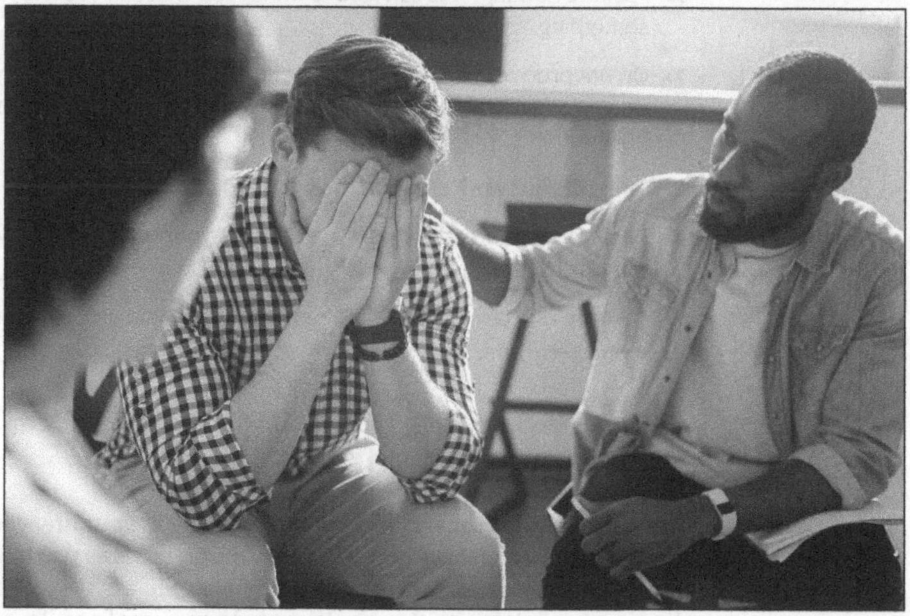

FIGURE 15-3: People need other people for support.

You need connectivity with other humans in your life. People you can laugh with, cry with, and talk to. Being able to stay connected enables you to grow and nurture yourself physically, emotionally, and mentally. This is a vital part of thriving, not just surviving! (If you don't have people to share life with, check out Chapter 4 to read about creating long-lasting friendships.)

Living your life with supportive individuals can

- Improve and maintain your health
- Extend your life expectancy
- Make life more interesting and fun

TIP

Opening up to your life group of friends and family can help you face your trials and tribulations head-on. Just knowing people are supporting you is often the boost you need to move forward!

Addiction

We often think of addiction in relation to substances such as drugs or alcohol, but people can get addicted to anything — cigarettes, drugs, alcohol, caffeine, anger, food, gambling, phones, technology, sex, gaming, or work. No addiction is healthy, but many addictions can cause significant problems in your life.

Addiction is "a compulsive, chronic, physiological, or psychological need for a habit forming substance, behavior, or activity." Drugs and alcohol might be the scariest form of addiction because they can cause the most damage to your health and relationships with friends, family, and coworkers.

Recognizing signs of addiction

Someone experiencing addiction

- Is not able to refrain from the behavior or substance
- Struggles with self-control
- Ignores problems that occur as a result of their behavior
- May show a lack of empathy or emotion

Signs that you or someone you love suffers from addiction include

- An unrealistic assumption or justification that the activity or substance has more pros than cons
- Blaming others when people bring up the addiction

» Being anxious, sad, or depressed

» Being complacent or aloof to people and situations

Addiction is often born out of curiosity. It then moves to participating in the activity or using the substance regularly or during social gatherings. Addiction arrives at the problem phase when the substance or activity is done in an extreme way. Dependency occurs when the substance or activity is done several times a day without regard for the consequences or effects on one's health. When you are dependent on stimulants, depressants, hallucinogens, opioids, and other substances, this can compel you to do whatever it takes to get more.

WARNING

Any type of addiction can be scary. If it sounds like I am describing you or someone you know, reach out for help immediately at `https://www.samhsa.gov/find-help/national-helpline`. The first step toward healing an addiction can be the hardest one, but stepping on the road to recovery is very much possible. Catching addiction in the early stages is beneficial. Overcoming addiction is a long journey, but it can be done with the help of medical professionals, support groups, treatment plans, and addiction experts.

Craving technology

Do you go into a panic if your phone is not in your hand?

Do you feel uneasy if you do not have your device with you at all times?

Do you have FOMO (fear of missing out) if you aren't connected with your device?

Do you have to stop and look at your social media at every stoplight when you are driving?

Do you stay up until all hours of the night scrolling through Instagram or TikTok?

I'm sorry to be the one to tell you this, but you are probably addicted to technology.

Technology has a lot to offer, but having it at your fingertips *all the time* can be a little much. Having an addiction like this can limit your ability to be fully present in any situation. Take a look at the people in Figure 15-4. Why are they not talking to *each other* instead of scrolling on their phones? They're missing an opportunity for a real connection.

While dependence on technology may not require medical intervention for most people, it does still have mental consequences of its own. This addiction could

FIGURE 15-4: Don't miss an opportunity for an authentic in-person connection!

- Delay learning and development in younger individuals
- Contribute to a sedentary lifestyle
- Consume hours in the day that should be used for exercising, socializing, conversing, or working
- Put a hardship on relationships
- Contribute to feelings of low self-esteem
- Increase chances of sadness and depression

TIP

Stop what you are doing right now and assess your technology usage. What does your usage look like? Brainstorm some ways to limit the amount of time you spend on your phone.

It might be easier said than done, but you can put your phone down! Here are some ideas.

- You know how some people might utilize intermittent fasting from food? You can also take a screen fast. This means completely eliminating all screen usage for a set amount of time. Start with a 24-hour detox from your phone, then assess how you feel. Taking a step back from your device can help you gain control of the relationship with your phone moving forward. Pick a day of each week to practice phone fasting.

» Set realistic rules for your screen time. Some phones and other devices will let you set these regulations on the device and remind you when you have been staring at your screen for too long.

» Turn off your phone notifications. You control when you look at your phone; don't let it control you!

» Rearrange the apps on your phone to make it harder to mindlessly click on them.

» Keep your phone out of your bedroom. Charge it elsewhere in your house.

» This might seem a little drastic, but if you *really* struggle with screen time, get an old-school flip phone!

5 Completing Household Jobs

IN THIS PART . . .

Keep your space organized and make a plan to clean and do laundry regularly to give yourself an environment in which to flourish.

Figure out the basics of stocking your kitchen with tools to cook for yourself, which is healthier and less expensive than eating out.

Prepare for unexpected life events that will inevitably happen.

IN THIS CHAPTER

» Cleaning up your act

» It's laundry day!

» Making your clothes last

Chapter 16
Keeping It All Clean

Maintaining your home benefits everyone who lives there. Home maintenance includes decluttering, cleaning, making minor repairs, and keeping your home equipment in good working order. Having a plan is the best way to address small household issues before they become major problems. For example, not cleaning up your food and drinks properly can eventually lead to an insect infestation, or not keeping your floors clean in the kitchen could lead to grease buildup that causes scary falls.

In this chapter, I not only cover the importance of keeping your home clean and tidy but I also include some tips for staying on top of your chores. I also explain how to do your laundry to keep your clothes looking newer for longer.

Taking Control of the Mess before It Takes Control of You

TIP

You can avoid most major issues by simply staying on top of keeping things clean and repairing issues while they're still minor. Joining forces with everyone who lives with you will help each person take responsibility for the working order of the house. Figure out what needs to be done daily, weekly, and occasionally, and then each person can pitch in. If you live alone, it's all on you to organize the plan, but it is doable! Following are some benefits of a clean house:

- Provides a more relaxed household because mess contributes to stress
- Prevents pests from invading
- Minimizes the risk of home accidents
- Enables you to find what you need when you need it
- Keeps dust, germs, and allergens at bay
- Is visually more appealing

REMEMBER

By identifying what should be done to keep your house clean, you're already taking responsibility for the state of your home. That's a great start!

Tidying up

Daily cleaning is inevitable. Having a clean home helps you to stay safe and healthy. Keeping your home clean every day is much easier than waiting until it's dirty. A few minutes a day can save you hours on the weekend. The following tasks should be carried out daily to help your home stay tidy:

- Wash the dishes! Make it a habit to clean up the dishes right after breakfast, lunch, and dinner. If you leave dirty dishes around the house or in the sink, bacteria can build up and create some pretty nasty germs. You could take turns with other members of your household to wash, dry, and put away the dishes and utensils. If you wash the dish (see Figure 16-1) or put it in the dishwasher right after you use it, you save time in the long run. Put on some music or use the time as a mental break; after all, washing dishes is a simple process that you don't have to think too hard about.

  1. You can fill your sink three-quarters full of soapy water, but most sinks are rather large. To conserve water, use a plastic dish pan that won't take near as much soapy water to fill up.
  2. Place your dishes in the sink and let them soak for a few minutes.
  3. With a sponge or a brush, scrub the dish.
  4. Rinse that dish with clean water.
  5. Set the dish on a drying rack or dry with a clean towel.
  6. Repeat Steps 3–5 with the rest of the dishes.
  7. Pour the dirty sink water down the drain.

8. Rinse and wipe dry your sink.
9. Once the dishes are dry, put them away in your kitchen cabinets or designated spot.

» Wipe down kitchen and bathroom counters with soap and water or an all-purpose cleaner.

» Sweep or vacuum the kitchen floor and other high-traffic areas, like the entryway.

» Take the trash out. Don't wait until it's overflowing. Get rid of the garbage because it can begin to smell really bad and create some gross germs and attract pests.

» If you spill any food or beverage, clean it up right then and there.

» Keep your clothes, shoes, accessories, or any other clutter picked up off of the floor. I know it can be tempting to kick your shoes off as you come home and ignore where they land, but there is nothing more frustrating than tripping over them the next day! Keep your dirty clothes in a laundry hamper, and put your shoes and clean clothes away in your closet or wardrobe.

» Make sure each of your belongings has an appropriate spot to "live." If you take it out of that spot to use it, put it back as soon as you're done.

» Make your bed each morning. This makes your room feel much cleaner and gives you a feeling of accomplishment!

FIGURE 16-1: Wash the dishes daily.

TIP

I recommend natural-based cleaning products you can purchase or mix yourself. Vinegar mixed with a little bit of water is a great all-purpose cleaner. Baking soda mixed with warm water is a great kitchen deodorizer that can be used on stainless steel. You can also put a couple of teaspoons of baking soda down your garbage disposal or drain to clean it and keep it from having a bad odor.

TIP

Keep a set of cleaning supplies in each bathroom to make it easier for daily wipe downs.

TIP

If you're having trouble getting motivated to tidy things up, try setting a timer for 15 minutes. During that time, get as much cleaning done as you can — 15 minutes can go a long way!

WARNING

There are some pretty strong chemicals in certain cleaning products. Most are perfectly fine to use alone, but you should never mix them, especially bleach and ammonia. That mixture creates a toxic gas that can cause breathing issues and chest pain! Read the labels on your cleaning products to verify the ingredients, keep the cleaning products in the original container or one that is clearly labeled, never store cleaning supplies near food, and keep them in a locked cabinet out of the reach of small children.

Becoming a chore conqueror

So now that you have the hang of daily cleaning, let's look at some tasks that should be done once a week:

- Your kitchen should be in great shape if you wash the dishes and wipe the countertops daily. At least once a week, you should clean the microwave, clean the stovetop, and mop the floors.
- Clean out your refrigerator! Have you ever lost those leftovers in the back of the fridge only to discover a really bad odor about a month later? Once you found the smell, you might even have deemed yourself a scientist for all of the mold you grew! But this is not a good thing. Clean out your fridge weekly and throw all expired food away immediately. You should eat leftovers within three or four days; if you do not eat them within that time frame, they are considered expired.
- Vacuum, sweep, or mop all the floors in your house once a week.
- Launder your towels once a week. Bath towels should be washed after three uses and kitchen towels the same, unless they were heavily soiled in the food preparation process. If you are not going to launder the towels immediately, make sure they air dry before throwing them in a laundry basket. This will help prevent mildew.

- Clean and disinfect your toilet with a toilet cleaner. Don't worry, you can wear gloves and use a handled scrubbing brush. Nasty microorganisms like E.coli can be lurking around if you do not clean weekly.
- Wash your toothbrush holder.
- Clean your bathtub or shower to stop mildew stains.
- Wash your sheets weekly to kill dust mites.
- Dust your shelves and other furniture with a microfiber cloth to trap the dirt. Did you know dust is made up of your hair and skin cells, as well as pollen, dust mites, and dust particles? This should give you more motivation to keep the dust in your house limited!

TIP

You should also clean and disinfect your cell phone, computer/laptop, and earbuds each week. Use a technology wipe or alcohol wipe to kill those germs.

If you have pets in the house, you will need to take a few extra cleaning steps. Use baking soda to deodorize the places your pet hangs out the most, even their cozy bed. Use a lint roller or bathroom squeegee to clean up the pet hair and if your pet has an "uh-oh" accident, clean it up immediately with vinegar and water.

REMEMBER

You and your housemates need to agree on an acceptable standard of tidiness and abide by the rules that are set.

Gathering dust

Certain items need to be cleaned occasionally. "Spring cleaning" is a term that is often used for this. It refers to cleaning out the old and starting fresh, and you don't have to wait until spring to do this type of cleaning. You can do it any time of the year.

Occasional or seasonal chores are tasks that include

- Washing walls, ceiling fans, and baseboards to get rid of cobwebs.
- Cleaning curtains and blinds.
- Dusting furniture legs and cleaning upholstery.
- Cleaning or washing light fixtures and lampshades.
- Cleaning home decor and art on the walls.
- Using furniture polishing oil on wood furniture. Trust me, it's like giving your furniture a tall drink of water!

» Deep cleaning your oven and other kitchen appliances.
» Cleaning behind the refrigerator, couches, chairs, and under your bed.

Decluttering the clutter

Decluttering is something that you should complete at least once a year. No matter how large the space you live in, you will essentially fill it to the brim. You might not know how it happens, but it will! Let me explain how to take some time to declutter it all:

1. **Mark a large chunk of time on your calendar to declutter.**

   Since this is a chore done only occasionally, it might take a longer period of time. A good decluttering session takes longer than 15 minutes.

2. **Begin by going through your drawers and closets.**

   Find a spot to create a keep pile, a give-away/sell pile, and a trash pile. Ask yourself, "Have I used this in the past year?" If the answer is no, it's time to get rid of it. There are a few exceptions like memorabilia and old letter jackets that you want to hang on to, but for most of your items, if you haven't worn it, used it, or decorated with it in the past year, it's time to move on.

3. **Try on your clothes to see if they still fit.**

   Get rid of duplicate items. Do you really need four of the same black shirt? Keep what is in the best shape and donate the rest.

4. **Hang your clothes with the hangers going the same way.**

   As you wear something, turn the hanger the opposite way. After a few weeks, you'll be able to see what items you actually wear and what items you could get rid of.

5. **Buy or reuse some nice boxes, trays, and containers to organize what you do keep.**

   Make sure everything has its place.

6. **Label the items you're putting in storage.**

   There is no way you can remember what you put in every container, so labeling will help you find what you need.

7. **Utilize every inch of storage you have.**

   Store items in the area where they are used and store frequently used items where they can be reached more easily than less used items. If items have a designated storage place, you're more likely to put them away regularly.

8. **Plan to declutter again; it's not a one-time chore.**

TIP You can make things a little easier on yourself by controlling the clutter in your house year-round. Keep a "donate" bag hanging in your laundry room or closet where you can place items when you decide you no longer need them.

Airing Your Dirty Laundry

Imagine you're trying to get ready for work or school. While trying to put together an outfit, you realize all of your go-to shirts are either dirty or wrinkled, your favorite jeans have a stain on them from the last time you wore them, and you have no clean underwear. You think to yourself, *Hmmm, maybe I can turn my underwear inside out. That would be OK, right? No one would notice this stain, and who really cares about wrinkles?*

Wrong! Don't do it! Just like that, you would be airing your dirty laundry and hygiene for everyone to. . . well. . . smell. I know washing your clothes seems like an overwhelming task, but it's not. It is, however, a *never-ending* task.

Laundry day should come weekly. If you let it go much further than a week, it will take you an inordinate amount of time to catch up, and you might find yourself in the predicament I described.

Between laundry days, there are some tricks you can use to take care of your clothes and keep them looking better longer:

- Check for stains right after taking off your clothes. This way you can treat them sooner. The longer the stain stays on, the harder it is to get off.
- Take your shoes off before stepping in and out of your pants, shorts, or skirts to avoid rips and tears.
- Check your clothes for rips, loose seams, or missing buttons. Keep reading this chapter to learn how to fix them.
- Put dirty clothes in a laundry hamper away from your clean clothes.
- Hang up or fold your clothes to store them.

Caring for your garments

If you have been doing your laundry for a while now, kudos to you! It's a skill that only has to be taught once for you to become an expert. It's not a difficult job, but it is not effortless. You need to put some thought into it so you don't end up ruining your favorite sweatshirt.

One of the first things you need to look at is the clothing care label. This label, which the federal government requires be included in any garment, is usually sewn into a seam in your clothes, and it gives you the best source of information on your article of clothing. Reading the care label can save you many headaches in the future. The label tells you

- The fiber content in your clothing. Examples are 100% cotton, or 65% acrylic/35% Spandex, or 100% polyester, and so on. The fibers for your clothing can be synthetic or natural fibers or a combination of both. There are many different combinations of numerous fibers that your clothing can be made out of; each one of them requires different care.
- The country in which the article of clothing was made. The garment industry encompasses the entire world.
- The manufacturer or brand of clothing. This is the identifying factor of who designed your clothing. Some garments also include a hang tag, which is separate from the clothing label to better showcase their design and explanation of the garment.
- The care instructions. The care instructions give you symbols that show you how to wash and care for your garment. The symbols are the same all over the world. Figure 16-2 shows the various symbols for clothing care.

TIP

If a label says to hand-wash the item, fill a tub with lukewarm water (or whatever temperature the label says), add about a teaspoon of detergent, submerge and soak the item, gently swish the item around with your hands, and rinse the garment with cool water until all the soap is removed. Repeat if necessary.

TIP

If the label shows the "lay flat to dry" or "dry flat" symbol, lay your garment on a nonwooden surface such as a countertop to air dry. Arrange it nicely so it will dry with fewer wrinkles.

WHERE IT'S MADE

There is a direct connection between consumers in developed countries and workers in developing countries. Your clothes might be manufactured in other countries because they have lower manufacturing costs. In some countries, this helps produce jobs and brings the poverty rate down, but some have been said to have very poor working conditions. Paying attention to *where* your clothing is made and researching *how* it's made can help you make more informed decisions about what you purchase.

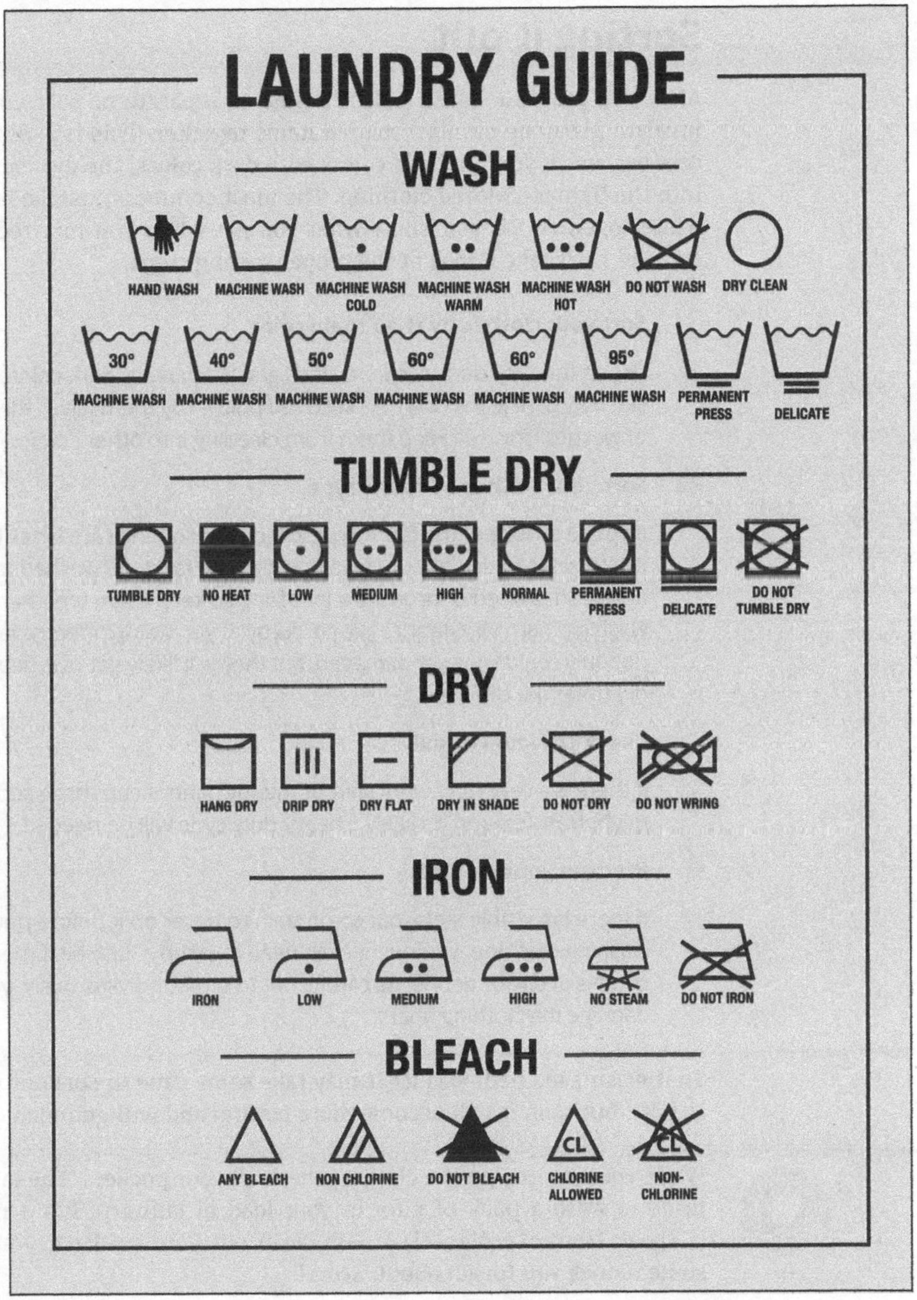

FIGURE 16-2: Clothing care symbols.

Sorting it out

After you read the care label, it's time to separate or sort your clothes, which involves grouping similar-colored items together. This is a vital step in the process because if you put light colors with dark colors, the dye can sometimes bleed into the lighter-colored clothing. The most common mistake is washing red and white together. Do you know what you get when you mix red and white? Pink clothes! Let's take a look at the proper sorting steps.

1. **Sort your clothes by their main color.**

   Group them by dark, medium, and light. Wash *really* dark-colored clothing — like new dark jeans or a new solid red polo — by themselves for the first couple of washes. This will keep them from bleeding into other colors.

2. **Sort your clothes by fabric type.**

   If you're unsure of the fabric type, check the clothing care label. Heavy items like towels can actually damage fine, delicate fabrics if washed together. Towels also tend to shed or produce a lot of lint, so keep them together and avoid washing them with fabrics like corduroy. If you wash different fabrics together, not only could they get damaged, but they will likely get overheated because dry times are different.

3. **Check the level of soil.**

   If there is a very dirty work shirt or muddy pants, keep those separate. The dirt might transfer, and it's likely a heavy-duty cycle will be needed.

4. **Pretreat your clothes.**

   If there is a visible stain, put some stain remover on it before putting it in the washing machine. You might even need to scrub a little bit if there are large chunks of dirt or debris. Be careful not to scrub too vigorously; you could damage the clothing fibers.

That wasn't too bad, was it? It may take some time to sort out your dirty clothes at first, but soon it will become more natural and will go much quicker.

TIP

While you're sorting your clothes, check all your pockets. The last thing you want to do is wash a pack of gum in your load of laundry. It's a mess to clean up. (I speak from experience!) If you clean out your pockets, you might also find some money you forgot about. Score!

TIP

Before washing, button all of your shirts or pants, zip up all zippers, and untie any ties. If you have something like an apron with a long tie or strap, you might consider washing it separately because it will tangle up all your other clothes in the load. Another trick to washing something with long ties is to wind up the tie, place a rubber band around it, then wash. This will prevent tangling.

Doing the ol' wash, rinse, repeat

Detergent is used to remove dirt from your clothes. It can be in dry or liquid form. Read the detergent carton to measure the correct amount for the level of soil and the number of clothes you're washing. Also, determine whether your washing machine uses a certain type of detergent. You use bleaches with detergent to remove tough stains from 100% cotton fabrics. Beware, though, because even one drop of bleach will leave spots on darker-colored clothing. Fabric softener reduces static cling, makes fabrics softer, and helps clothes come out less wrinkled. Fabric softeners can be added to the rinse cycle in a liquid form or the dry cycle in a dryer sheet form. Before you begin a load of wash, choose the laundry products that are appropriate for your laundry load.

Refer to Figure 16-2 to verify what the symbols on your clothing label mean before setting up your washing machine. Compare your washing machine to the clothing label and choose the appropriate setting. Most washing machines allow you to set the soil level, choose the temperature of the water, and offer other settings such as

- Cotton/Normal
- Heavy Duty
- Bulky/Bedding
- Permanent Press
- Delicate
- Wools
- Sanitize

TIP

Avoid overloading the washer. The clothes will not be cleaned properly if they are stuffed into the washing machine. A washer is fully loaded if the garments are loosely placed and about three-quarters of the way from the top.

TIP

Don't forget to add the detergent before beginning the cycle!

Spot cleaning

Random spots or stains on your clothing can ruin your vibe. Just because you spill tea or coffee on a t-shirt doesn't mean it's ruined. Many stains like this will come out if you rinse vigorously with water immediately after you make a spill. However, most of the time you're out and about, and this solution isn't practical. In those cases, pretreat the stain with a stain remover as soon as you can, and then throw it in the wash.

Some stains, such as the following, are especially tough to get out:

- Nose bleed? No problem. Treat a fresh blood stain by soaking it in cold water. Do not use hot water because it will set the stain. Watch the stain fade away from the cold soak, then launder as usual.

  A dried blood stain is a little more difficult. Cover the stain with hydrogen peroxide or vinegar, then blot it with a sponge. If the stain is still visible, add a stain remover pretreatment, and then wash as usual.
- Oil and grease can be difficult stains. Treat them by sprinkling baking soda on the affected fabric and letting it sit for 24 hours. Scrub with soap, then rinse. Another technique is to scrub the area with dish soap for about five minutes. This will usually cut through the grease stain. Then you can wash as usual.
- Grass stains can be annoying, but you can easily get them out by using distilled white vinegar mixed with water. Coat the stain with the vinegar; then let it sit for 15–30 minutes. Next, scrub and rinse. Repeat if necessary.

WARNING

Heat from the dryer sets in the stain further, so do not dry your stained clothes in the dryer until you have completely removed the stain.

Drying time

After you wash your clothes, you have options for drying them. Most clothes can be air-dried or dried in a drying machine. It's important to check the care label (again) and follow the symbols. Usually whatever was washed together can be dried together, but sometimes that's not the case. Use these important tips to ensure your clothes are dried properly:

- Shake out your wet, laundered clothes before adding them to the dryer. This helps them dry faster.
- Do not overload the machine. Overloading can cause uneven drying, wrinkles, and longer drying times.
- Set the dryer for the type of clothes you place inside. Most dryers allow you to choose the temperature, dry level, and load type. Some are autosensing, and others require you to set a timer.
- Do not over-dry your clothes. This can cause heat damage and shrinkage.
- When your clothes are dry, remove them promptly. It can be tempting to leave your clothes in the dryer until you need them, but this interrupts the whole laundry process and only causes more work for you later on, plus they get pretty wrinkled.

TIP

Many clothes that you wash and dry still come out wrinkled. Ironing your clothes is important so you look presentable. Do not be intimidated by using the iron and ironing board. Ironing simply involves moving the hot iron back and forth over the fabric. Start with the small areas and move to the larger areas. Check the care label before ironing to see if the fabric can withstand the heat and to determine what setting is appropriate for the fabric.

TIP

If you have an item with a "dry clean only" label, it needs to be cleaned with chemicals in a professional environment. There are many dry cleaning services available; just check out one near you to help explain your options. Keep in mind that you have to pay for this service, so if this is not something you're interested in, check the care tag next time before you buy.

Sharing the secrets of the folding gurus

The last crucial part of doing laundry is folding it and putting it away! If you fold your clothes correctly, they won't have any wrinkles when you're ready to wear them.

Here's an easy way to fold a t-shirt to prevent wrinkles:

1. **Lay the shirt out with the back of the shirt facing you and fold the arms neatly at the sides.**
2. **Fold one side toward the center; then fold the other. Your shirt will look like a long rectangle.**
3. **Fold the top of the shirt and the bottom of the shirt to meet in the middle.**
4. **Fold in half one more time to form a neat tight square.**

Folding a long-sleeve collard dress shirt is similar to folding a t-shirt, but you need to keep the collar out of the fold. Take a look at Figure 16-3 for an illustration of folding this type of garment.

Some of your clothes most likely need to be hung up. Here are a few tips for keeping your closet organized:

- Hang similar clothes together so they are easier to find. Hang pants with other pants and shirts with other shirts.
- Fold pants neatly over hangers or hang them by the bottom of their legs so they keep their shape.
- Hang skirts by the waist.

- Button the top button on shirts to help them keep their shape and prevent them from slipping off the hanger.
- Keep your shoes at the bottom of the closet in pairs to avoid wasting time looking for a shoe's mate when you need it.

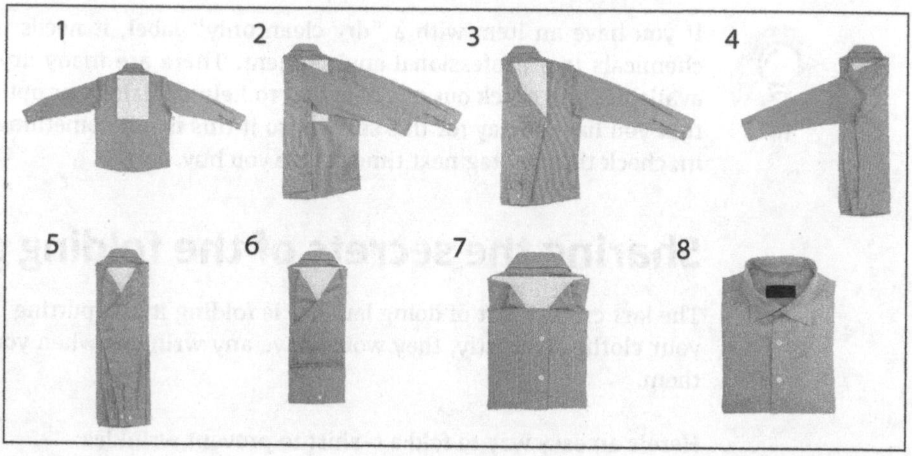

FIGURE 16-3: The perfect fold for a dress shirt.

TIP Whenever the dryer buzzes, stop what you're doing to take the clothes out to fold and put away. If you don't tackle it when you hear it buzz, your clothes might end up staying in the dryer for another week, and you will drive yourself crazy looking for your favorite shirt.

REMEMBER Create a dedicated folding space. Take the time to match up your socks after they come out of the dryer. Trying to find a matching sock on a busy morning can slow you down tremendously.

Giving New Life to Old Threads

Billions of discarded articles of clothing are currently sitting in landfills around the world. Your clothes can take up 200 years or longer to decompose in a landfill, adding greenhouse gases and toxic chemicals to the air and soil. This harms the environment! You most likely already donate clothing that you have outgrown or that you just don't reach for anymore, but what if your clothing has rips, tears, stains, broken zippers, or missing buttons? Clothing with these issues would not be taken as a donation, but your clothes should never end up in the trash!

Calculating cost per wear

One technique you can utilize to avoid discarding your clothing often is to purchase clothing that is well-made with quality materials. Think *quality* instead of *quantity*. That $5.00 shirt might be on-trend, but the cost is probably very cheap for a reason. The materials and textiles used are not made to last. Your trendy shirt might last for a couple of wears, but after you wash it twice, it's almost unrecognizable due to the lack of quality and durability. When shopping, keep in mind the equation of cost per wear (CPW):

CPW = Total Cost of the Item ÷ Number of Times You Wear It

Here's an example: If you buy a winter coat that costs $20.00, and you only wear it 5 times before it wears out, you would divide $20.00 by 5, and your CPW= $4.00. This means each time you wore that coat, it cost you $4.00.

However, if you save up and buy a higher-quality coat that costs $100.00, and it lasts you through at least three winter seasons when you wear it a total of 80 times, your CPW = $1.25. Your nice, quality winter jacket is still ready to wear more winter seasons in the future, and it ended up being cheaper than the $20.00 jacket in the long run. The more you wear it, the more money you save!

REMEMBER

Next time you're shopping, remember to consider a garment's cost per wear and how much you will wear the item. Purchasing high-quality clothing is less expensive in the long run than buying cheap and less-durable counterparts.

Embracing the reuse, repair, recycle philosophy

Reusing or repurposing your clothing is a great option to limit how often your clothing ends up in a landfill, which causes havoc in the environment. Consider the following ways you can reuse or repurpose your clothing:

- You can collect all of your high school, college, or special event t-shirts, sew them together, and make a blanket of memories. You can also sew them together to make a pillowcase or decorative pillow.
- With a few snips here and there, you can turn an old sweater into a cozy pair of gloves.
- Put on a stretchy long-sleeve t-shirt, slide the neckline to your waist, wrap the arms around and tie them in the front or back, and voilà, you have a fresh new skirt. Get creative with your clothing!

- Cut your old t-shirts into reusable grocery bags.
- Cut your t-shirt into a scarf.
- Cut and sew a stuffed toy out of old jeans or shirts.
- Make your old jeans into a nice, heavy comforter.
- Cut out the design graphic from a t-shirt, and put it in a matted picture frame.
- Pass clothing on to someone who can continue to get use from it.
- Sell your clothes on a social media site to give them new life and earn a pretty penny in the process.
- Learn basic hand sewing to mend holes in your clothing, or iron on patches or designs.

Did you know that your clothing can be recycled into fiber that is used in all sorts of manufacturing products? Carpet padding, wall insulation, and various rubbers are only a few of the ways your clothes can have their next life. Just like you can recycle paper and plastics, textiles can be recycled as well. So instead of throwing out your clothing, recycle your clothing at your local collection site.

TIP

Old cotton socks and soft cotton t-shirts make great rags for removing makeup, dusting or polishing furniture, and doing mechanical work.

Tackling a hot-button topic

One of the most common issues with clothing is having a button pop off. It's such a problem that the manufacturers include an extra button with the garment! If you buy a garment with buttons in the design, the hang tag includes an extra button, or an extra button will be sewn into the side seam. Don't believe me? Go take a look in your closet at one of your dress shirts or blouses, and I bet you will find an extra button sewn inside toward the bottom.

If you have discarded an article of clothing because a button popped off, I'm here to help! You are very capable of sewing the button back on, and many times, the button *you* sew on will end up being more secure than it was before.

TIP

It gives you a great feeling of pride and accomplishment when you can take action to repair your favorite item.

Knowing how to sew on a button will give you a newfound lease on life. OK, maybe that's a bit extreme, but it will make you feel good that you can add extra wear to your favorite shirt. The following are the steps to sew on a button, and Figure 16-4 gives a good visual to aid you through the process:

1. **Gather your supplies.**

   You need a needle, a button that matches your garment, thread that matches your button, and scissors.

2. **Unwind enough thread to match the length of your arm and then cut the thread.**
3. **Place a pin or dot where the missing button is to be replaced.**
4. **Put the tip of the thread into the eye of your needle and move the needle to the middle of your entire thread length, then knot the ends together.**
5. **Place the button on the fabric and hold it with your nondominant hand.**
6. **With your dominant hand, thread the needle through the underside of the fabric to pierce the fabric and come through one of the buttonholes; pull the thread all the way through.**
7. **Thread the needle down through the opposite buttonhole, ending on the back side of the fabric; pull the needle completely through.**
8. **Bring the needle back up through the opposite buttonhole, making sure to pull the thread all the way through again.**
9. **Repeat Steps 7 and 8 several times or until your button feels secure, making sure to pull the thread all the way through each time.**
10. **Bring the needle back to the wrong side of the fabric and slide the needle through your previous stitches to secure the thread.**
11. **Cut your thread and marvel at your finished button! You did it!**

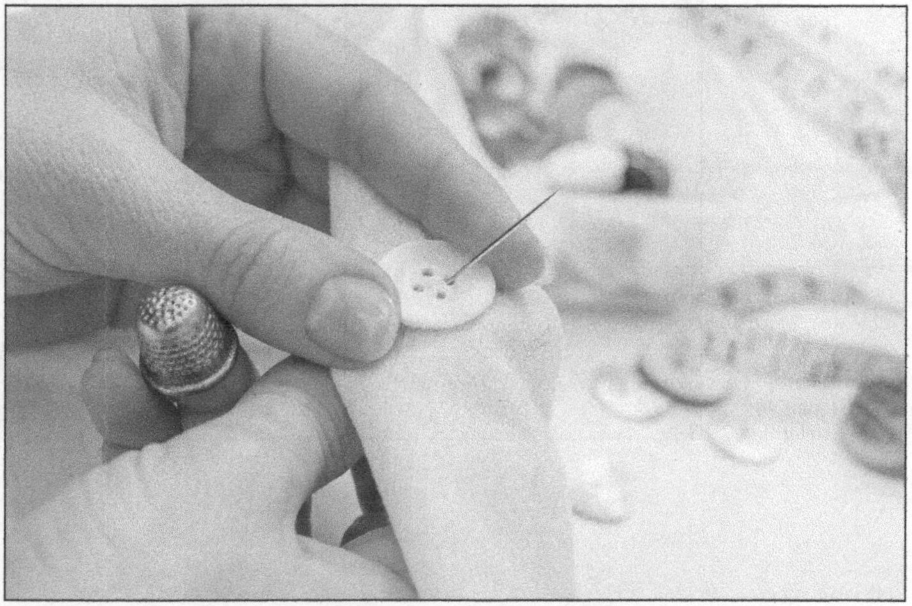

FIGURE 16-4: Sewing on a button.

TIP

You can find tiny travel-sized sewing kits that contain extra buttons and threaded needles at most convenience stores in case you find yourself in a fashion emergency.

Patching things up

It happens to everyone. You bend over to pick up your keys and *riiippp*, a tear down the back of your pants. You're probably mortified and run away as fast as you can grabbing your . . . ahem . . . behind! Once you get the pants off, the reality sets in that your favorite pair of pants are ruined — or are they?

By repairing your clothing, you take ownership and control of your wardrobe and extend the life of your favorite clothes. One of the simplest ways to repair a hole in clothing is to purchase a decorative patch and iron it over the hole. Not only can you wear your clothing again, but you can make a fashion statement as well.

You can also mend your own clothes. *Mending* is a broad term that refers to simple repairs for your clothing. A small rip or tear isn't the end of the world. Figure 16-5 shows an example of how you can repair your clothing.

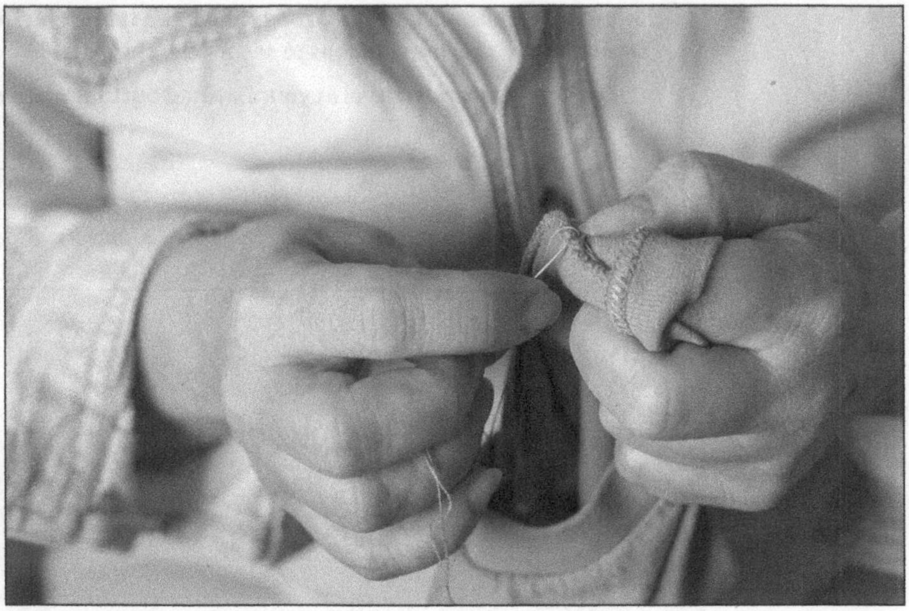

FIGURE 16-5: Repair your clothing.

You can fix a small rip or tear by taking the following steps:

1. **Pin the torn pieces together to close the hole.**
2. **Thread a needle with a matching thread color.**
3. **Tie a knot at the ends of the thread, away from the needle.**
4. **Beginning at the end of the rip, bring the needle through both layers of fabric and pull completely through and tight.**
5. **Repeat Step 4 until the hole is closed.**
6. **Tie a knot at the end of the seam you just sewed and cut off the excess thread.**

TIP

Craft stores sell fabric glue and hem tape that you can use to quickly fix unraveling edges from your clothes. You might consider having some on hand.

REMEMBER

You can save money and make your wardrobe last longer by getting creative with your clothing by patching it up yourself!

IN THIS CHAPTER

» Putting (kitchen) tools in your toolbox

» Staying on the safe side

» Giving compliments to the chef

Chapter 17 Stirring Things Up in the Kitchen

In this chapter, I cover how to be independent in the kitchen and how to successfully cook for yourself. Knowing your kitchen equipment, understanding kitchen safety, and knowing how to follow a recipe will help you get on your way to prepping and cooking meals to provide for yourself and others.

Knowing Your Equipment

Being an adult means providing basic needs for yourself, which includes food! I discussed healthy food for your body in Chapter 12, and eating fast food or convenience food is not always the best choice. Being able to cook meals for yourself and others is a skill that will stick with you for the rest of your life and can greatly affect your overall health and wellness.

To do any job correctly, you need the right tools. An artist needs the correct paint and brushes, a carpenter needs a hammer and nails, and a doctor needs a stethoscope. These professionals need appropriate tools just like you need the right tools to be successful in the kitchen.

Kitchen equipment varies from large kitchen appliances to small kitchen appliances and cooking utensils. Some appliances you might use more than others, but they all play a part in successfully preparing meals and snacks.

TIP

The right kitchen equipment can help you maintain a clean and orderly kitchen.

REMEMBER

Having the correct tools for the job —including cooking — can make your life easier. Understanding the differences among kitchen gadgets can help you feel more confident as a budding chef.

I need coffee!

You do not have to spend $5.00 on a cup of coffee every morning; I promise. You can make it at home and save yourself a significant amount of money! There are many options for making your coffee at home, the most common being a coffee pot.

Small kitchen appliances are generally powered by electricity, can be set on your countertop, and can be moved easily. There are tons of small appliances available for purchase, but before you buy, ask yourself if you will actually use them. Do you really need something called the "Garlic Zoom Garlic Chopper"? Or could you just chop garlic with a knife?

Figure 17-1 shows some of the following common small kitchen appliances that can make your time in the kitchen more productive.

FIGURE 17-1: Small kitchen appliances.

- **Slow cooker:** This is used to cook foods for long periods on a lower heat setting than traditional methods such as baking and boiling. Slow cookers usually have low, medium, and high settings. One way you can use a slow cooker is to pop 4 uncooked chicken breasts and 2 cups of your favorite salsa into it before you leave for work in the morning. Set the slow cooker to the low setting. When you come home six to eight hours later, you'll have some yummy chicken for tacos or nachos!
- **Food steamer:** You use this small appliance to cook foods with steam heat by surrounding a food basket with boiling water that produces steam. Some foods you can cook with a food steamer include rice, vegetables, and seafood.
- **Blender:** A blender is a jar or pitcher that sits atop a motor with various speeds for chopping and mixing. You can use a blender to make salsa, sauces, dressings, frozen desserts, smoothies, and much more. Here's a recipe you can make in a blender for a yummy snack!

  You need

  1 cup of frozen strawberries (or other berry of choice)

  1 banana

  1 cup of milk

  Place all the ingredients in your blender. Put the lid on the blender; you don't want blended goo exploding everywhere in your kitchen! Blend on low speed until smooth. Serve immediately with a tiny umbrella. You just made yourself the best *Strawberry Smoothie* ever! Look at you, using your small appliances already!
- **Food processor:** A food processor has different styles of blades and cutting disks that you can use for various cutting and mixing tasks including chopping, slicing, shredding, grinding, or pureeing foods.
- **Electric water kettle:** With an electric kettle, you can boil water quickly without turning on the stove. In about three minutes you have boiled water you can pour straight from the kettle into a bowl or mug to make oatmeal, instant soup, tea, or hot chocolate.
- **Waffle maker:** You pour waffle batter into to this appliance to cook waffles that are fluffy on the inside and crispy on the outside.
- **Toaster:** This appliance toasts nice, crispy bread slices to put your butter and jelly on for breakfast. You can get either a two- or a four-slice toaster, depending on the size of your family. You can use a toaster for many types of bread, as well as toaster pastries and frozen waffles and pancakes.
- **Toaster oven:** A toaster oven is similar to a toaster, but the food you're preparing lays flat on a rack to toast or bake. You also have more temperature

options. Things you can bake in a toaster oven include grilled cheese sandwiches, small pizzas, bacon, quesadillas, and biscuits.

- **Handheld mixer:** This is a lightweight mixer that enables you to mix cake batter, whip cream, and prepare whipped potatoes faster than using a wooden spoon. The appliance does all the hard mixing work for you!
- **Air fryer:** This appliance cooks food very quickly by a convection current that is circulated rapidly by a fan. It produces a crispy coating on your food using minimal oil, which is healthier than pan frying or deep frying.

REMEMBER

Small kitchen appliances are available to make your life a little easier. Consider investing in a few that will assist you by lessening the stress and time constraints of cooking your favorite meal.

Is this thing on?

Your kitchen most likely has the basic large appliances such as a stove and refrigerator. You need to know how to use them properly since appliances like these are often major purchases. Large appliances are kind of like cars; there are luxury versions of kitchen equipment as well as "I just need to get where I am going" versions that do the needed job without any bells and whistles. It's up to you to decide what style, size, and features you want, but know that upgrades come with a hefty price tag.

Aside from a stove and refrigerator, other large kitchen appliances include the following:

- Microwave
- Dishwasher
- Chest freezer
- Garbage disposal
- Beverage refrigerator
- Ice maker
- Oven hood and vent
- Warming drawers
- Stand mixer
- Deep fryer
- Electric grill

TIP

Take care of your large kitchen appliances by familiarizing yourself with the owner's manual, using them correctly, cleaning them properly, and protecting them when they are not in use.

TIP

If your refrigerator full of food suddenly stops working or there is a power outage, work quickly to keep your food from spoiling. Put your frozen foods at the bottom of an ice chest, then layer them with nonfrozen foods that need to be kept cold. Add layers as you work your way to the top of the ice chest. This should keep your food cold until you can get your refrigerator up and running.

Measure, mix, and cut. Oh my!

Your kitchen does not need to be overflowing with supplies for you to be a successful cook, but you do need to have basic supplies to be able to follow recipes and prepare dishes. You need measuring utensils, mixing utensils, and cookware. Without utensils, you would not be able to measure, mix, or prepare foods. Make sure you invest in some well-made utensils so they'll last you many years. Figure 17-2 and Figure 17-3 show some of the utensils I've listed here:

- **Measuring utensils**
  - Dry measuring cups (bottom of Figure 17-2): Use to measure dry ingredients like sugar and flour in ¼ cup, ⅓ cup, ½ cup, and 1 cup.
  - Liquid measuring cups (top left of Figure 17-2): Use to measure liquid ingredients in cups, ounces, and milliliters.
  - Measuring spoons (top right of Figure 17-2): Use to measure small amounts of dry or liquid ingredients in ¼ teaspoon, ½ teaspoon, 1 teaspoon, and 1 tablespoon.
- **Mixing utensils**
  - Mixing bowls: Available in different sizes to mix your ingredients in.
  - Mixing spoon: Use to mix dry or wet ingredients; these have long handles and are made of metal, plastic, or wood.
  - Pastry blender: Use to cut shortening into flour for biscuit and pie crust recipes.
  - Wire whisk: Use for beating and blending ingredients like eggs.
  - Plastic or rubber scraper: Use to scrape bowls and mix ingredients.
  - Sifter or mesh strainer: Use to break up lumps in dry ingredients to make them easier to mix thoroughly.

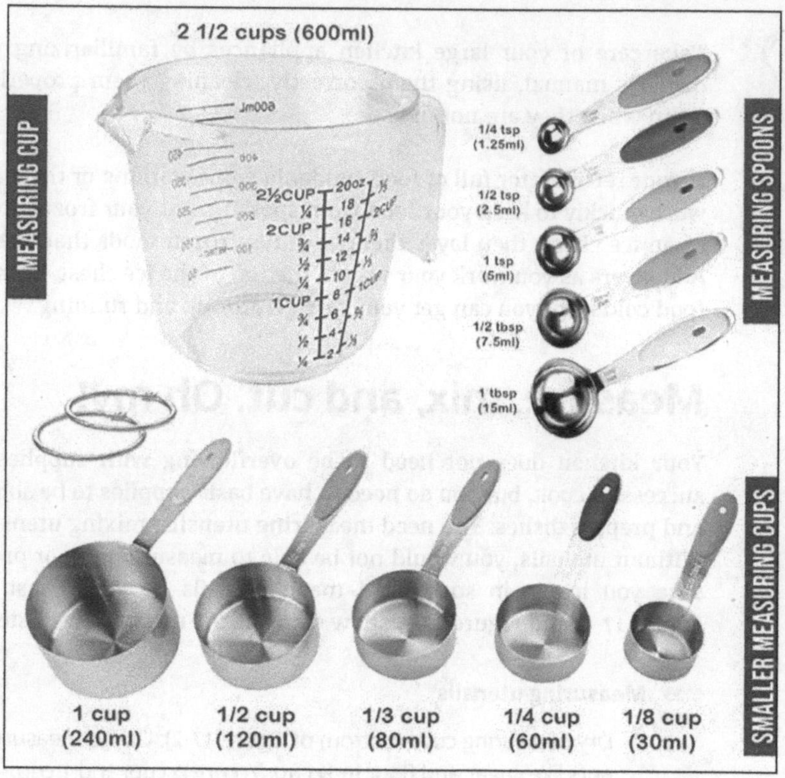

FIGURE 17-2: Common measuring utensils.

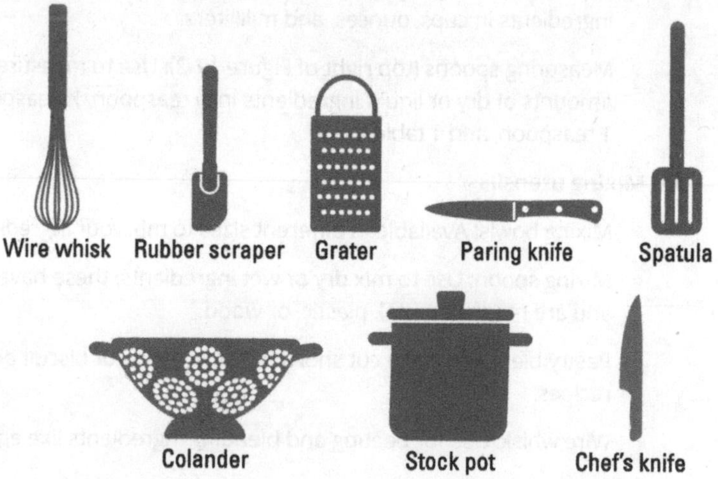

FIGURE 17-3: Common knives and cooking utensils.

» **Kitchen utensils**

- Cutting board: A board of wood or plastic that keeps sharp knives from ruining your countertops
- Paring knife: A smaller knife used for fruits and vegetables
- Utility knife: An all-purpose knife used for cutting and slicing
- Chef's knife: A larger knife for cutting, mincing, and dicing
- Bread knife: A knife with a serrated blade used for slicing bread
- Grater: A tool with holes with raised edges for shredding cheese and vegetables
- Kitchen shears: Sharp scissors for cutting food items
- Peeler: A swiveling blade on a handle for peeling vegetables and fruit
- Potato masher: A tool used for mashing cooked potatoes
- Colander: A bowl with holes to drain liquid from foods
- Slotted spoon: A spoon for lifting solid food from liquid
- Spatula: A long-handled utensil with a broad blade for flipping pancakes and hamburgers
- Tongs: A tool kind of like giant tweezers for grabbing and holding foods
- Ladle: A scoop on the end of a long handle for serving liquids like soup or punch
- Cooling racks: Wire tray that allows air to circulate around food to provide even cooling

» **Cookware**

- Saucepan: A one-handled pot that comes in various sizes, measured in quarts or liters
- Stockpot: Double-handled pot measured in quarts or liters
- Cake pans: Metal pans that come in round, square, or rectangular shapes that can be used for baking various foods, not just cakes
- Loaf pans: Metal pan used for bread and meat loaves
- Baking dishes: Deep glass or ceramic dishes use for baking; often come with a cover
- Skillet: Shallow pan with a long handle, used for sautéing, pan-frying, and searing

- Baking sheet: Rectangular, low-sided pans used for baking cookies and roasting vegetables
- Pie pans: Round metal or glass pan with sloping sides for baking a pie or quiche
- Muffin pan: Metal pan with 6 or 12 wells for baking muffins or cupcakes

TIP

Cooking utensils are often sold in sets, which can make them more cost-effective.

TIP

Take care of your kitchen items by paying attention to the materials they are made of. If you have nonstick pans, use nylon or wooden utensils to stir or mix items.

Playing It Safe

Getting ready to cook might seem like it requires a lot of prep work, but that's because it does! Not only must you shop for ingredients and have the right mixing and cooking utensils, but you must also prepare for a safe and sanitized experience. Many injuries can happen in the kitchen. Cuts, bruises, burns, fires, shocks, or foodborne illnesses can all be prevented by working safely in the kitchen. Many accidents can be avoided by having proper food handling techniques and proper sanitation.

Have you ever eaten a meal, then a little while later you have an upset stomach with diarrhea and vomiting? Something you ate most likely made you sick. When you cook for yourself or other people, you do not want to be the one who makes everyone sick! Your best bet is to learn how to prevent injuries in the kitchen and learn to control foodborne illnesses. Keep reading to learn some ways to keep everyone happy and healthy in the kitchen.

REMEMBER

Thinking ahead and working safely in the kitchen can prevent accidents from happening.

TIP

Each person you live with needs to understand kitchen safety and sanitation. It can be dangerous if they do not. After reading this chapter, share your newfound knowledge with them.

An accident waiting to happen

Accidentally cutting yourself in the kitchen is pretty easy to do because of all the sharp knives and utensils you use. Do the following to help prevent cuts, bumps, and bruises:

- Wash knives and other sharp objects separately from your other dishes. Do not place knives in a sink full of soapy water. You could easily cut yourself when reaching into the suds.
- Store your knives in a safe spot, separate from your other utensils.
- Do not leave your knives laying around. As soon as you are done with the knife, put it back into its spot.
- Use a cutting board and keep your fingertips away from the knife. To prevent the cutting board from slipping, place a wet towel underneath it.
- Don't stick your hands down a drain that has a garbage disposal. If you dropped something down the drain that needs to be retrieved, unplug the disposal first.
- Close cabinet doors when not using them. The last thing you want to do is turn around and bump your head on the cabinet you left open. Ouch!
- Use a step-stool to reach high places in the kitchen. Don't climb on the countertop.
- Wipe up spills from the floors and countertops right away.

TIP

Sharp knives are safer than dull knives. The sharper a knife is, the easier it is to control the cuts you make with it.

TIP

The best place to store your knives is in a countertop knife block or a magnetic strip mounted to the wall. Returning knives to their proper storing place immediately after using and washing them makes your kitchen a much safer place.

Don't play with fire

You may have heard the saying, "If you play with fire, you're gonna get burned." This is true. The fire used in the kitchen is not for play; it is used as a tool. You cannot be too careful when working with gas and electric appliances.

Here are some precautions to take while you cook:

WARNING

- Avoid cooking in loose-fitted clothing that can get caught in appliances or catch fire.
- Keep towels and cords away from the stovetop and oven.
- Use a dry potholder or oven mitt to handle hot cookware. If the potholder or oven mitt is even the slightest bit wet, you could get a steam burn!
- Balance your pots and pans on top of the range to keep them from tipping over.
- Turn the handles of your cookware and utensils to the inside of the range so they cannot be knocked off when someone walks by.
- Remove the lid of your pot by tilting it away from you to keep the hot steam from flowing toward you.
- Don't use your fingers when removing items from hot water or hot oil. Use tongs instead.
- Keep a fire extinguisher in the kitchen. Examine it once a month to ensure it is still in good working order. See Figure 17-4 for an example of how to properly use a fire extinguisher.

WARNING

If a grease fire starts, *do not* throw water on it. The flames will spread! Smother the grease fire with a pan cover or baking soda.

FIGURE 17-4: Using a fire extinguisher.

TIP

Put foil or a liner in the bottom of your oven so if you have a spill, you can replace the liner instead of scrubbing burned food off the oven. If spilled food is left at the bottom of the oven, it could lead to a fire.

It's all quite shocking

The electrical equipment in your kitchen should be checked regularly to ensure it is in good working order. Electrical shocks can be common in the kitchen, so prevention is key.

Keep the following things in mind to protect yourself from electrical shocks:

- Don't use wet hands when touching electrical equipment in the kitchen.
- Keep forks and knives out of the toaster. If something gets stuck in the toaster, unplug it and try to shake it out.
- Do not plug in a kitchen appliance while standing on a wet floor.
- Disconnect an appliance by unplugging it with the plug, not pulling on the cord.
- Do not submerge appliances in water. If you have to clean a small appliance, unplug it and wash the area that was in contact with the food without submerging the electrical cord in the water.

WARNING

Keep appliances unplugged when not in use. They can be fire hazards if left plugged in.

Healthy clean fun

You have a new recipe you want to try, so you go to the store to buy the ingredients. Great! Once you buy them and get them home, food safety becomes your responsibility. Did you know that bacteria live in and on your foods? Bacteria can double every 30 minutes under the right conditions.

If items need to be kept cold, put them in the refrigerator, or more bacteria will grow, and the bacteria can cause foodborne illness. If you are even a little bit careless, cross-contamination can occur. This is where harmful bacteria are transferred from one food to the other. This usually happens because your hands and utensils are not washed properly.

Taking the time to sanitize and clean to get rid of harmful bacteria in the kitchen is the first step toward preventing foodborne illness. Here are some tips for keeping a sanitary kitchen:

- Wear clean clothes and a clean apron when working with food.
- Always wash your hands with warm, soapy water before handling any type of food and after you work with raw meat such as poultry, beef, and fish.
- If you need a restroom break while cooking, take off your apron and wash your hands after using the bathroom.
- Use separate towels for drying your hands and your dishes. Keep them color-coded to tell the difference.
- Keep all kitchen surfaces clean by using a disinfecting cleaner.
- Wash raw vegetables and fruits under cold running water, even if they look clean. Bacteria cannot be seen with the naked eye.
- Wash prepackaged salad and vegetable mix even if the label says they are prewashed.
- Thaw frozen foods in the microwave or refrigerator. Do not leave them sitting on the counter all day to thaw out. This is a bacteria breeding ground!
- After using a cutting board for raw meat, sanitize it with bleach and water.
- Thoroughly wash all utensils used to avoid cross-contamination.
- Use a clean spoon every time you taste food while cooking. No double-dipping is allowed.
- Cook beef to an internal temperature of 160 degrees, chicken to 165 degrees, fish to 145 degrees, and eggs to at least 158 degrees to kill any harmful bacteria. A meat thermometer is the best way to measure the internal temperature.
- Hot foods should be served hot, at or above 140 degrees, and cold foods should be served cold, at or below 40 degrees.
- Once you have enjoyed your meal, place leftovers in the refrigerator or freezer within two hours.

TIP

Even though you may be tired from all that cooking, clean up your kitchen immediately after you eat. Don't wait until the next morning, or you might find that the bacteria in your kitchen has doubled.

FOODBORNE ILLNESS

Foodborne illness affects one in six people every year. There are many forms of food poisoning, but there are some common ones that can easily be avoided:

- **Norovirus:** This type of illness presents itself as the stomach flu after you have eaten. The norovirus is resistant to freezing and hot temperatures and can survive on different surfaces. It is very important to sanitize consistently to kill this bacteria.
- **Salmonella:** Salmonella can contaminate almost any food. Salmonella is killed by cooking and pasteurization. If you cut raw chicken on the same cutting board as your lettuce for a salad, you have just contaminated your lettuce. You will kill the bacteria when you cook the chicken, but the lettuce will not be cooked, therefore you will be consuming raw chicken juice that touched the lettuce. Yikes! Salmonella can make you very sick for at least four days.
- **E. Coli:** This is usually found in undercooked ground beef and items made with unpasteurized milk and juices. It can also be found on raw fruits and vegetables; this is why it is so important to wash them with cold water before eating.
- **Staphylococcal food poisoning (Staph):** This is contracted from items that are not properly refrigerated or left out too long. Meats, creams, and pastries should all be stored at the proper temperatures to prevent illness.

Cookin' up a Storm

Making your first dish in the kitchen can be intimidating, but trust me, you can do it! You will feel a newfound sense of confidence by preparing your own meals. Once you know how to use your equipment and can practice safety and sanitation skills, you are ready to begin.

A recipe is a set of ingredients and directions used in cooking. You may have heard someone say, "Oh, I love this recipe," or "My grandma had a secret recipe for her spaghetti sauce."

The recipe tells you what ingredients to use and what steps to take to get to a final product. There are thousands of cookbooks that contain many recipes you could use, and you can easily search the internet for some yummy recipes.

If you are just beginning to cook, there are a few things you should consider when deciding on a recipe:

- Does this recipe have ingredients in it that you like?
- How long will this recipe take and how many will it feed?
- Do the steps make sense and do you have the skills needed?
- Do you have the necessary equipment and utensils?
- Can you find all the ingredients?

Here's my mother's secret No-Bake Oatmeal Chocolate Cookie recipe. OK, it's not really a secret, but she told us it was. This would be a great recipe to start with!

No-Bake Oatmeal Chocolate Cookies

PREP TIME: 10 MINUTES	COOK TIME: 3 MINUTES	YIELD: 24 COOKIES

INGREDIENTS

1 stick butter or margarine

2 cups sugar

½ cup milk

2 tablespoons unsweetened cocoa powder

2½ cups quick-cooking oatmeal

1 teaspoon vanilla

2 tablespoons peanut butter

DIRECTIONS

1. Place the butter, sugar, milk, and cocoa powder in a medium saucepan over medium-high heat. Bring to a boil and let boil for 3 minutes.

2. Remove from the heat and use a wooden spoon to stir in the oatmeal, vanilla, and peanut butter until completely combined.

3. Drop tablespoonsful of the mixture onto wax paper and carefully shape them into a round cookie shape. As they cool, they will begin to harden. Enjoy!

Whenever you find a recipe you like, make notes on it and keep it handy so you can make it again. Who knows, maybe one day you can put together your own cookbook.

TIP

When you are first beginning to cook, choose recipes that have just a few ingredients and steps. They are usually easier to prepare. Once you get more experienced, you can choose more complex recipes to follow.

TIP

Cooking your meals instead of going out can save you money! Try to plan your meals for each week and make a list of what you need at the grocery store.

Measuring twice, pouring once

Much of your success in the kitchen is determined by the way you measure and combine ingredients. Recipes usually use abbreviations of measurements and methods to save room. Memorizing the abbreviations and terms is a great idea to help you become a pro at making your meals. Figure 17-5 is a helpful guide for units of measurement.

FIGURE 17-5: Kitchen measuring conversions.

Did you know that the ways you measure dry ingredients and wet ingredients are different? Dry ingredients include items such as sugar, flour, salt, and baking powder. For dry ingredients, you use the measuring cups shown on the left in Figure 17-6. For wet ingredients such as milk, water, or oil, use liquid measuring cups. Liquid measuring cups are clear so you can place them on the counter and read the measurement at eye level. Figure 17-6 explains how to accurately measure dry and wet ingredients.

TIP

Measure your ingredients over the canister or wax paper to avoid any spillover into your mixing bowl or cooking pot, which would throw off the proportion of ingredients.

TIP

Before you begin mixing, line up your ingredients on the counter in the order in which they will be added according to the recipe. This helps you keep track of what you have used and added.

WARNING

Be mindful of the recipe ingredients. If it says 2 cups of *sifted* flour, you must sift it before measuring it. If you sift after measuring, the quantity is a different amount than the recipe is asking for. Once you have added the flour to the measuring cup, use the spine of a butter knife to level off the top.

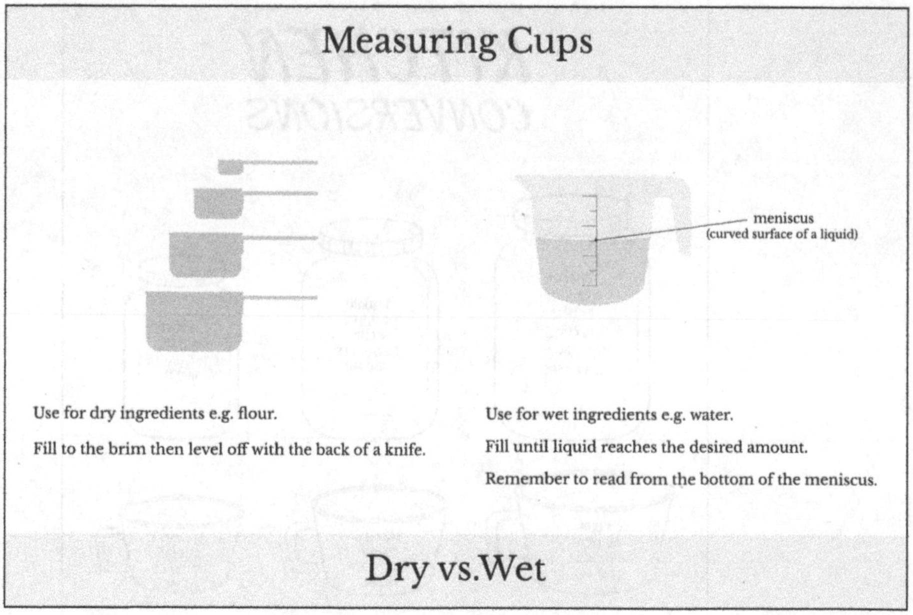

FIGURE 17-6: Dry versus wet measuring.

Boiling, basting, baking, and BBQ-ing

Have you ever read a recipe and wondered what the heck it was saying? Mince. Fold. Beat. Whip. It's almost as if cooking has a language all its own.

No fear. In this section, I share the most common mixing, cutting, and cooking terms, some of which are illustrated in Figure 17-7. The next time you read a recipe, you will know what to do!

» **Mixing terms**

- Stir: Use a spoon to make circular motions or figure-eight motions.
- Blend, mix, or combine: Use a spoon to stir two or more ingredients together completely.
- Beat: Use a quick over and under motion with a spoon, whisk, or electric mixer to create a smooth consistency.
- Whip: Beat ingredients rapidly to bring in air and increase the volume, as with whipping cream. Use a whisk or electric mixer.
- Cream: Use a spoon, beater, or mixer to combine ingredients until smooth and creamy.
- Fold: Use a rubber scraper to gently combine ingredients delicately.
- Cut in: Use a pastry blender or two knives with a cutting motion to mix solid fat with dry ingredients.

» **Cutting terms**

- Chop: Cut food into small, irregular pieces.
- Cube: Cut into evenly shaped pieces, approximately ½ inch.
- Mince: Chop food into the smallest possible pieces; often used for garlic.
- Dice: Cut food into evenly shaped pieces, approximately ¼ inch.
- Pare: Cut off the outside skin of a fruit or vegetable.
- Grate: Rub food over a grater to get small fine pieces, as in grating Parmesan cheese.
- Shred: Cut or tear food into long, thin pieces with a food grater or food processor, like shredded cheese.

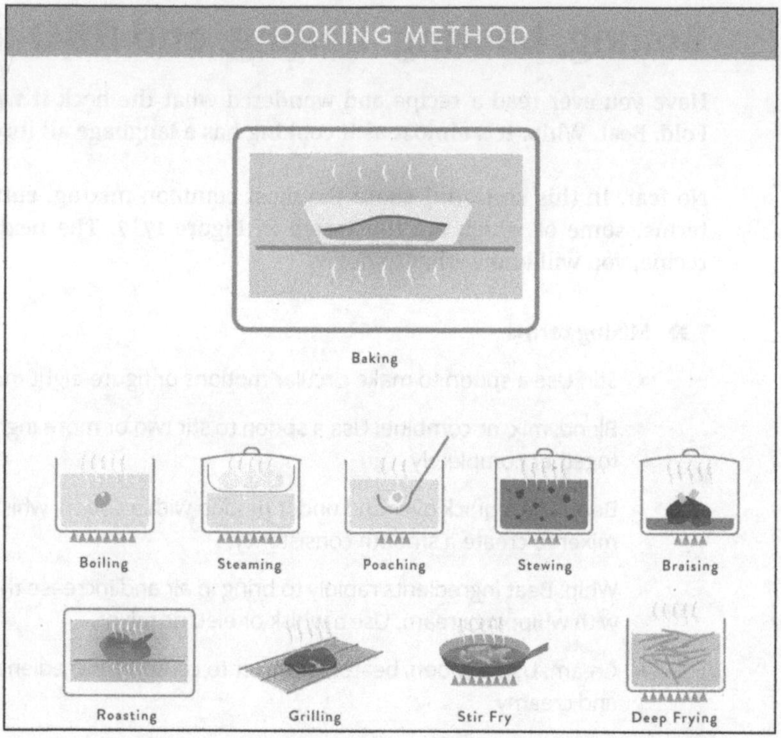

FIGURE 17-7: Cooking methods.

» Cooking terms

- Boil: Heating a liquid to 212 degrees Fahrenheit.
- Bake: Cooking with dry heat, typically in an oven.
- Poach: Cooking food directly in liquid at a temperature lower than the boiling point.
- Roast: Cooking with dry heat, similar to baking but at higher temperatures.
- Baste: Moistening foods while cooking them to add flavor and prevent the food from drying out.
- Grill: Cooking food at high heat directly over burning coals or a gas flame.
- Smoke: Flavoring food by cooking it at a low temperature for a long period. You can generate natural smoke with an off-set grill, or you can purchase liquid smoke as an additive to your food while cooking it.
- Grease: Rubbing lightly with oil, butter, margarine, or cooking spray.
- Simmer: Heating liquid to just below boiling point until the bubbles show on the surface.

- Steam: Cooking food over water rather than in the water.
- Braise: Browning food in a small amount of fat, then simmering in small amounts of liquid.
- Stew: Cooking food that has been cut into small pieces in a small amount of liquid, similar to braising.
- Deep fry: Cooking with food submerged in a type of fat.
- Stir-fry: Cooking quickly over high heat in a skillet by stirring small pieces of food in a small amount of fat.
- Drain: Removing excess liquid by placing food in a colander or strainer.

TIP

You can use a toothpick to check cakes and bread. Stick the toothpick in the center, and if it comes out clean, your baked good is done!

TIP

To make sure your food is cooked thoroughly, use a thermometer and take notice of the color of your food after it has been cooked. Fully cooked meat and poultry should not be pink on the inside.

Getting on the same wave length

The microwave is an amazing invention! Microwaves are convenient and easy to use, they are much faster than other cooking methods, and there is less risk that you'll burn yourself. Always follow package directions for microwaving your food, but I have a few suggestions to ensure you get the best results from using your microwave.:

- » Before cooking, pierce potatoes (and other items with skin) with a fork to allow steam to escape.
- » Cover foods to prevent drying out or a splattered mess in the microwave.
- » Check for doneness at the shortest recommended time. You can add more time if needed.
- » Let the food stand in the microwave for the recommended amount of time. The food is continuing to cook, and then cooling down during this resting period.

TIP

There are so many things you can cook in the microwave. A couple of my favorites are Omelet in a Mug and Baked Potato Soup.

Omelet in a Mug

PREP TIME: 5 MINUTES | COOK TIME: 3 MINUTES | YIELD: 1 OMELET

INGREDIENTS

2 large eggs

½ bell pepper (any color), diced

2 slices deli ham, diced

¼ cup chopped fresh spinach

Salt and pepper

DIRECTIONS

1 Place all the ingredients in a microwavable mug and mix well.

2 Cook on high in the microwave for 2–3 minutes, stirring halfway through the process.

Baked Potato Soup

PREP TIME: 5 MINUTES | COOK TIME: 15 MINUTES | YIELD: 4 SERVINGS

INGREDIENTS

1 pound baking potatoes (about 2), peeled and cubed

1 (14½-ounce) can chicken broth

1 cup milk

3 strips bacon, cooked, crumbled, and divided

1 cup shredded cheddar cheese, divided

1 green onion sliced, divided

¼ cup sour cream

DIRECTIONS

1 Microwave the potatoes in a large microwaveable bowl on high for 5 minutes, stirring after 2½ minutes.

2 Stir in the broth and milk. Microwave on high another 10 minutes, stirring halfway through.

3 Use a potato masher to mash the potatoes.

4 Reserve 2 tablespoons each of the bacon and cheese and 1 tablespoon of the onions for topping. Stir in the remaining bacon, cheese, and onions.

5 Serve topped with the reserved bacon, cheese, and onions, and the sour cream.

TIP

Understanding cooking terminology, methods, and abbreviations can help you successfully read and prepare a recipe. Taking the time to read the recipe step by step will help your dish to turn out great. Your stomach thanks you!

IN THIS CHAPTER

» House and home

» Making lemonade out of lemons

» A helping hand

Chapter 18
Preparing for the Unexpected

Unexpected things or events will happen in your life. You don't know what those things will be, but it is guaranteed that surprises are going to happen.

How you handle unexpected events can tell a lot about your character and your maturity. What happens when your roof begins to leak or your water gets shut off? Do you panic and run away? No! You problem-solve and handle the situation. Maybe your problem-solving involves reading this book for ideas, in which case, I have you covered.

In this chapter, I help you understand the important reasons for maintaining your home, planning for the unexpected, and knowing when you need to ask for help.

Caring for Your Home's Health

Let's first look at how to ensure your home is taken care of properly. If you can properly maintain your home, you can prevent more serious issues that could arise unexpectedly. You should routinely complete the following:

- » Test your smoke alarms, carbon monoxide detector, fire extinguishers, and alarm system.
- » Keep drains in sinks, tubs, and showers clear to avoid the pipes becoming clogged.
- » Clean the garbage disposal with hot water and baking soda.
- » Rake leaves and aerate your lawn.
- » Inspect roofing for missing or damaged shingles and potential leaks.
- » Power wash windows and siding.
- » Clean windows and screen doors.
- » Fix squeaky handles and hinges.
- » If the weather looks like it might freeze, wrap insulation around your outdoor faucets.
- » Change your air conditioning filter.
- » Change your water filter.
- » Remove leaves and debris from your gutters.
- » Prune trees and shrubs.
- » Professionally clean your carpets.

TIP

During the growing season for your grass, you need to cut it once a week to keep it healthy.

TIP

If you are not in a position to handle some of these home maintenance tasks on your own, there are professional services that can help you take care of them.

The magic of electrons

You walk into your home after a long hard day. You feel the cool air conditioning, flip on the light switch, and turn on the ceiling fan. If it weren't for electricity, none of these conveniences would be possible. Electricity is often taken for granted. You might become well aware of this if you forget to pay your electricity bill and it gets shut off or if you are moving and the service isn't on in the new place by the time you get there. *Before* you move to a new place, contact the electric company to ensure you have electricity up and running for moving day.

Utilizing electricity probably seems like second nature to you. But beware, electricity can be very dangerous and can even start fires. Here are a few safety tips.

- If you need electrical work done in your home, hire a qualified electrician. It is too dangerous to try and fix it yourself.
- Do not use your cell phone around water when it is plugged in. Do not sleep with your cell phone under your pillow or close to your sheets while it is plugged in and charging. This could start a fire.
- Major appliances such as refrigerators, stoves, and microwaves should be plugged directly into the wall. Do not use extension cords. When unplugging, grasp the plug part, not the cord.
- Do not run electrical cords through doorways or under carpets.
- Use a light bulb with the correct number of watts for the lamp or light.
- A fire can begin if heat builds up near flammable objects. Keep paper or fabric away from light bulbs and other heating elements.
- If you have flickering or dimming lights, replace the light bulb ASAP.
- Call a qualified electrician if you see sparks from an outlet, smell a burning smell coming from an appliance, or experience continued problems with tripping a breaker.

WARNING

Make sure appliances and their wiring do not come in contact with water. Also, if an electrical cord is visibly damaged, throw out the item that has the damaged cord!

TIP

If you have children in your household, cover the outlets with tamper-resistant baby-proof outlet covers to keep little hands out of the outlets.

Flood zone

If you live near a body of water or a high-risk flooding area, you will most likely be *required* to purchase flood insurance for your home. But water can get in your home and cause flooding even when you don't live in a flood plain, which might be reason to choose to buy flood insurance even if your lender doesn't require it. Your house could flood due to broken pipes, a poor drainage system, malfunctioning appliances, poor floor and wall sealing, sewer backup, or many other reasons. If your home floods due to a natural occurrence or a household issue, flood insurance will cover the costs of the damages.

Even though you may not want to pay extra money each month for something you cannot "see," it is too expensive *not* to have flood insurance. Just one inch of water in your home can cause more than $25,000 worth of damage. There are some things you can do to minimize the damage flooding causes and get a jump-start on repairs:

- **»** Turn off the water! If the flood water is not from a natural occurrence, find the water source and turn it off. Most likely you will need to shut off the water valve to the entire house. Find the main water valve and figure out how to shut it off *as soon as* you move into a new house. The last thing you need is to be searching for the water shut-off while a water emergency is occurring!
- **»** After the water has stopped, turn off the electricity. If you find yourself standing in water and in front of the fuse box at the same time, call an electrician and evacuate. Water and electricity do not mix!
- **»** Call for help. If you are renting, call the property manager or proprietor to let them know what is happening. If you own the home, call your insurance company to make them aware. Take pictures for your insurance company to document the mess.
- **»** Begin the cleanup process. Check out `www.redcross.org` for a guide on cleaning up water damage from flooding.
- **»** Prevent mold damage as much as you can. Black mold or toxic mold can affect your overall health. After the water has been cleared, work to keep the flooded areas as dry as possible. Keep a running fan over the damp areas and use a bleach cleaner to kill bacteria.

REMEMBER

Failed plumbing systems within your home can lead to pipe leaks and bursts, resulting in water damage.

TIP

A waterproof safe for your valuables and documents is a good investment. Passports, social security cards, and birth certificates should be placed in the safe.

Take Murphy's Law to Heart

You may have heard one of many variations of Murphy's Law, such as this one: "Anything that can go wrong will go wrong and at the worst possible time." You may also have felt that this statement is true, like everything is going wrong in your life and there is no end in sight. I know I have.

However, if you expect the unexpected or leave room in your "plan" for things not to go according to the "plan," then you will feel more in control when things do go a bit haywire, thus easing your stress in many situations. Being flexible is key.

TIP

Do not expect things or events in your life to go a certain way. Do not assume anything about the circumstances.

TIP

Worrying and visualizing unexpected events are two different things. Worrying carries no solution, whereas visualizing can lead to finding a solution.

Brainstorming the storms

An optimist is a "person who tends to be hopeful and confident about the future or success of something." An optimist sees the positive side of things. Instead of saying, "Why does this always happen to me?" an optimist would say, "Let's turn this situation upside down and see it from a different, positive perspective."

Considering many possible scenarios in life will help keep you from a lifetime of disappointment. An optimistic person has usually visualized different life scenarios, which enables them to be proactive instead of reactive. If you tend to look at the negative side of things, here are a few tips for shifting your mindset:

- Acknowledge and notice good things as they happen. For example, if you don't catch any red lights on your morning commute, let yourself be happy about it. At the end of the day, write down all the things you are grateful for. Before you know it, you will be *intentionally awaiting* amazing things to happen every day.
- Believe that you can make great things happen. For example, you might say to yourself, "If I work hard, I will get a promotion." Or "If I study more, I will get a better grade." Confidence that things will work out for the good contributes to successful outcomes.
- When something good happens or you achieve a goal, give yourself credit. Think back on the steps you took to be successful and be thankful!
- Don't be too hard on yourself when things go wrong. Positive self-talk helps you get through the tough times. Just because you failed the test or didn't get the promotion doesn't mean you are stupid. It just means you get another chance to review the material and think outside the box.
- Setbacks are temporary. As soon as you fail, mess up, or something unexpected occurs, plan your next move forward.

REMEMBER

Optimism can be learned. It might take a while to become more positive in your disposition, but be patient.

TIP

Sometimes the people you are around can add negativity to your mindset. If you are with people who complain all day, you are likely to join in. Surround yourself with others who are positive and who want to see you succeed.

Evaluating risk versus reward

Risk is much more than mathematics and statistics. Every person has a different risk factor based on their personality and what challenges their current situation can withstand.

Do you remember those TV shows that had blindfolded people stick their hands in jars that could be full of something scary, like venomous snakes, or something harmless like fluffy feathers? The individuals on the show would be scared or psych themselves out thinking about the risk involved. But what about the reward? If they successfully held their hands in the jar for 30 seconds, they could win thousands of dollars! So does the risk outweigh the reward or does the reward outweigh the risk? Only you can decide what risks you're willing to assume.

It is the same way in life. Yes, there will be risks involved in different situations. Some risks result in amazing things; others will not. Some risks put you on a path to success; others may not. By making educated decisions and calculating your risk versus reward, you are partaking in the amazing, exciting journey of life!

REMEMBER

Greatness requires risk. No guts, no glory!

TIP

Learn from your mistakes. Reflect on the risks you take and assess how you can improve your decisions for next time.

Being prepared

You hear someone around you say, "It looks like it's supposed to snow this week." Someone else says, "Yes, the news says there'll be major snowfall like we haven't seen in a while around here." You think to yourself, "Cool, snow! I can't wait to see snow; it's been a while." After work, you head to the grocery store to grab a couple of small items for dinner and notice it's much busier than normal. You don't think much about it and head home to eat and get a good night's rest. You wake up the next morning, and more than 10 inches of snow have fallen! You cannot even open your front door, and it looks like you aren't going anywhere for several days because another storm is on the way.

If this scenario had played out for you in real life, what could you have done differently? You knew about the snowstorm, but you seemed to be in denial as to what might happen. This is where you need to expect the unexpected. You didn't prepare!

The following are some suggestions for preparing for events such as this one:

- Stock up on food. Buy food that requires no refrigeration because you might find yourself without electricity. Canned foods, bagged snacks, nuts, peanut butter, water bottles, dry cereal, granola, and beef jerky are a great start. Figure 18-1 is a shopping list to use to prepare your household for an emergency.
- Stock up on the essentials like toilet paper, soap, toothpaste, shampoo, and deodorant.

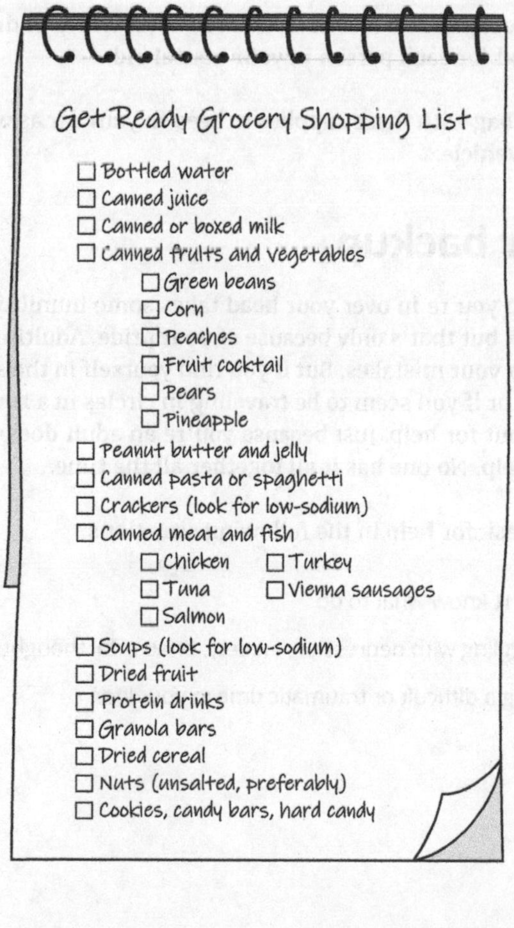

FIGURE 18-1: Stockpile shopping list.

» Be prepared with other emergency supplies:
  - Flashlight
  - Batteries
  - Radio
  - Matches or lighter
  - Paper goods such as plates, utensils, cups, and napkins
  - Trash bags
  - Pet food
  - Scissors
  - Hand-cranked can opener
  - First aid supplies

TIP

Make sure your stockpile includes at least three days' worth of drinking water and nonperishable food for each person in your household.

TIP

Fill a small duffle bag with these supplies to keep in your car as well. You could get stranded in your vehicle.

Calling for backup

Recognizing when you're in over your head takes some humility. Asking for help is not always easy, but that's only because of your pride. Adulting is hard, and you have to learn from your mistakes. But if you find yourself in the same rut you have been in for years, or if you seem to be traveling in circles in a rough spot, it might be time to reach out for help. Just because you're an adult doesn't mean that you don't ever need help. No one has it all together all the time.

You may need to ask for help in the following situations:

» If you just don't know what to do.

» If you're struggling with depression, anxiety, or suicidal thoughts.

» If you're facing a difficult or traumatic time in your life.

Asking for help can be difficult. Here are some tips for asking for help from others:

- Decide on the best person to ask depending on your unique situation.
- Be assertive about what you need help with. Don't dance around what you need; be clear.
- Determine the best time (from their point of view) to ask.
- Pick a time to ask when you can speak privately.
- When a person agrees to help, let them.

REMEMBER

Asking for help is not easy, but to be your best self, it is necessary. Your friends and family want to see you succeed and would most likely give you the shirt off of their back if you asked. Allow people to help you.

TIP

If you know you need help, do not waste time. Ask for help as soon as you can. Whether that means help at work or help in your personal life, sitting idly by and watching your life stand still is not positive or productive.

6 The Part of Tens

IN THIS PART . . .

Do your part to be a responsible citizen.

Keep up with general maintenance to keep your car running in tip-top shape.

Avoid the most common rookie mistakes of adulting.

IN THIS CHAPTER

» Understanding the importance of integrity

» Giving back

» Being courageous

Chapter 19 Ten Ways to Be a Responsible Citizen

Being a good citizen comes with responsibility. Learning about your community, state, and country enables you to be a more informed citizen, which makes you better equipped to contribute to society and make a positive difference. Citizenship is the way you handle your responsibilities to allow your community to run smoothly and serve the needs of the people. Part of adulting is being a productive citizen in society. Here are 10 ways to make that happen.

Having Integrity

Having integrity means living your life with your deepest values in place:

- You are honest and trustworthy.
- You behave ethically for yourself and others.
- You do the right thing, not matter who is watching.

» You are reliable.

» Your moral compass stays the same through thick and thin.

Integrity is an admirable trait that comes with being a good citizen.

Being Productive

Get out in society and be productive! Become an employee in an industry you are passionate about or own your own business that provides a good or service for others. The possibilities of what to do with your life are endless. Whatever you decide, get out there, be productive, and be a role model for the next generation.

Helping Make Improvements

Don't just complain; provide a solution. Fix situations that aren't working! If you see a problem or issue you are passionate about in your neighborhood, workplace, state, or country, work toward a solution.

It only takes one individual to make a difference, and that person can be you! Research, learn, advocate, and educate. People do not like to hear someone complain about everything that happens. No one wants to listen to you complain about your responsibilities; all adults have responsibilities and requirements in their life. Make improvements to your situation by changing your attitude or by changing your situation.

Staying Informed

Stay up to date with local, state, and national policies. Know who is in charge. What are their plans for your community? Subscribe to a reliable news source to gain knowledge about day-to-day issues. A reliable news source clearly marks opinion articles, discloses conflicts of interest, and is transparent regarding where the information was obtained and how the source was verified. When it comes time to vote on policies, do your research and vote. Do not just let things happen to you. Be a part of the decision-making process for yourself and others.

Exhibiting Patriotism

Think back to your history class. The information that was covered will help you understand the history of your local community, state, and nation to make decisions about the future. To exhibit patriotism, you could work to make your country better, advocate for issues you are passionate about, and vote for officials who share your beliefs. As an adult, you need to learn respect, love, and devotion for your culture and country.

Living up to High Standards

A good citizen is accountable for their actions and takes ownership of mistakes and wrongdoings. Set high standards for yourself and those around you. Keep each other accountable and hold your elected official to that same standard. Hold yourself to a high standard when it comes to protecting or conserving resources for the future of your community. You can practice this by recycling, composting, picking up trash, buying local produce, and conserving water and energy.

Showing R-E-S-P-E-C-T

A good citizen follows the golden rule: "Treat others the way you want to be treated." Ask yourself if you would approve if someone treated you the way you treat them. If you wouldn't like someone disrespecting you, then don't do it to them. Show respect to your parents, siblings, friends, elderly individuals, authority figures, and those who are just trying to do their job. You have a choice: you can either make or break someone's day. That is a lot of power to have.

Making Judgment Calls

Use good judgment. Use the decision-making process I discuss in Chapter 2 to avoid making rash decisions that can have some pretty rough consequences. It is OK to show your emotions, but don't base the choices you make purely on how you feel. Have a clear mind before making a judgment call that could affect your life. Do not judge other people. You have no idea what they are going through, and their life likely looks drastically different than yours. Do not be selfish in your decision-making; consider others.

Facing Your Fear

Show courage. Having the courage to do the moral thing, even when it might seem risky, is part of being an adult. Standing up for your values and what you believe in shows maturity. When the going gets tough, it is easy to give up. Showing courage and determination to finish the race will get you a long way in society; others will notice and respect your choices. Showing courage helps you to chase those goals that are most important to you. There are no handouts in life, so continue to face your fear of failure, believe in yourself, and work hard. You got this!

Paying It Forward

When someone does something nice for you, return that favor to them and someone else. Have you ever driven up to the window in the drive-through at your favorite fast food place and been told, "The car in front of you has paid for your meal!" How did that make you feel? Shocked and excited? It has happened to me, and it made my day! If you are ever in this position, consider paying for the car behind you; this is called paying it forward. It is your job to make the next generation better than yours. Volunteer often by giving your time, money, or energy to those less fortunate than you. Volunteering not only helps others, but it can help you improve your self-concept by showing positive character traits as discussed in Chapter 2. Take care of the environment, and continue to pay it forward.

IN THIS CHAPTER

» Getting your car on the road

» Making sure the brakes don't break you

» Giving it a polish

Chapter 20

Ten Tips and Tricks for Car Maintenance

A car is a huge investment and a privilege to have. It gets you where you need to go and keeps you safe. Caring for your car means taking care of your livelihood, freedom to travel, and financial investment. Maintaining your car can lower the stress in your life, make your driving experience more enjoyable, increase safety, save money, and ensure your car performs to its fullest ability. Keeping your car fully functional can be intimidating, but you can do it. Just follow these tips and tricks to help you maintain your car.

Paying Attention to Spare Parts

When buying a vehicle, pay attention to the extra parts that come with the car, especially the spare tire. Try to purchase a vehicle that has a full-size spare tire. Tires are an investment in themselves, so having a full-size spare tire can help if you end up getting a flat. Emergency tires or "donuts" as your spare tire will only get around 50 miles of travel time. Depending on where you have a blowout, this might not be enough to get you to a service station.

Going for the Good Oil

Your car's motor oil keeps the engine running properly. Going for the good oil means purchasing the type your specific car needs. Check your owner's manual or oil cap to see what type of oil is required for your car and to figure out how many miles your car can go between oil changes. Knowing what you need can help avoid price hikes when you get your oil changed. Synthetic oil can cost four times as much as regular oil, so double-check if this is really what your manufacturer requires for your car.

Caring for the Car Battery

Your car will not start without battery power. The battery also stabilizes the energy supply to your car to keep it running. Car batteries usually last for approximately two years. To make your battery work better for you, drive your car to keep it charged, turn off electronics and interior lights when using auxiliary power, and pay attention to battery warnings such as

- Clinking sounds from the engine when you turn the key to start the car
- A corroded battery
- Your battery dying intermittently
- Dimmer-than-usual lights

Breaking for New Brakes

Pay close attention to your brakes. If you notice that you have to push harder on the brake pedal to stop or you hear squeaking or creaking when you brake, it is time to get them replaced. Brake pads are relatively inexpensive and fairly easy to replace. Getting your brakes fixed as soon as you feel the wear and tear on them will keep you and others on the road safe!

Keeping the Air Clean

Change your air filter once a year. Your air filter keeps dirt and debris from entering the engine. A clean air filter

- » Increases your car's fuel efficiency. You know how expensive gas is, so make sure the gas works at its best.
- » Reduces emissions contributing to environmental pollution.
- » Prolongs your car's engine life.

Maintaining a Squeaky Clean Windshield

Where you live determines how often you need to change your windshield wipers. If you live in a rainy environment, you need to change them more often than someone who lives in a dryer climate. A good rule of thumb is to change your blades each year at the start of the rainy season.

Working Those Shocks, Struts, and Springs

Looking good! Strut your stuff . . . oh wait, not that kind of strut!

Shocks and struts for your car help to stabilize turns, braking, and accelerating. Your ride would be rough and shaky without them. The springs in your car absorb the bumps and jolts that arise when you drive on uneven roads. Your shocks, struts, and springs wear out around 30,000 miles or so; keep an eye on them.

Talkin' about the Car Wash

Reasons to clean your car weekly include

- » Maintaining a higher resale value
- » Feeling less stress and embarrassment when you have an unexpected passenger

- Preserving your paint job
- Protecting your car from rust that can occur after salt is used to treat ice on the roads
- Having better visibility through your windows
- Keeping clear headlights to see better at night
- Feeling pride in your vehicle

Running on Empty

Don't get caught with an empty gas tank. First of all, it's not good for your car, and second, it could leave you stranded. A best practice is to keep your gas tank at least half full to keep the fuel pump primed.

Doing a Tire Check

Labeled on the side of your tires is the proper pounds per square inch (PSI) range to which your tires should be inflated. Once a month, look for uneven tire tread, punctures, and improper inflation. If you find issues, take the tires to get serviced or replaced ASAP. Healthy tires are key to safety on the road.

IN THIS CHAPTER

» Watching for common pitfalls to avoid

» Gaining knowledge through trial and error

» Learning from your mistakes

Chapter 21

Ten Rookie Mistakes

It is important to learn from your mistakes, and sometimes that takes a little trial and error. In this chapter, I include some common mistakes or predicaments that I hope to help you avoid in the future.

Maxing Out Your Credit Cards

If you cannot afford something now, you most likely cannot afford it later. When you max out your credit card, you have reached the limit, or sometimes even gone over. If you do not pay it back promptly, you get hit with tons of fees and possible damage to your credit score. Carefully think about your use of credit cards so you do not end up in this situation.

Staying in a Relationship Even When You Realize It Will Not Last

Sometimes it might seem easier *not* to deal with things in your life, but that line of thought is a slippery slope. If you realize that your relationship with a friend or romantic partner does not have a future, it is better to deal with it sooner than later. If you already know the outcome, you will end up wasting precious time in your life in a toxic or less-than-stellar relationship. Let the other person know you are ready to end the relationship rather than just disappearing.

Not Putting Verbal Contracts in Writing

Working with your friends and family can be an exciting process, but it can turn south very quickly. Since you have a special relationship with friends and family, each business move could be taken personally. Even though it may seem like you can trust those closest to you, get business deals and agreements in writing. This will help protect everyone involved.

Breaking Up, Then Trying to Remain Friends

Yes, you *can* remain friends with an ex, but most of the time it is not a good idea. If there are children involved, I urge you to remain cordial and friendly to be able to co-parent, but if there are no children involved, the best step is to separate fully from the person you break up with. If you continue to be around your ex, you could get back together, then break up again when you remember why you separated in the first place. It becomes a vicious cycle of toxicity.

Putting Dish Soap in the Dishwasher

The ingredients in liquid dish soap and dishwasher detergent are very different. Liquid dish soap makes soap suds to help scrub away debris when you hand-wash dishes. Dishwasher detergent uses chemical enzymes to clean the dishes in the dishwasher but does not produce soap suds. The two types are not interchangeable. If you put dish soap in the dishwasher, you will end up with soap suds all over the kitchen floor! Time to get a mop and towels!

Buying Too Much Furniture

Actually, my full title for this section is "Buying Too Much Furniture, Not Having Room to Carry It Home in Your Car, and Forgetting You Actually Have to Put It Together Yourself," but my editor said that was too long. All three of those things go hand in hand, though. It's a common mistake, and it can be a real problem.

You head into a store and buy something rather large without considering how you will get it home. Trust me, trying to tie something like that to the top of your car will end very badly. Wait to purchase large items until you have a way to transport them safely. Also, read the instructions thoroughly before trying to put together furniture or other items you purchase. It will save you time in the long run if you read first. There is nothing like getting to the end of the building process and realizing you put one piece in backward. You have to start over completely. How frustrating!

Dropping Out of School and Thinking You Will Have Time to Go Back

I realize there may be circumstances where dropping out of school is a necessity, but dropping out because it is too hard or you are just not "feeling it" is not a good reason to quit. Stick with it and persevere. Once you have dropped out, you'll find it hard to start again. Your life will continue and finding the time to resume school will seem hopeless.

Moving Locations and Realizing You Haven't Solved All of Your Problems

Your problems will follow you wherever you go. Yes, moving to get away from toxic people is good, but if you are moving from one job you don't like to a similar one, or you are having financial problems, or you are not motivated, the grass isn't greener on the other side. Your old problems will remain or be replaced with new ones. Confront your issues and tackle them head-on.

Washing a Red Sweatshirt with Your White Clothes

You might like the color pink, but you probably don't want all of your white socks and undies to be that color. Separate your clothes before washing them! Place light colors together and dark colors together when you wash. If you have a brand-new item of clothing that has deep-colored dye, like jeans, wash it separately for the first couple of washes to make sure it does not bleed into the rest of your clothing load.

Forgetting to Preheat the Oven

Time to bake a cake! You've worked in the kitchen tirelessly preparing the cake batter. It's time to put it in the oven to bake. But wait. The oven isn't hot, and you have to wait another 30 minutes before your cake can even begin to bake. This is a bummer, especially if you're in a time crunch. If you put the cake in the oven before the oven is the correct temperature, the cake doesn't cook evenly. Turn on your oven before you even begin getting your ingredients out; that way it is ready when you are.

Index

D

G

H

R

S

About the Author

Gencie Houy is an expert in family and consumer sciences education (FCSE). Her expertise comes from years of high school classroom instruction, school administration, writing curriculum, and postsecondary instruction and administration. She has a bachelor's degree in FCSE from Texas Tech University, a master's degree in educational administration from Lamar University, and a PhD from Texas Tech University in FCSE. Her position at Texas Tech University has allowed her to educate students in family and consumer sciences education and professionalism in the classroom. Dr. Houy's research has identified an important need for diverse populations of college-age individuals to learn essential life skills needed to become successful adults. She has been able to meet that need by researching, creating, writing, implementing, and teaching a course curriculum entitled Adulting 101: Real Skills for Real Life for Texas Tech University.

Dr. Houy and her husband, Scott, reside in Lubbock, Texas. God has blessed them with four daughters: Hattie, Elsie, Bonnie, and Winnie. Her family inspires her to become a better person daily. When Gencie is not writing or educating others on adulting, she enjoys dancing with her daughters and going through the ups and downs of life with her family and friends!

Dedication

To all of my students: past, present, and future.

Author's Acknowledgments

First, I would like to thank my Lord and Savior, Jesus Christ, for the blessings you have sent my way. Thank you for enlarging my territory to be able to show others their worth and that they are loved! I would like to thank my husband, Scott, for his unwavering support and witty ideas for the book. Hattie, Elsie, Bonnie, and Winnie, thank you for showing me so much love and compassion during this journey. You girls are my inspiration, and everything I do is for you! Clint and Shalan — aka Mom and Dad — thank you for loving me and raising me to follow in both of your footsteps. I wouldn't have it any other way. Chris and Dawn, thank you for the life advice; and Dan and Sheila, thank you for all of the silver-haired wisdom. Kelly, Lindsey, and Shannon, thank you for your emotional and mental support through this endeavor. Tanner, thank you for your mechanical expertise, and Luke, your financial expertise for the book was appreciated. Dr. Alexander, thank you for allowing me the opportunity and platform to research essential life skills in individuals and for allowing my creativity in that path. To all of my colleagues, thank you for allowing me to bounce ideas off of each of you and reinforcing my ability for success. And finally, as an educator, I would be remiss not to thank all of my students who have trusted me and helped me to become the person I am today.

Publisher's Acknowledgments

Acquisitions Editor: Jennifer Yee

Project Editor: Charlotte Kughen

Copy Editor: Amy Handy

Technical Editor: Melanie Schmitt

Sr. Editorial Assistant: Cherie Case

Production Editor: Pradesh Kumar

Cover Image: © PeopleImages.com – Yuri A/Shutterstock

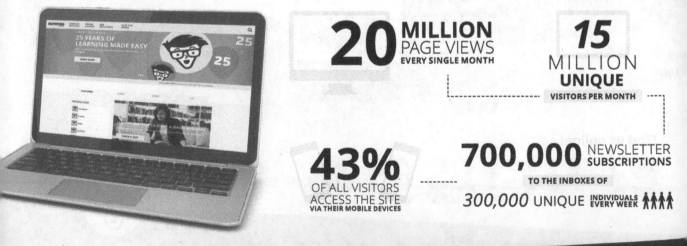